IMPERIAL LYRIC

PENN STATE
ROMANCE STUDIES

EDITORS
Robert Blue (Spanish)
Kathryn M. Grossman (French)
Thomas A. Hale (French/Comparative Literature)
Djelal Kadir (Comparative Literature)
Norris J. Lacy (French)
John M. Lipski (Spanish)
Sherry L. Roush (Italian)
Allan Stoekl (French/Comparative Literature)

ADVISORY BOARD
Theodore J. Cachey Jr. (University of Notre Dame)
Priscilla Ferguson (Columbia University)
Hazel Gold (Emory University)
Cathy L. Jrade (Vanderbilt University)
William Kennedy (Cornell University)
Gwen Kirkpatrick (Georgetown University)
Rosemary Lloyd (Indiana University)
Gerald Prince (University of Pennsylvania)
Joseph T. Snow (Michigan State University)
Ronald W. Tobin (University of California at Santa Barbara)
Noël Valis (Yale University)

IMPERIAL LYRIC

*New Poetry and New Subjects in
Early Modern Spain*

LEAH MIDDLEBROOK

THE PENNSYLVANIA STATE UNIVERSITY PRESS
UNIVERSITY PARK, PENNSYLVANIA

LIBRARY OF CONGRESS
CATALOGING-IN-PUBLICATION DATA

Middlebrook, Leah, 1966–

Imperial lyric : new poetry and new subjects in early modern Spain / Leah Middlebrook.
p.   cm.
Includes bibliographical references and index.
Summary: "Examines poetry and ideology in Early Modern Spain. Includes eight representative Peninsular writers and one poet from the Americas to demonstrate the shifting ideologies of the self, language and the state that mark watersheds for European and American modernity"
—Provided by publisher.

ISBN 978-0-271-03517-8 (cloth : alk. paper)
ISBN 978-0-271-03518-5 (pbk. : alk. paper)
1. Ballads, Spanish—History and criticism.
I. Title.

PQ6081.M53 2009
861'.0440903—dc22
2008045779

Copyright © 2009 The Pennsylvania State University
All rights reserved
Printed in the United States of America
Published by The Pennsylvania State University Press,
University Park, PA 16802-1003

It is the policy of The Pennsylvania State University Press to use acid-free paper. Publications on uncoated stock satisfy the minimum requirements of American National Standard for Information Sciences—Permanence of Paper for Printed Library Material, ANSI Z 39.48–1992.

This book can be viewed at
http://publications.libraries.psu.edu/eresources/978-0-271-03517-8

CONTENTS

Acknowledgments vii

Introduction 1

1
Sonnetization:
Acuña, Boscán, Castillejo, and the Politics of Form 14

2
Otro tiempo lloré y ahora canto:
Juan Boscán Courtierizes Song 59

3
Imperial Pastoral:
Gutierre de Cetina Writes the Home Empire 103

4
Heroic Lyric 138

Coda: The Tomb of Poetry 175

Bibliography 181

Index 189

ACKNOWLEDGMENTS

IN QUOTING POETRY IN THIS BOOK I have consulted modern critical editions as noted, modernizing some of the spelling. Unless otherwise noted, all translations are my own. One important exception is Petrarch; the translations are Durling's and are used by permission. Parts of Chapter 3 were published in the *Bulletin of Hispanic Studies* 78, no. 3 (July 2001). I am grateful to the Comparative Literature Program and the Romance Languages Department at the University of Oregon for granting me leaves to work on this book in 2003 and 2006, and to the Oregon Humanities Center for a research fellowship in 2005. In addition to this valuable material support, this book has benefited from a rich intellectual climate. I extend my thanks to Barbara Altmann, Juan Barja, John Bender, Emilie L. Bergmann, Anthony J. Cascardi, David Castillo, Marsha Collins, Alicia Colombí-Monguió, Robert Davis, Carl Djerassi, Cecilia Enjuto Rangel, Leonard Feldman, Karen Jackson Ford, Dian Fox, Lisa Myobun Freinkel, Edward Friedman, Pedro García Caro, Leonardo García Pabón, Lynn Glaser, Roland Greene, Timothy Hampton, Elise Hansen, Gina Herrmann, Jill Kuger-Robbins, Herb Lau, Herbie Lindenberger, Emily Taylor Meyers, Sophia Middlebrook, Keely Muscatell, Michole Nicholson, Amanda Powell, Max Rayneard, Erin Rokita, Daniel Rosenberg, Laura Schattschneider, Jill Stauffer, Michael Stern, and David Wacks. The membership of the Society for Renaissance and Baroque Hispanic Poetry provided helpful feedback on parts of this project presented at meetings in 2003 and 2005. The University of Oregon EMODS gave stiff readings and crucial advice over many extended evenings. Thomas Dolack and Ignacio Navarrete each provided useful suggestions about translating some of the thornier passages quoted in the book. Any remaining tangled syntax is the result of my own slow-mindedness. Anonymous readers for the Pennsylvania State University Press gave thoughtful readings and incisive feedback on the first draft of the manuscript, and I am grateful to the Press and series editors for steering the book to completion.

Special thanks are due to a number of people whose careful reading, tact, support, and cheer extended far beyond what anyone should be allowed to ask, although this did not keep me from asking, or from receiving ... and receiving. I owe great debts to Nathalie Hester and to Fabienne Moore as readers and as friends, and to my husband, Norio Sugano, for support and patience. Diane Wood Middlebrook read, considered, and talked over sentences, pages, and chapters of this book, patiently and at all hours. The book will stand as a testament to the emotional and intellectual generosity she extended me during the closing months of her life, as well as during the forty or so years that preceded it. Jonathan Middlebrook, his hands full with other matters, set down his framing hammer and picked up his pen to address himself to the manuscript's final complete draft. To each of my parents, then: *Escrito 'sta en mi alma vuestro gesto.* This book is dedicated to my family—all of them.

INTRODUCTION

line-forms, and verse forms in general, are fundamentally discussable as mediations of relationships, as rules and orders of polities
—Allen Grossman, *The Sighted Singer*, 283

THIS IS A BOOK ABOUT POETRY and ideology in early modern Spain. Set in the era when Spain was developing from a peninsular monarchy to the seat of a pan-European and global empire (roughly 1526–1600), this book addresses a curious phenomenon in early modern studies: despite the fact that in the 1990s and the early 2000s the humanities began to move beyond the traditional focus on Europe to develop a global reach, and the role of imperial Spain in the Renaissance became central to our reinvention of cultural history, the scholarly conversation about early European and global modernity has yet to fully "place" the significance of Spain and Spanish cultural production.[1] *Imperial Lyric* demonstrates the importance of peninsular letters to our understanding of shifting ideologies of the self, language, and the state that mark watersheds for European and American modernity. As a second but not insignificant point, this book also aims to complicate the historicizing turn we have taken in the field of early modern studies by considering a threshold of modernity that was specific to poetry, one that I believe was inscribed in Spanish culture when the genre of lyric poetry attained a certain kind of prestige at the expense of the epic. The terms *new poetry*, *new art*, and *new lyric* refer primarily, in the context of sixteenth- and seventeenth-century poetry, to erudite sonnets and songs that were based on Italian models but composed in Castilian. In the pages that follow, I take up the conundrum that emerged when this new kind of poetry, composed

---

1. One recent and suggestive exception is Helgerson's 2007 study of Garcilaso, Boscán, and the idea of poetry and empire, *A Sonnet from Carthage*.

in the "minor" genre that was the lyric in the sixteenth century, became synecdochic with the courtly Spanish elites.

Until the early modern era, poetic prestige had been determined either in accordance with the ideas set forth in Aristotle's *Poetics,* which privileged epic and tragedy, or through a discourse of plenitude of the type framed by Dante when, in the *De vulgari eloquentia,* he elevated the *canzone* over all other poetry on the grounds that only that form could capture "all that has flowed from the heads of the illustrious poetic minds, down to their lips" (2.3.41).[2] Whether a given writer followed Aristotle, Dante, or various combinations of the two, poetic excellence was judged based on a given form's abilities to preserve and transmit the traditions of a culture from its origins in the native past to the present moment of utterance. The "greatness" of "great poetry" thus resided in its length, in addition to its subject matter and the register of its diction. Meanwhile, the various forms of poetry that fell into the loose and shifting category of "the lyric" were referred to in a number of ways, as *vario stile, poemi brevi,* and *poemi piccoli.*[3] The very indeterminacy of their naming indicated their relative lack of importance, and I will demonstrate that this aspect of the lyric concerned aristocratic writers as much as its foreign provenance did. In the wake of Petrarch, and with the onset of the humanist Renaissance, the beauty and adaptability of the poetry of the *Canzoniere* clearly influenced the popularity of the practice of writing in the "small style." Furthermore, Bembian theories of poetic reform increased poets' interest in Petrarchism. However, writers remained ambivalent about the status that should be accorded to these short forms whose Italian and classical provenance lent them authority, but whose absence from the texts of Aristotle suggested that they were lacking in nobility.

Of course, the concept of "nobility" itself was undergoing a transformation during the period in question. In Hapsburg Spain, the country's grandees were drawn away from the battlefield and into the court, where they were seduced and subjected into identifying with new discourses of nobility and new regimes of prestige and power. Within this context, the criteria by which to measure a nobleman's virility and excellence changed. Previously associated with the force of his sword arm as he fought to secure the Iberian Peninsula for Christianity (during the so-called Christian Reconquest), his worthiness now became linked to equally violent and powerful acts of suppression that

---

2. In a related vein, see Agamben, *The End of the Poem,* 1–22, on the poetic thresholds crossed by Dante with his turn to comedy.

3. See Maria José Vega, "La poética de la lírica," 15–43.

were directed inward, against the self, in the manner described by Norbert Elias in his discussions of the process of "courtierization" and by theorists of early modern courtiership and courtliness.[4] Over the following pages I will argue that the lyric's rise to privilege was conditioned by this radical revision of the social role assigned to the aristocracy in early modern Spain. I will demonstrate that the legitimation of short forms of poetry took place in conjunction with the symbolic and actual abbreviation of the modern courtier's access to power and agency. Furthermore, I will show that writers examined here understood the complex and self-reflexive utterances forced by the rules of the sonnet form, in particular, as allegories of the intricate psychological operations they had to perform in order to reconcile their traditional senses of identity with the postures and the discourses imposed on them by the imperial state.

Another way of framing the forthcoming argument, then, is that *Imperial Lyric* links the "new lyric" with that emergent modern figure, the individuated, "split," and interpellated subject.[5] But this book is also fundamentally about *poetic* modernity. The cultural acceptance—more than that, the elevation to a place of privilege—of a poetic genre that was cut to the dimensions of the self at the expense of the expansive forms of poetry whose purpose was to secure a native cultural continuum reflects a passage from what Allen Grossman has referred to as the poetics of Homer to those of Horace, from a notion of poetry as the art that serves to memorialize images of "Achilles and other great persons of value" in an ongoing record of civilization, to a cosmopolitan poetry that appropriates the special privileges assigned to poetic discourse—the privileges of *poiesis*, of unique linguistic contact with the origins of culture and the orders of the mythic and the supernatural that are represented by references to prophecy and the muse—"on behalf of . . . individual personhood, taking the great privilege

---

4. On "courtierization," see the discussion in Elias's *Power and Civility*, especially pages 104–16. On the self-reflexivity of the courtier, see Harry Berger Jr., *The Absence of Grace*, as well as the classic study by Daniel Javitch, *Poetry and Courtliness*.

5. My discussions of the subject in this book tend to quote Judith Butler, *The Psychic Life of Power*. Her emphasis on "thinking the theory of power together with a theory of the psyche" (3) is useful when we are considering the category of the subject in its origins in early modern culture and discourse. Another important text in this regard is Paul Smith, *Discerning the Subject*. Smith compares the uses of the term *subject* in phenomenological, psychoanalytic, Marxist, and juridical discourses. His study has been particularly useful to critics working on the early modern period because of Smith's critiques of the term *subject* as it overwrites the more flexible and precise discourse of agency (see Smith, xxxiii–xxxv and 24–30, as well as José Antonio Mazzotti, on the terms *sujeto* and *agencia* in *Agencias criollas*, 8–16).

of the hero, the privilege of continuity of image, and bestowing it upon himself, declaring that his poetry was a monument to his own selfhood."[6]

Grossman invokes a long-standing preoccupation: it was Horace himself who first drew this distinction. Furthermore, as humanist writers took Horace up as a model, they, too, confronted the question of relevance: does poetry remain *poetry* when it is turned to the ends of memorializing and elaborating a self that is produced, traversed, and sustained by the discourses and practices of a state regime?[7] Contemporary critics are not the only ones to perceive cultivated sixteenth-century lyric as passing along a trajectory that fixes it as a static icon of monarchic power.[8] Spanish courtiers, perhaps especially, were attuned to the stakes of what the new lyric was empowered to overwrite.[9] As an introductory example, consider the following poem, composed sometime in the mid-sixteenth century by Francisco de Aldana (1537–1578):

---

6. Grossman, *The Sighted Singer*, 7–8. He writes: "The most passionate advocacies for the art of poetry in sophisticated late periods, such as the period of Horace, turn upon the function of poetry as keeping alive, across the abysses of death and of the difference between persons, the human image. Horace says, for example, that there were many heroes who lived before the heroes whom Homer recorded, but since they lacked a poet, they are overcome in darkness—they cannot be remembered. . . . Horace is recording a fact of his civilization and of our civilization: that Homer was the principle of the recovery of the image of Achilles and of other great persons of value who are the subject of his poems" (6–7). Susan Stewart elaborates on Grossman's reference to the darkness of forgetting in *Poetry and the Fate of the Senses*. See chapter 1.

7. Grossman continues: "I began by alluding to the use of poetry for conserving the human image—because I think that function constitutes the singular importance of poetry now and also specifies the particular dangers within the practice of poetry to which we are heir. When the poem ceased to conserve information about how to till the fields, about what flood-plains could be inhabited because they were free from cyclical dangers of inundation, when poetry ceased to be the principal instrument for conserving human laws (—it must be remembered that Solon wrote his laws in poetry, and that the Delphic oracle uttered its prophecies in poetic form, and that it was felt by most of Western civilization that the laws of Moses and the agonies of Job were embedded in poetic structures—) what was left for poetry was that fundamental function to which Horace refers: the function of making persons present to one another in that special sense in which they are acknowledgeable and therefore capable of love and mutual interest in one another's safety. It is the function of poetry as making persons present, of modeling the conditions under which persons can be present, that seems to me to survive to us and to justify the prestige of poetic art." Grossman was speaking of the state of poetry in 1981. His subsequent doubt reproduces the early modern conundrum: "In part, I believe the immense equivocalness of poetry at the present time is a consequence of the use of poetry as an instrument of private self-legitimation" (9–10).

8. See, for example, the work of John Beverley on Sonnet 23 of Garcilaso de la Vega (*Against Literature*, 25–39).

9. Anthony J. Cascardi identifies a similar question informing the famous ode, "Ad Florem Gnidi": "the project of lyric self-creation involves a dramatization of the poet's anxieties concerning the efficacy of his own powers. . . . the hypothetical 'if' that opens the ode . . . remains always in force in Garcilaso's verse" (*Ideologies of History*, 256).

Sonnet 45

Otro aquí no se ve que, frente a frente,
animoso escuadrón moverse guerra,
sangriento humor teñir la verde tierra
y tras honroso fin correr la gente;
éste es el dulce son que acá se siente:
"¡España, Santiago, cierra, cierra!"
y por suave olor, que el aire atierra,
humo de azufre dar con llama ardiente;
el gusto envuelto va tras corrompida
agua, y el tacto sólo apalpa y halla
duro trofeo de acero ensangrentado,
hueso en astilla, en él carne molida,
despedazado arnés, rasgado malla:
¡oh sólo de hombres digno y noble estado![10]

[Here one sees nothing but, face to face, / the animated squadron fomenting war, / a bloody humor stains the green earth, / and the people race toward their honorable end; / this is the sweet sound which here is heard: / "España! Santiago! Charge! Charge!" / and in place of a delicate fragrance that falls to earth from the air / there is sulfurous smoke, released by the burning flame; / taste seeks corrupted / water, and touch palpates, and finds / a harsh trophy of the bloody steel, / shattered bone, lined with ground flesh, / fragments of armor, torn mail: / Oh dignified, noble state, known only to man!]

Aldana was celebrated in his time as an ideal example of the Spanish man of arms and letters.[11] As a fighter, he participated in some of the notable battles of his era before losing his life while fighting at Alcazarquivir at the age of forty-one. As a writer, he was prolific and complex. He spent his youth in Naples and Florence, where he would have been exposed to Ficinian thought; critics identify this influence in his skillful manipulation of the Italian style, and the unusual sensuality with which he elaborated Neo-Platonic and Stoic philosophies, as well as orthodox Christian doctrine.

---

10. Francisco de Aldana, *Poesías castellanas completas,* ed. Lara Garrido, 344–45. Unless otherwise noted, all translations into English are my own.
11. On Aldana's life, see Rivers, *Francisco de Aldana.*

Stylistically, Sonnet 45 displays a baroque aesthetic and a masterful grasp of rhetoric. It delivers its shock—the encounter with the mangled flesh of the fallen soldier in line 12—by deftly mobilizing the poetic device of the hierarchy of the senses, perhaps, as Elias Rivers has suggested, with reference to the *Spiritual Exercises* of Ignatius of Loyola.[12] We are *shown* the green earth (lines 1 and 3), we *hear* a harsh sound (line 5), we are led to smell, taste, and, finally, touch. This progress "down" through the order of the senses is encouraged by a skillful deployment of sonorous and rhythmic devices. Assonance between the "l" and "a" sounds in lines 10 and 12 brings the act of touch (*apalpar*) together with its object (*astilla* and *molida*), across the speaker's editorial gloss in line 11, while the enjambment between lines 10 and 11 underscores the theme of seeking, drawing the action of apalpar across the border of its own line into the next. The reader conjoins in the artifice as he or she engages in the physical act of moving the eyes over and down. The result of Aldana's artistry is a series of intertwined appeals to a reader's sensual and intellectual faculties, so that we are primed for an experience of disgust upon encountering the mangled flesh and bone, the "hueso en astilla, en él carne molida" in line 12. They are contained neatly in their syntax, and they startle us all the more for that fact.

Sonnet 45 is in keeping with the dramatic sensibility that informs later key works of the Spanish baroque, such as the bloody handprint on the nobleman's new coat of arms at the close of Calderón de la Barca's *El medico de su honra,* or the *vanitas* paintings of Valdés Leal. In fact, the poem encompasses both poetry and the visual arts, inasmuch as it is structured as an emblem. The sonnet, the emblem, and the epigram were all closely associated in the sixteenth and seventeenth centuries. Here, the poem's organization as a visual scene accompanied by a moral gloss—"¡Oh sólo de hombres digno y noble estado!"—provides a strong cue to read it as an emblem, and this cue is supported by the apostrophe in the final line. The speaker's exclamation, "¡*Oh* . . . !" draws him out of the visual scene and into a middle ground between the landscape and the viewer. The effect is to cast him as a *beschouwer,* the figure—often a man or a boy—in emblem and in painting, who gestures to an onlooker from the foreground of the image, inviting us to gaze "in" on a significant scene.

But what are we gazing on? The most conventional message of the beschouwer is *Ecce homo*. The device is common in religious paintings wherein early modern viewers were guided to contemplate biblical events such as

---

12. See Rivers, *Francisco de Aldana*.

the Nativity, the Crucifixion or the Assumption of the Virgin. Sonnet 45 contains a register of religious allusion, in the echo of St. Paul, Corinthians: "For now we see through a glass, darkly, but then we will see face to face" (1 Cor. 1:13). However, religion is not paramount in this poem. Paramount is the scene of devastation where, heaped at the "bottom" of the visual frame that is created by the rectangular shape of the sonnet, that bloody mass of flesh, bone and mail fixes our attention and invites us to interpret it.

In this reading—and over the course of this book—I argue that we are summoned to gaze on the scene because it represents the clash of two Spanish cultures: the traditional order of Castile represented by the war cry "¡Santiago!" in line six versus the culture surrounding that cry, the culture that supports both the poetic speaker's arts of demonstration and the artifact of the sonnet itself, that is, the culture of the modern courtier. As carefully as the first thirteen lines of the poem work to describe the battlefield, they also build up an image of the speaker who is showing it to us. We see that he is well educated in the conventions of rhetoric and the visual arts (painting, emblem),[13] and we find that he knows the principal tropes and forms of the Renaissance poetic tradition: he describes a scene that alternates between a battlefield and a Petrarchan *locus amoenus*. The tone of his final commentary, bitter but accepting, identifies him with the dissembling and ultimately passive masculine behavior that came into fashion with the coalescence of the early modern state and the politicization of the aristocracy into creatures of the court. From Castiglione to Gracián, a principal sign of the courtier's skill was his Stoic capacity to deflect passion into art. The poem's speaker exhibits his courtliness by waiting until line 14 to unleash his vehement—but cultured, and ironic—lament about the degrading practice of modern war and the disaster that has befallen the second estate.[14] Thus while critics have tended to read Sonnet 45 as a protest against war, I would suggest that we refine that view, and find the speaker disgusted by two phenomena associated with contemporary battle.[15] First is the rise of gun warfare through the middle part of the sixteenth century, as refinements to the harquebus made

---

13. On "painting with words" in the sixteenth and seventeenth centuries, see Bergmann, *Art Inscribed*.

14. "Vehemence" was a quality privileged by mannerist rhetoricians. For example, Herrera employs the term throughout the *Annotations*.

15. Criticism of Sonnet 45 has turned around the question of whether it is or is not an antiwar poem. Rivers and Silva each view it in this way; Walters focuses on its religious nature. These two ways of interpreting the poem are reconciled if we see it as framing a statement of disgust at modern Spanish war. In response to modernity, Aldana here, as in other important poems, such as the "Epístola a Arias Montano," turns to his worldly and Stoic Christianity for solace.

it the weapon of choice in the European wars after Pavia (1526).[16] Second is the *symbolic* violence that the gunpowder revolution and the turn to a mercenary fighting force enacted on Spain's elite warrior caste.[17] As the nobility were moved away from the front, their place was taken by a combination of professional soldiers and commoners bought or coerced into military service.[18] This shift protected the lives of the scions of the noble houses, but it also greatly diminished the traditional role of the aristocracy within Spanish society. This bit of historical context helps us explain Aldana's reference to corruption (*corrompida*, line 9) and his use of *noble* in line 14. The noble practice of war is no longer noble when it is fought in modern terms, even if one is fighting the infidel and charges to the traditional Castilian shout of "¡Santiago!" The speaker invites us to reflect on this fact as he sets the corrupted scene before us.

But he also invites us to contemplate how the tensions between traditional and contemporary culture are identified with specific kinds of poetry. Sonnet 45 represents two genres of poetry in contention for control of its landscape. The conflict manifests itself, first, in the speaker's style of description, which, phrased as contradictions ("otro aquí no se ve que"), contrasts our expectation of a lover's meadow with a stinking, muddy field that is more proper to the gory scenes that enliven epic and ballad than it is to the sonnet. But it is in line 12, in our encounter with the mass of flesh and bone that transfixes us after the speaker has skillfully led us to "touch" it, that the clash emerges most clearly. The courtly Petrarchan tradition contains a discourse of fragmented bodies, but conventionally those bodies are

---

16. On the impact of the harquebus on poetry, in particular, see Murrin, *History and Warfare*, who focuses on the epic but whose study is also useful to thinking about the lyric.

17. Cascardi discusses the early modern period and the changeover from a society based on caste to one of class (*Ideologies of History*, 1–4).

18. Albi de la Cuesta discusses the shifts in the makeup of Spanish military forces in the fifteenth, sixteenth, and seventeenth centuries (*De Pavía a Rocroi*, 13–43). He observes that firearms were used earlier and more widely among Spanish forces than they were in the militaries of France, Italy, and England and argues that the position of the nobility within the battle lines and the fighting strategies of Spanish troops came under significant revision in the last quarter of the fifteenth century and the first quarter of the sixteenth, as squadrons of Swiss pikemen displaced the *caballeros:* "Agrupado en gigantescos cuadros de gran profundidad y formados por miles de hombres, equipados con largas picas, pone fin a siglos de predominio de la caballería noble. La solidez de estas tropas, que durante cincuenta años nunca volvieron las espaldas . . . contribuyó a hacer de ellas las más temidas de Europa. España y Francia pagaron a precio de oro sus servicios" ("Grouped in gigantic squadrons of great depth and formed of thousands of men, equipped with long pikes, it puts an end to centuries of predominance by the aristocratic cavalry. The solidity of these troops, which for fifty years never turned their backs . . . contributed in making them the most feared in Europe. Spain and France paid in gold for their services"); ibid., 16.

female and appear as eroticized fragments represented through proliferations of comparison to jewels, metals, stars, and the sun.[19] The body part we find in line 12 almost certainly belongs to a man, since it is wearing chain maille. Furthermore, it is represented without recourse to metaphor. Finally, we encounter it through the base sense of touch, as opposed to through the exalted sense of sight that is the key to Petrarchan tropes of Neo-Platonic sublimation. All of these elements contribute to the sense that line 12 is playing with a reversal of Petrarchan expression and that the pulverized bone and the clumps of flesh represent a deliberate inversion—or perhaps it is better to say *perversion*—of sonnet-speech, an "anti-blazon."[20] This reversal of conventions in turn invites us to notice another significant structuring feature of the sonnet, namely, that it is a work of anamorphosis that inscribes two perspectives, one keyed to the tradition of Santiago and the noble Castilian warrior, the other to a new age of the courtier, the sonnet, and Petrarchism.[21] This modern culture is the stronger one. This is evident from the fact that the poem is a sonnet, the form is most clearly identified with modern European court culture. Moreover, a clear aim of this sonnet is to represent the courtier's view of warfare. But these aspects of the poem allow us to make one more interpretation of line 12. Viewed from the alternate sight line of Castilian tradition, the mass of flesh and bone suggests itself as the remains of the heroic fighting arm, the *diestro braço* wielded by the noble Castilian knight. From the modern perspective, the *diestro braço* is perceptible but not legible. For one thing, it has been exploded by guns. For another, it is irretrievably distorted by the culture of the courtier and the conventions

---

19. *Blazon* is the poetic technique of describing isolated parts of the (generally female) body, often through comparison to natural phenomena such as the sun and the stars and often through comparison to precious objects. On Petrarchan blazon and the fragmenting effects of the erotic gaze, see Vickers, "Diana Described."

20. Fox ("Frente a Frente") reads line 12 as a blazon within the context of homoeroticism. I make a different interpretation above, but her discussion of the possible homoeroticism of King Sebastian of Portugal, and possibly of Aldana as well, is informed and provocative.

21. David Castillo has recently discussed the phenomenon of literary anamorphosis in early modern Spanish texts, especially in the picaresque. Using the definition of anamorphosis offered by César Nicolás ("una variación del ángulo de mirada transforma el objeto: la imagen 'deforme' supone un doble proceso . . . de estructuración y reestructuración sucesivas" [a variation in the angle of viewing transforms the object: the "deformed" image assumes a double process . . . of successive structuring and restructuring]; Nicolás, 17, cited in Castillo, 1), Castillo points to the suitability of the device to the nascent absolutist, "guided" culture of early modern Spain, in which nature is overwritten by politics such that everything is subject to interpretation. In a manner analogous to lived experience at court, the spectator confronted with a work of anamorphosis is "invited to distance himself or herself from fixed interpretations, and to reflect on the uncertainty and artificial or constructed nature of meaning" (*[A]Wry Views*, 1–2).

of his speech. Despite the formal brevity of the "new" Italianate lyric adopted into Spanish courtly society in the sixteenth century, writers such as Juan Boscán or Fernando de Herrera would defend it as endlessly capacious ("capaz de contener cualquier tipo de materia" ["capable of containing whatever material whatsoever"], as Boscán put it in his "Letter" to the Duchess of Soma[22]). In fact, as we will see over the course of this book, the new lyric was not all-inclusive. Rather, it substituted the plenitudinous, expansive "all" that was preserved and transmitted within Castilian culture in bardic song, epic, and ballad with "all that was necessary" to speak and write in order to be viable and legible as a subject within the coalescing Hapsburg state. Ultimately, Sonnet 45 represents Petrarchism, the mode of poetry that is aligned with modernity and with courtierization, as imbued, through its association with these forces, with the power to suppress Castilian tradition and its principal poetic formulas. Aldana's sonnet testifies to that transformation, even as its speaker accepts the violence and manages it with the grace expected of the courtier, transforming his disenchantment into art and revealing the resulting scene to us with his good arm. But the *diestro braço* still subtends the vision, as so many deformed but seductive objects strewn across the field.[23]

Having decoded the dense, elaborate, and highly rhetoricized poem that is Sonnet 45 and having identified it as offering a vision of a joined crisis in Spanish masculine identity and in poetry, we are in a position to

---

22. Boscán, *Obra completa*, 119.

23. In *Writing and Vulnerability in the Late Renaissance*, Jane Tylus distinguishes late sixteenth-century subjectivity as a period of shifts in notions of how the classical ideal of *invulnerabilis* could be achieved. Noting that the ideals of courtiership propounded by Castiglione's early imitators were from the outset exposed as untenable within the matrix of patronage and dependency that determines the early modern subject's life, Tylus focuses on a substratum of writers and artists who, "far from being mere accomplices of the social and political orders . . . attempt[ed] to manipulate those orders while seeking legitimation for their voices through different and, in their own eyes, higher authorities. In so doing, they refuse to permit their own creative strategies of immunity to be appropriated by those for whom, ostensibly, they write" (27). This description fits Aldana's strategies for managing the conditions of modern courtiership, at least as these strategies are represented in his poetry, and here I refer not only to Sonnet 45 but across the spectrum of his work, which combines a deep knowledge of ancient and modern philosophies and sciences (particularly Stoicism, Ficinian Neo-Platonism, and, it would seem, the writings on nature by Pliny) with an equally profound and complex religious sense (Rivers, *Francisco de Aldana*; Walters, *The Poetry of Francisco de Aldana*, especially page 116). The final point of the invitation to readers to look on the scene of the disaster of modern warfare, courtiership, and poetry that is represented in Sonnet 45 may be to lead us to grasp the meaning of the St. Paul line, since it is invoked as part of the poem's opening ("frente a frente," or face to face). Such a reading would fit in with Tylus's notion of the pragmatic courtier who seeks meaning in communities and alternate social constellations that fall outside the dominant institutions and practices of his immediate surroundings.

review our attitudes about both the early modern sonnet and the wider phenomenon of the new lyric. Over the course of this book I will consider the impact of this genre, which, in the second half of the century, especially, became a virtual emblem of state and imperial power. In addition, I will reflect in particular on the sonnet, arguing for how this minor and apparently stable—even lifeless—form came to be associated with the forces of subjection, courtierization, and restraint in the early modern era.[24] Chapter 1 examines how the writers Hernando de Acuña (1514–1580), Diego Hurtado de Mendoza (1503–1575), and Cristobal de Castillejo (1490–1550) engaged with the ideologies and the implicit politics inscribed within the new lyric by means of a trope I call "sonnetization." In Chapter 2, I consider these same ideologies as they inform an attempt by Juan Boscán (1487–1542) to constrain and rationalize song. In the final part of the chapter, I take up Elegy 2 and Sonnet 33 by Garcilaso de la Vega (1500–1536), both of which systematically dismantle these constraints and thereby demonstrate another aspect of the new art, namely, the opportunities for resistance that are inscribed within discourse by the forces of poetry, even when this poetry is the reformed and abbreviated "new lyric." Chapter 3 examines another mode of address to the mandates of imperial lyric, a collection of poems by Gutierre de Cetina (1514–1557), which I argue represent an incomplete pastoral text, most likely modeled on the *Arcadia* of Jacopo Sannazaro. Like Boscán, Cetina was engaged by the multiple levels of narration and allusion that were facilitated by the structure of the lyric sequence, and like Boscán, he sought to adapt the Petrarchan model to the specificities of modern Spanish courtier's subjectivity. Unlike Boscán, Cetina figured the imperial courtier as subject to a complex and divided desire that was more suitably accommodated in a hybrid text than it was within the unifying schema of the Petrarchan *Canzoniere*.

Chapter 4 presents the heroic struggles that Fernando de Herrera (1534–1597) carried on with the various subgenres of the lyric as marking a literary, if not a chronological, endpoint to the interpellation of poetry by institutions of early modern politics and power. Herrera is often framed as a belated Petrarchan; in U.S. and British criticism, especially, his 1580 *Poesía de Garcilaso con anotaciones* (Annotations to the Poetry of Garcilaso) and his

---

24. Roland Greene observes in the opening pages of *Unrequited Conquests*, "Lyric poetry ... has a special purchase ... because it engages the subjective positions of speaker and reader not to drive out society and politics—this is the Romantic notion—but to deliver a closely calibrated reassessment of both those subjective positions and their social contexts, a mutual and self-interrogation" (3).

richly illuminated and embellished sonnets and songs are treated as attempts to rival Italian poetic glory by instituting a new Spanish canon.[25] In a departure from this view, I discuss Herrera's writings in the context of the messianic triumphalism that was rife during the reign of Philip II, arguing that his elaborate mannerist aesthetics represent an attempted solution to what had become an impossible task, namely, representing the heroic Spanish virility of men who were radically subject to the Hapsburg political regime and the religious doctrines of the Counter-Reformation. Despite Herrera's efforts, by the seventeenth century, many writers considered poetry to be a stale and outmoded discourse. This study concludes with a brief reading of a poem by Cervantes that presents the sonnet as the tomb of poetry.

This is a book about politics, about identity, about subjectivity, and about Spain. But most of all it is a book about poetry. I quote and discuss a great deal of poetry in this book. I do so, first, because with respect to the questions I am raising here, the poets "got there first." Horace, who will emerge in these pages as the Roman father of courtierized lyric, forged his style and his poetic voice under the protection of his patron Maecenas, after having fought on the wrong side in the civil war. But in addition, one of my aims in this book is to shift the image that many non-Hispanists have of sixteenth-century peninsular lyric, as a genre devoted to Petrarchism and represented by the figure of Garcilaso de la Vega (some Hispanists hold this view as well). Petrarchism matters to this book. We will observe how writers drew on the *Canzoniere* as a resource as they negotiated their relationships to the shifting social and cultural circumstances in which they found themselves in the mid-sixteenth century.[26] Garcilaso also matters. He will appear as a man of arms and letters who engaged the noble and the ignoble circumstances of warfare with the best poetic resources available to him at the time. But generally this book presents noncanonical poems that, while (nearly) all in print and available in reasonably modern critical editions, may not be familiar to readers. I foreground them to broaden the sample of Spanish lyric available to non-Spanish-speaking readers. To this end, I have provided paraphrases—if not fully literary translations—of the poems discussed here, and have done my best to convey their tone and

---

25. Some of these discussions are highly informative, even if, as will emerge in Chapter 4, I disagree with the emphasis they place on belatedness and rivalry with Italy. For the most comprehensive reading of Herrera's Petrarchism, see Navarrete, *Orphans of Petrarch*.

26. Roland Greene defined the tradition of "post-Petrarchans," writers who draw on the *Canzoniere* to "represent specific solutions to local cultural and aesthetic problems" (*Post-Petrarchism*, 1).

style. Where a writer has employed a double meaning, I have provided both meanings in a note.

This study is not comprehensive. I pay close attention to a select group of writers, omitting others who, although I wanted them to find a place in these pages, did not engage with the lyric tradition in a way that made it possible for me to include them. What did seem important was to take a category of cultural production that has in recent years been considered resolved as "merely" literary or aesthetic and to show what happens when we read it back into its social and ideological contexts. The results call attention to the fundamental role played by poetry in the reorientation of Europeans toward modernity.

1

SONNETIZATION:
ACUÑA, BOSCÁN, CASTILLEJO, AND THE POLITICS OF FORM

THE KIND OF POETRY WE CATEGORIZE as lyric was only just becoming established as a genre during the early modern period. Despite the prevalence of Petrarchism as a compositional praxis, canzone, sonnets, and the other poetic forms that Spanish, French, and English poets adopted from Italy were viewed by many writers as *poemi piccoli*—poetry that was "small" both in length and in scope. It was often taken as poetry dedicated to the representation of trivial and frivolous themes instead of the great matters contained in epic and tragedy.[1] In this chapter I argue that the lyric rose to privilege within the context of the transformation of ideas about men as Spanish society shifted from a military to a courtierized culture—from a culture that celebrated its aristocratic warrior-heroes to one in which the agency and the physical prowess of the nobleman were suppressed, curtailed, and deflected into the courtliness associated with Italian *sprezzatura*. That is, I will be arguing for a reciprocal, mutually conditioning relationship between new ideals for poetry and for men in the early modern era. Moreover, I will speak for the essential modernity of this new poetry whose function was not to inscribe the present order within a continuum of culture (the function of ballad) or to recount Castilian greatness (the function of epic), but rather to rehearse and elaborate the image of the courtier as the new masculine ideal.

One of the Spanish writers whose work supports these claims most clearly is Hernando de Acuña (1514–1580). Born into a noble family in Valladolid, Hernando de Acuña understood courtierization. The younger brother of one celebrated fighter (Pedro de Acuña) and the precocious favorite of another (Antonio de Leiva, the Marquis of Vasto; after the marquis's death Acuña remained on close terms with his son), he also knew of the

---

1. For an excellent discussion of the status of the lyric in sixteenth- and seventeenth-century treatises on poetry, see María José Vega, "La poética de la lírica."

ambivalent rewards of prestige within the Hapsburg court. Successful both in fighting and in cultivating the right patrons, Acuña was singled out for favor when he was assigned the captaincy of a Milanese fort at the young age of twenty-four. He frequently traveled in the emperor's retinue during the 1540s and 1550s. Under Philip II in the 1550s, he carried out missions in France. But he also suffered periods of misfortune and disgrace, as when he was captured and imprisoned in France (three of his sonnets are headed "sonetos en prisión de franceses") and when he lost the fort in Milan in 1546. Furthermore, near the end of his life, he seems to have shared a fate common to captains and fighters throughout the European kingdoms: the *Memorial* of his life and service, from which much of our information about Acuña's life and career is drawn, was composed in order to convince Philip II to pay arrears for the years of service that he had provided to both the emperor and the king.[2]

Acuña is often mentioned in passing in discussion of Spain's generations of fighter poets, but his work is rarely read in any breadth or depth. Yet two of his sonnets, in particular, illustrate that the rules of poetic form can be analyzed for what they reveal about the changing ideologies within a culture. Poems 45 and 30 demonstrate that the "courtierization" of the warrior was imagined as a phenomenon that took place in poetry, as well as in politics. In Acuña we find the clearest representation of a trope that we will encounter repeatedly in this book; we might call it "sonnetization":

Sonnet 45

Atenta al gran rumor la musa mía
del armígero son de Marte fiero,
cesó el dulce estilo que primero
en sujeto amoroso se extendía;
mas hora, con la vuestra en compañía,
me vuelve al sacro monte, donde espero
levantarme más alto y, por grosero,
dejar con nuevo canto el que solía.

---

2. Most biographers use Acuña's *Memorial,* a summary of his service to emperors Charles V and Philip II, written for Philip II in an attempt to receive greater acknowledgment of and compensation for his labors on behalf of the empire, as the basis for documenting his military career. The few biographical studies of Acuña's life and work are summarized and corrected by Díaz Laríos in the introduction to the 1982 edition of the *Varias poesías*. Short but comprehensive, this is the most up-to-date biographical sketch we have of Acuña.

Así sus horas con la espada a Marte,
y los ratos del ocio con la pluma
pienso, señor, enderezar a Apolo;
dando a los dos de mí tan larga parte,
y tomándola dellos tal, que en suma
no me cause tristeza el verme sólo.

[My muse, attentive to the great rumor / of the warlike sounds of fierce Mars, / ceased the sweet style in which she at first / extended herself on the subject of love; / but now, in company with yours, / she returns me to the sacred mount, where I hope / to rise still higher and / with my new song abandon as crude that one I used to sing. / Thus to Mars his hours with the sword, / and in periods of leisure, with the pen / I plan, sir, to make right with Apollo; / giving of myself so large a part to each, / and taking so much from them, that, in summary, / to find myself alone will not cause me grief.][3]

Most who study early modern literature think of sixteenth-century sonnets in terms of Petrarchism and evaluate them based on their success in representing an introspective self (generally masculine, generally courtly), whose utterances, whether they are perceived as allegories of political relationships, transactions in the social currency of patronage, or genuine expressions of love, should flow smoothly toward their object. The aesthetics of the sonnet dictate that it mimic the "artlessly artful" cadences of sprezzatura, but this poem does not appear to do that. On the contrary, Acuña's workmanlike progress through the principal rules of the sonnet form makes for heavy sledding, particularly in lines 7 through 9, where an awkward use of the poetic technique of hyperbaton causes the word *grosero,* or "crude" seem to at first modify the speaker. The fact that a reader must pause to untangle line 9 and then double back to read the quatrain again to have it make sense makes this poem a good example of exactly the kinds of darkness and difficulty that scholars and humanists of Acuña's day counseled poets to avoid. There are other rough spots, as well: the jerky accents of line 3 ("cesó el dulce estilo que primero," where the accent on the "ó" of "cesó" forces a pause between it and the "e" of "el," and thus disrupts the flow of the line) and wordiness in line 13 ("y tomándola dellos tal, que en

---

3. All poetry by Acuña quoted in this book is taken from the Díaz Laríos edition.

suma"). At the level of content, the poem contradicts our expectations of a Renaissance sonnet by framing neither a statement of love nor a readily apparent allegory of the court.

Sonnet 45 may fail to meet conventional expectations of what a *good* sonnet is, then; but it is nevertheless an interesting sonnet, and a useful one with which to begin to consider the ideologies that were attached to the new Italianate lyric forms adopted by Spanish courtiers in the sixteenth century. In the first place, the poem foregrounds the relationship between forms of poetry and forms of men. Its plot is the speaker's trajectory from medieval lover to warrior hero to courtier, as each of these identities is conferred and described by lyric discourse: the epic and ballad that inscribe "armígero son" (lines 1–2), the courtly *dolce stil nuovo* ("el dulce estilo;" 3–4), and finally, the poetry of arms and letters, the cycle of "now the sword, now the pen" that is the ideal for the Renaissance courtier (9–14). Along the way, the poem stages a comprehensive statement of what Norbert Elias would call the "courtierization" of a Spanish knight. In his classic series of essays on "the civilizing process," Elias described a late medieval European tendency in which formerly independent knights were induced and coerced into renouncing their rights to raise private armies and wage internal wars, handing the "monopoly on violence" over to the king (*Power and Civility*, 104–16, 258–69). In Acuña's Sonnet 45, the speaker narrates a version of this process as a seemingly natural progression,[4] the maturing of a rough-and-tumble man's taste as it develops under the guidance of a thoughtful friend. However, closer examination of the poem reveals that his metamorphosis is not at all natural. On the contrary, it entails the self-conscious and deliberate *naturalization* of a set of discourses and practices that have been imposed from the outside and that are formed in response to the political structure and the ideologies of

---

4. This progression anticipates Elias's narrative, in that it posits a tension in lines 2 and 3 between the *dolce stil nuovo* and the poetry of the unrestrained knight-warrior. Elias discusses the rise of the discourse of *fin amours* and chivalric service as a model of "pacifying conduct" whose purchase on the culture of knighthood in the eras leading up to the full flowering of European absolutism in the seventeenth century is a discontinuous process: "the web of interdependence into which the warrior enters at first is not yet very extensive or tight . . . At court, towards the mistress, he may deny himself violent acts and affective outbursts; but even the *courtois* knight is first and foremost still a warrior, and his life an almost uninterrupted chain of wars, feuds and violence" (*Power and Civility*, 260–61). Elias's reading of the ideological function of court poetry stops at the Middle Ages and the early Renaissance, with the "sweet" love song. What Acuña adds is the later stage of the courtier's pacification, in which his embrace of a Stoicism that is modeled variously on Cicero and Seneca further refines his techniques of self-restraint. Acuña associates the complete interpellation of the modern courtier with the humanist sonnet.

the nascent modern court.[5] These discourses and practices condition the speaker's status as "sólo" at the poem's close. Moreover, as we will begin to see shortly, they inflect his position with the types of double meanings that are generally attributed to the subject of modernity. In particular, he is attributed with a solitude that is not isolated and a self-sufficiency that is in fact radically dependent. The ingenuity with which this process has been framed (and masked) in Acuña's composition offers us a new way to evaluate Sonnet 45's relative success as a poem, although doing this requires shifting our expectations out of the conventions of Petrarchism to think a little more broadly about the ideological capacities of the sonnet form.

Courtly Subjects

Perhaps the best way to begin is by noticing the strong subtext of subjection and liberation that accompanies the speaker's self-reported narrative of his progress. His experience of medieval love and of war beats is described in terms of dependency. Writing in those forms, he follows the dictates of his muse, who is herself subject to the shifting attractions of different types of sound patterns, martial and sweet. Against this background, the sonnet is portrayed as the form that enables autonomy: from line 6, as the speaker begins writing sonnets, the verbs shift into the first person: "espero . . . levantarme . . . [espero] . . . dejar" (lines 6–7) and "pienso . . . enderezar" (11). This resituates agency from the muse to the speaker himself. Furthermore, the actions these lines convey portray him, first, as exercising mastery over his utterances and his labors and, second, doing so in a balanced way that we can associate with the judgment and sense of proportion that are a principal characteristics of the modern sixteenth-century courtier. The opening word of the poem's sestet, "así," or "thus" (9), establishes the reticent, moderate tone of the new ideal, and the second half of the poem continues to be marked as the voice of the quintessential Renaissance man, the stand-alone,

---

5. Among these discourses is that of perfect masculine friendship. As Ullrich Langer has discussed, sixteenth-century writers developed a rich discourse on the idealized relationship, more perfect even than Neo-Platonic heterosexual desire, "a relationship of good men with each other through their goodness" (*Perfect Friendship*, 20). Among the poetic conceits elaborated around perfect friendship is the play of presence and absence, solitude and accompaniment that we find represented in Acuña's "no me causa tristeza el verme sólo," for example. Friendship is central to the constitution of the subjectivity of the courtly speaker in Juan Boscán's lyric sequence as well. See my discussion in Chapter 2.

masculine-singular "I" represented by "sólo," which is, we might notice, the poem's last word.

On first pass, then, the orientation of the poem seems to be toward the production of the self-possessed modern courtier, the man "of arms and letters" idealized by Castiglione and adopted with particular fervor as a model by both traditional Spanish aristocrats and the new nobility made up of groups such as the *letrados*. However, several elements of the poem undercut such a reading. First of all, although the speaker lays claim to the position of a sovereign subject at the end of the poem, his autonomy is in fact entirely contingent upon the conventions of the sonnet form. If the poem had been composed as anything other than a sonnet—as a Provençal *cant*, a Castilian *romance*, a fragment of epic, or a last will and testament for that matter—the speaker might have been knocked from his position of "sólo" and swallowed up by the momentum of language as it proceeded on around him. It is the forced rule of sonnet closure, *in* syllable eleven, *of* line fourteen, *with* rhyme E, that positions him to have, and in fact, to *be*, the last word.

As a second point that undermines the speaker's autonomy, Sonnet 45 reflects the humanist fashion for lyric composition based on researched and scholarly imitation of literary models (*imitatio*).[6] Many of these models were ancient (Horace, Catullus, Ovid); others were more recent (Petrarch) and even roughly contemporary (Sannazaro, Bembo). But all of them were debated and subject to approval by scholarly authorities before they were admitted as legitimate sources for contemporary expression. Therefore, when Acuña's speaker identifies with the formula "con la espada a Marte . . . con la pluma . . . a Apolo" ("with the sword to Mars . . . with the pen . . . to Apollo") (9–11), this is an ambivalent act, a self-assertion that is enabled by a primary submission to linguistic, as well as political, authority. Sonnet 45 thus shifts the ground on which the poet stands, from traditions of poiesis to discursivity, or the imperative that a man be legible within a given social order. Poiesis implies the long continuum of the poetic creation of the world from its divine origins to the present, as that tradition is memorialized by *vates* and singers who preserve it in their songs.[7] In Sonnet 45,

---

6. On *imitatio*, see the classic study by Thomas M. Greene, *The Light in Troy*. On the applicability of Greene's ideas in Spain, see Cruz, *Imitación y transformación*.

7. "The Greek word . . . *poiesis* . . . conveys two kinds of creation: the inspired creation that resembles a godlike power and the difficult material struggle, the . . . *techne*, of making forms out of the resources available. . . . Poetic form made of language relies on rhythm and musical effects that are known with our entire bodies, carried forward by poets working out of tradition and carried over by listeners receiving the work" (Stewart, *Poetry and the Fate of the Senses*, 12).

the speaker presents himself as initially inhabiting this domain, as he and his muse are caught up in the martial beats of native Spanish war ballads and epic. But he breaks with it when he abandons song in the second quatrain to take up the modern poetic practice of imitatio.[8] Furthermore, as I have been suggesting, this account is aligned with a radical and equally modernizing change in his identity, which he represents as being shifted from nature to culture, so to speak, and reconstituted along the lines of the subject of discourse. The change becomes especially clear when we take into account that, despite what he says about his condition at the end of the poem, from line 5 forward the speaker is in fact *not* alone. In lines 1 through 4, he has been isolated with his muse, in the monadic state of the man who maintains a one-to-one relationship with the divine. But in line 5 he is joined by his friend and drawn into a circle of courtly peers. From that point forward, their attitudes and practices induce him to change his behavior, and they go on to condition his actions and his desire whether they are present or not. That is, the speaker *states* that he is not lonely because of how he spends his time (i.e., in the cycle of service to Mars and Apollo). The reason that this is not experienced as solitary service, however, is that it is completely socialized, structured through the formula that unites all modern courtiers under their new rubric as men of the sword and the pen. Thus the speaker's emergence into his masculine identity of sólo is actually his statement of having been absorbed into their ranks.

The connection that Acuña assumes between kinds of poetry and kinds of men may take a bit of explanation. Sonnet 45 builds on a tension that critics have long noted, namely, that in Spain, "Petrarchan forms had acquired a near-hegemonic cultural status, but . . . the power of the heroic Spanish past, whose lyric forms were not at all Petrarchan in nature, remained also to be reckoned with."[9] In medieval Castilian

---

8. Sixteenth-century defenses of poetry read references to the muse as attributing of poetry to the order of the divine in an ere "before" composing poems landed in human hands, and in human practices of fiction-making and imitatio. Encina, in the *Arte de poesía castellana,* refers to: "la dinidad de la poesía, que no en poca estima y veneración era tenida entre los antiguos, pues el esordio e invención de ella fue referido a sus dioses, así como Apolo, Mercuiro y Baco, y a las musas, según parece por las invocaciones de los antiguos poetas" (9) ("the dignity of poetry, which was held in no little esteem and veneration among the ancients, for the exordium and the invention of it was attributed to their gods, such as Apollo, Mercury, and Bacchus, and to the muses, or so it seems from the invocations of the ancient poets").

9. Cascardi, *Ideologies of History,* 248. Cascardi addresses the conundrum of poetic authority in the cultural era of exorcising the heroic tradition from poetry. See especially pages 247–85, which focus on Garcilaso de la Vega.

poetry of the type that the speaker abandons in line 5, the identity of the great Spaniard is based on his sword fighting. He fights for the ultimate benefit of the king and Christianity, but in an independent and sovereign way, as in the following scene in the *Poema del Cid,* in which the Cid comes to the aid of his friend in a battle with the Moorish king:

>Viólo Mio Çid, Ruy Díaz el castellano,
>acostóse a un aguazil que tenía buen caballo,
>dióle tal espada con el su diestro braço
>cortólo por la cintura, el medio echó en campo.
>A Minaya Álvar Fáñez íbalo a dar el caballo:
>"¡Cabalgad, Minaya, vós sois el mio diestro braço!
>Hoy en este día de vós abré grande bando;
>firmes son los moros, aún nos van del campo."
>Cabalgó Minaya, el espada en la mano,
>por estas fuerzas fuertemente lidiando
>
>(748–57)

[My Cid, Ruy Díaz the Castilian, saw this, / he seized a vizier who had a good horse, / he gave him such a blow with his right arm / that he cut him through the waist, he left half of him on the open field. / He went to give the horse to Minaya Álvar Fáñez: / "Gallop, Minaya, you are my right arm! / On this day, today, I have great need of you; / the Moors are strong, although they depart from the field." / Minaya galloped, his sword in his hand, / fighting with strength through their forces]

After winning the battle, the Cid sends Minaya to deliver the customary tribute to the king, but the poem makes clear that the decision to respect this custom lies with the Cid and that his choice to do so accrues to his honor:

>"¡Oíd, Minaya, sois mio diestro braço!
>De esta riqueza que el Criador nos ha dado
>a vuestra guisa prended con vuestra mano.
>Enviárvos quiero a Castilla con mandado
>de esta batalla que habemos arrancada,
>al rey Alfonso que me ha airado

quiérole enviar en don treinta caballos,
todos con sillas y muy bien enfrenados"

(810–17)

["Listen, Minaya, you are my right arm! / From this wealth the Creator has given us / take to your taste, with your own hand. / I want to send you to Castile with news / of this victory we have seized, / to the king Alfonso, who has affronted me / I wish to send him thirty horses as a gift, / all with saddles and very well bridled"]

In contrast to *diestro braço,* "now the sword, now the pen" is an early modern aesthetic topos conditioned by the political and social strictures that were being levied on where, when, and how far the courtierized aristocrat could raise his arm. As Acuña frames clearly in Sonnet 45, to identify with the formula implied a primary subordination to power, both in the form of the dictates of humanist imitatio and in the form of the new courtly fashions and codes of behavior that had been formed in response to the consolidation of crown control over its formerly spirited and unruly noble subjects.[10] Therefore, the courtier, generally, and the Spanish courtier, specifically, was a figure for the subjection of the aristocrat. It thus makes sense that his arm, the former symbol of his honor and his sovereignty, would be interpellated into an ever more stylized and ritualized formula in language. Nor is it surprising that the modern, sixteenth-century articulation of arms and letters would become a site for the emergence of symptoms of anxiety and ambivalence about the repositioning of the nobility within Spanish culture. In addition to Acuña's deployment of the topos, there is another telling example at the head of Sonnet 21 by Diego Hurtado de Mendoza (1504–1575):

Ahora en la dulce ciencia embebecido,
ahora en el uso de la ardiente espada,
ahora con la mano y el sentido
puesto en seguir la caza levantada

(1–4)

---

10. As we saw in Sonnet 45, to voice the term sealed a nobleman's embrace of the mediated existence that was the condition of his acceptance into the society of the nascent modern court, a society that was organized, in great part, to strengthen the bonds of mutual interdependence among aristocrats and make violence an ever less appealing recourse. See Elias, *Power and Civility,* 263–65.

[Now absorbed in the sweet science, / now in the use of the shining sword, / now with the hand and the mind / set upon following the roused hunt][11]

Mendoza's phrasing represents the speaker as entirely absorbed (*embebecido*) into a poetic discourse that governs the cycle of his activities: fighting, hunting, and writing sweet poetry. His wording serves as a counterpoint to Acuña's Sonnet 45, in which the speaker recounts the process of his absorption into precisely the mode of being that Hurtado de Mendoza's speaker describes.

In Sonnet 45, then, the speaker's adoption of the discourses and practices that are associated with the early modern court, and with the "new" lyric compositional techniques of Renaissance imitatio, is attributed with two effects: first, it deracinates the speaker, cleaving him off from native traditions and from the archaic and divine origins of culture that are represented by poetry understood as poiesis; second, it reconstitutes him from a state I earlier referred to as monadic into the split, dissembling figure of the courtier, whose legible exterior (legible via the established phrase "man of arms and letters") masks an interior that is subject to contradictory, hidden operations of motivation and meaning. These motivations are only partially available to view, when they appear in details of his speech. For example, in lines 7 and 8, the speaker does not simply leave off composing his love and war songs; he abandons them as *grosero,* or "crude." This elaboration of opinions we can assume he has received from his friend (who has, after all, drawn him into sonneteering in the first place) demonstrates the depth of his identification with the new culture of courtiership.[12] In a similar vein, the evocative word *armígero* (line 2) invites attention, as the speaker recalls how his muse was "Atenta al gran rumor . . . del *armígero* son" (1–2). *Armígero,* or "martial," is, as a rippling tetrasyllable, both the most elegant word in the poem and, as Díaz Laríos tells us, a relatively new one in Castilian usage (*Varias poesías,* 263, n. 2). This makes it a good candidate for reading as a sign of the speaker's ambivalence about his new posture of moderation and courtierized self-restraint.

---

11. Hurtado de Mendoza, *Poesía,* 276.
12. The detail is especially telling because of what Cascardi has noted as the "particular authority of judgments of taste" in early modern Spain. Taste, he notes, "depends upon the internalization of forms of authority that once were located elsewhere in the social sphere" (*Ideologies of History,* 12). For the complete discussion, refer to pages 133–60.

All told, as we begin to examine the complexity of the figure of the speaker as it is presented in this poem, we see that he begins to respond more and more to the paradoxical logic of the subject of power, as described by Judith Butler: "We are used to thinking of power as what presses on the subject from the outside, as what subordinates, sets underneath, and relegates to a lower order. . . . But if, following Foucault, we understand power as *forming* the subject as well, as providing the very condition of its existence and conditioning the trajectory of its desire, then power is not simply what we oppose but also, in a strong sense, what we harbor in the beings that we are" (2). In fact, the process that the speaker undergoes over the course of the poem tracks fairly systematically along the lines of post-structuralist accounts of the constitution and investiture of subjects, as this is theorized by writers such as Butler, Žižek, and, before them, Althusser and Foucault. In particular, the Althusserian scenario of interpellation—in which people are "hailed" by the law and "turn" to accept the terms of that hailing (Althusser's famous "Hey you!"), thereby simultaneously identifying with a summoning authority and performing their submission to it—corresponds to the process by which the speaker in the sonnet is hailed by his courtly friend and drawn into the fellowship of modern courtiers. Like the Althusserian subject, Acuña's speaker turns from a state of being that exists outside the social order (in that it is associated with the supernatural, asocial order of unmediated, one-to-one contact with the muse), accepting a new set of terms through which to define himself. And like the poststructuralist subject of discourse, once he has done this he inhabits a new mode of being, one that is profoundly mediated in that it is structured by the power relationships in the early modern court, as these relationships are disseminated through the fashionable discourses of arms and letters. Hence following Butler's formulation of the paradox of the subject, we can say that Acuña's speaker becomes "fundamentally dependent on a discourse . . . [he] never chose but that, paradoxically, initiates and sustains . . . [his] agency" (*The Psychic Life of Power*, 2). Furthermore, the Renaissance courtly imperative of sprezzatura dictates the graceful masking of the effort that it takes to participate in the life organized by these terms.[13]

Despite this dissembling, however, and despite the pressure that the speaker's new subject position exerts on the view he takes of his past experience, reframing it, as we have seen, into a narrative of liberation and autonomy, Sonnet 45 portrays an independent knight's subjection. This is

---

13. See the important rereading of sprezzatura in Berger, *The Absence of Grace*, 9–33.

thrown into relief by the condition of actual sovereignty he enjoyed in the first quatrain, the sovereignty of a poet who receives his inspiration from the muse and not from the select canon of writers whom his society deems appropriate for imitation in modern practice. By analogy, this is also his sovereignty as a warrior who fights when and where he wishes, and on his own behalf. In one respect, then, Sonnet 45 is an account of a poetic conversion that resembles the Italian trope of *vita nuova* that was popularized by Dante and Petrarch; however, the comparison extends only so far. In place of the metaphysics elaborated by the Italian humanists, Acuña inscribes a specifically worldly situation: the Spanish nobleman as he is caught up by two powerful and conflictive social orders, each of which bears a heavily freighted set of poetic conventions at its heart.

Rational Subjects

The structuring conceit that lies at the heart of Sonnet 45 is therefore the radical transformation of the identities of both the courtier and his poem as they are summoned into the dispositions of early modernity. Acuña aligns the disavowal of traditional song in favor of the short, discursive new lyric form with the nobleman's internalization of the notion of agency as "power on loan" from the authorities that surround him. Indeed, one additional signal of this internalization is his reduction of the diverse poetry traditional within Castilian culture to the single category of "armígero son." Another important poem, Sonnet 30, thematizes the intersection of the Renaissance rational mind and the sonnet form as the two act together to derive civilized and constant subjects out of a chaotic state of nature. At the start of the poem, the poetic order runs amok:

Sonnet 30

> Cuando era nuevo el mundo y producía
> gentes, como salvajes, indiscretas,
> y el cielo dio furor a los poetas
> y el canto con que el vulgo los seguía,
> fingieron dios a Amor, y que tenía
> por armas fuego, red, arco y saetas,
> porque las fieras gentes no sujetas
> se allanasen al trato y compañía;

después, viniendo a más razón los hombres,
los que fueron más sabios y constantes
al Amor figuraron niño y ciego,
para mostrar que dél y destos hombres
les viene por herencia a los amantes
simpleza, ceguedad, desasosiego.

[When the world was new and produced / a people like savages, indiscreet, / and the heavens gave furor to the poets / and the song for which the crowd followed them, / they pretended that Love was a god, and that he had / as his arms fire, a net, a bow and arrows, / so that those wild, unsubjected people / would distance themselves from his company, and from treating with him; / later, when men came to more reason, / those who were the wisest and the most steadfast / figured Love as a child, and blind, / to show that from him, and from those other men, / descends, as an inheritance, to lovers / simplemindedness, blindness, restlessness.]

This poem builds on the tension between the sonnet and the poetic traditions of song that also appeared in Sonnet 45. A simple paraphrase might run: "In the old days when the world was new, people were in thrall to their poets and their passions, but later, men came to reason and understood that love is infantile and makes one blind and restless." Reason schools the "wisest and most constant" men to a new image of Love, cutting him down to size so that the formerly powerful god is recast as a blind child. But reason is supported in this action by the principal structuring feature of the sonnet form, the *volta*, or "turn" a sonnet takes conventionally (in Italianate sonnets), at line 9, which is to say, after the quatrains and before the tercets.[14] The word *razón* appears at line 9, as the poem takes its turn: "Después, viniendo a más *razón* los hombres." Thus, both reason and the volta secure the civilized order that reigns in the second half of the poem.[15]

---

14. The rules of the sonnet, including comments on the variations in the location of the volta, are given below.

15. It is probably unintentional that one effect of the civilizing process as it is worked in Sonnet 30 is the transformation of a society of ungendered "peoples" into one governed by men ("*viniendo a más razón* los hombres, / los *que fueron más* sabios," lines 9–10). On the other hand, while humanists of the stamp of Castiglione and Boscán took public feminist positions, both in their writings (the perfect courtier is ultimately a woman) and their lives (Boscán seems to have had a genuine intellectual partnership with his wife, who edited his poetry and supervised its publication

In its essence, Sonnet 30 expands upon an element left undeveloped in Sonnet 45, namely, the trade-off of the supernatural inspirational force of the muse for the new poetry whose composition is based in imitatio, not inspiration. While he is captivated by his muse and her taste for martial beats, the speaker in Sonnet 45 is subject to the forces that are associated with a mythic order of creation whose point of reference exists outside of the contemporary social order, in the province of the divine that is the terrain of the muse. By the end of the sonnet, he has embraced a poetics that is based on man-made social conventions. In Sonnet 30, the scenario unfolds on similar grounds, but the scene of divine poetic inspiration is more fully elaborated. The quatrains are charged with powerful energies—passions, gods, furor. Traditional song is thus figured not only as "crude," but as overwhelming and maddening. In this light, the poem indicates that the containing pressures of reason, of constancy, and of the sonnet form rescue and secure a population previously cast as poetry's victims. The quatrains are held in check by the volta, by reason, and by the curtailing force of the tercets, but they loom and threaten from their position "above" the circle of order that has been established by the wise and steadfast men inhabiting the smaller space of the poem's second half. Therefore, whereas Sonnet 45 presents interpellation in the guise of the pleasures of fellowship and participation, Sonnet 30 offers interpellation's other face, a scene of chaos and threat that can be escaped only through the subjection of "wild," "indecent" peoples to the forces of reason and civilization.[16]

But in the same manner in which ambivalence is inscribed in the staging of the perfect courtier in Sonnet 45, as his sólo position is exposed as anything but solitary, Sonnet 30 injects a destabilizing note by means of its final word. "Desasosiego" ("restlessness"), even as it seemingly puts paid to the powers that the uncivilized peoples of the quatrains formerly ascribed to Eros, also subverts this containment, first by means of the rhythmic propulsion of its assonance as it is extended over five syllables; second, because restlessness is a shifty idea, and not a good one to introduce when the aim is closure. The advantage to the modern order, in which meaning

---

after his death), Acuña's poetic persona was that of a man's man. It seems entirely in keeping with the rest of his poetic opus that he would view the well-ordered society to be governed, not only by "constant" Senecan Stoics, but, specifically, by men.

16. The New World subtext that is suggested in Sonnet 30 only highlights the fact that this poem is treating the topos of "then and now" / "state of nature, civilized" as ideological. A New World subtext plays beneath references to savage and indecent peoples tamed by the civilizing forces that topple their gods and instill a new order that must remain watchful for threats of rebellion.

is determined by the wisest and most constant men, is that people are no longer driven wild by their poets and their frenzied, divinely inspired *canto*. But the disadvantage is that there is no more dancing. The restless final feet of Sonnet 30 return us once again to a vision of the sonnet as a constraining form, one that delivers peace and equanimity on its own terms, which impose an uneasy fit.[17]

Form and Politics

Sonnets 45 and 30 offer an unusual display of Renaissance wit. Composed with clear attention to the tonal and intellectual as well as formal conventions of the new courtly lyric (which was not very new by the time that

---

17. Another set of concerns arose around the issue of "song" in the sixteenth century, and while it is not specifically relevant to Sonnet 45, which is clearly referring to war ballads and perhaps to epics, it bears mentioning here. The rise of the *jongleur*, or the court singer, coincided historically with early phases of courtierization (for example, see Elias, *Power and Civility*, 77, on the Minnesanger). The discussion by Jeffrey Kittay and Wlad Godzich indicates how this figure participated in the shift I am tracking in this book between the poetics of Homer and those of Horace: "the *jongleur*, by means of his trained memory and what it stored, represented an important cultural institution. The texts, epic and otherwise, that were his stock-in-trade constituted the cultural patrimony of the collectivity.... His function, particularly at the beginning, was not to innovate or add to his patrimony but to preserve it . . . the audience of a performed *chanson de geste* was looking not for novelty but for something it already knew, presented in an effective and entertaining manner. The *jongleur* was judged not on the content of his recitations and songs, which in any case the audience was familiar with, but on the style of his presentations.... He had to be a master at the complex task of performing a narrative, as well as of reciting other forms of discourse . . . the way in which he fulfilled these expectations . . . showed him to be a keeper of tradition . . . a person worthy of credit and, therefore, one whose authority is not put into question" (*The Emergence of Prose*, xvi). In this formulation, the singer/jongleur is an individual who has assumed the responsibility for assuring that the structuring customs, laws, and truths continue to circulate and be disseminated within a given culture. With the coalescence of incipiently modern formations in European society, however, the authority of this type of singer erodes, and we begin to see the kind of transfer of poetic privilege that Grossman has identified with Horace. Kittay and Godzich continue: "as soon as the earlier collectivities become stratified in a new order of estates and even emergent classes, there is no longer a locus that is universally agreed-upon for the *jongleur* to occupy. In this new social order, the *jongleur* is increasingly dependent on members of the seigneurial class, and he soon finds himself sought after by embryonic bourgeois communities as well. No longer able to function as the depository of the entire collectivity, he will be called upon by powerful private or municipal patrons.... In other words he sells his authority . . . [to] individuals who use for their own ends the fact that the *jongleur's* discourse had not up to that point been subject to question on the grounds of truth" (ibid., xvi). The erosion of the poet's authority and the impact of that erosion on poetry was a significant preoccupation for writers such as Sánchez de Lima, who will be discussed later in this chapter. Boscán and Acuña appear to have been more preoccupied with the rival claims of various poetic forms on the social imaginary, but all told, anxieties about the power and the prestige of song were overdetermined in the sixteenth century.

Acuña was writing it), these poems also show Acuña's clear insight with respect to the elaboration and the dissemination of modernizing ideologies through the vehicle of poetry. On the one hand, they thematize the derivation of the sonnet as a distinct poetic kind among the genres (Sonnet 30). On the other, they highlight the discursive production of the courtier on the threshold of political and cultural modernity (Sonnet 45). We can attribute Acuña's sensitivity to the politics of form, to a general attentiveness of highly placed courtiers of his era to the discursive nature of culture, and to the ideological capacities of form and of language to establish the terms by which men (especially) were "read" by their peers, by their monarch, and by his ministers. However, it is also the case that Acuña's career kept him close to the seats of power, both in Spain and in Italy. In addition, Acuña was a nuanced reader and writer of poetry. Across the spectrum of his work we find that he was familiar with the rules and the implicit meanings of form—meanings both political and poetic. Moreover, he appears to have been interested in experimenting with the suitability and the adaptability of the various poetic genres to the ingenious linguistic effects that were expected from a court favorite of his standing. His best-known work is his paean to imperial power, Sonnet 94, "Ya se acerca Señor, o ya es llegada" ("Now approaches, Sire, or now has arrived"). In this poem, written to commemorate the victory of the forces of Philip II at Lepanto (1571), Acuña deployed the compacting pressure of the sonnet form and a stately pattern of repetition to frame a statement of the fulfillment of earthly and divine will under the just Christian sway of "un Monarca, un Imperio y una Espada":

Sonnet 94

Ya se acerca Señor, o ya es llegada
la edad gloriosa en que promete el cielo
una grey y un pastor sólo en el suelo,
por suerte a vuestros tiempos reservada.
Ya tan alto principio, en tal jornada,
os muestra el fin de vuestro santo celo
y anuncia al mundo, para más consuelo,
un Monarca, un Imperio y una Espada;
ya el orbe de la tierra siente en parte
y espera en todo vuestra monarquía
conquistada por vos en justa guerra

que, a quien ha dado Cristo su estandarte,
dará el segundo mas dichoso día
en que, vencido el mar, venza la tierra.

[Now approaches, Sire, or now has arrived / that glorious age promised by heaven / in which there is one will and one shepherd alone on the earth, / this was reserved for your age. / Now this great beginning, on this day, / sets out for you the end of your blessed desire / and announces to the world, to its consolation, / one Monarch, one Empire and one Sword; / now the orb of the earth feels in part, / and awaits to experience wholly, your monarchy / conquered by you through just war; / for to him to whom Christ has given his standard / will also be given that second, more fortunate day / on which, having conquered the sea, he conquers the earth.]

Whereas in Sonnet 45 the figure of the unified subject is presented in order to be called into question, in this sonnet Acuña capitalizes on the blocklike, compact nature of sonnet structure and on the links between the sonnet form and Renaissance rhetoric to frame something akin to a well-ordered paragraph. The portentous, prophetic tone of the "ya" ("now") that opens each quatrain and the first tercet sets the progress of the poem at a stately pace as it leads up to the climax of line 8's "un Monarca, un Imperio y una Espada" and beyond, creating a monument to imperial universalism.[18] In its alpha-omega totality, the short poem is impregnable.

There are other works that provide evidence of Acuña's sensitivity to both poetic and political registers of meaning and to how they intersected at court. During his travels with the emperor, in the late 1540s or early 1550s, he was invited to versify the Castilian prose version of Olivier de la Marche's *Le Chévalier Déliberé* (The Steadfast Knight) (1480). This poem was a Burgundian favorite, and the emperor himself had translated it into Castilian prose. Acuña combined scholarship, his skills in the various verse forms, and courtly perspicuity in composing his version, *El caballero determinado,* completed in 1551. He added stanzas that praised the Catholic kings, Philip the

---

18. As detailed by Díaz Laríos in *Varias poesías,* critics and historians have argued over whether this poem was dedicated to Charles (he cites Cossio and Morelli), or to Philip II after Lepanto (he cites Elliott and Rivers) (328). The theme of "just Christian war," a discourse developed by Philip II and his propagandists promoting universal monarchy, suggests the latter.

Fair, and Charles himself. Moreover, in choosing the verse form in which to set the text, he selected native Castilian *coplas,* and the reasons he gave for choosing to do so reveal an interest in comparative Romance poetics:

> Hizo se esta tradución en coplas castellanas, antes que en otro genero de verso, lo uno por ser este mas usado y conocido en nuestra España, para quien principalmente se tradujo este libro. Y lo otro porque la rima Francesa, en que el fue compuesto, es tan corta, que no pudiera traduzirse en otro mayor sin confundir en parte la traducion (40)

> [This translation was done in Castilian coplas, and not in another kind of verse, first, because this is more used and known in Spain, for which this book is principally translated. And, second, because French rhyme, in which this was composed, is so short that it was impossible to translate it into longer rhyme without confusing the translation]

In other poems, Acuña showed himself to be a witty critic. His "lira de Garcilaso contrahecha" ("the lyre of Garcilaso, unstrung") takes a poet to task for his lack of skill with the Italianate style.[19] The lyric he writes does not correspond to the structures of authority that govern the practice of imitatio, but "mueve el discreto a ira / y a descontentimiento, / y vos sólo, señor, quedáis contento" (3–5) ("moves the discerning man to anger / and to discontent, / and you alone, sir, remain contented"). Interestingly, Acuña is taking this "bad poet" to task for his failure to write appropriate heroic song:

> el fiero Marte airado,
> mirándoos, se ha reído
> de veros tras Apolo andar perdido.
> ¡Ay de los capitanes
> en las sublimes ruedas colocados,
> aunque sean alemanes,
> si para ser loados

---

19. Díaz Laríos (*Varias poesías*) suggests that the poet in question is Jerónimo de Urrea, who had also published a version of *El caballero determinado* in addition to a Castilian version of *Orlando Furioso* set in hendecasyllables. Díaz Laríos suggests that in light of Acuña's comments in the preface of his own version of de la Marche's text, he might have considered Urrea's work to be an abuse of the Italian style, 40–41.

fuera a vuestra musa encomendados!
. . . .
Que vuestra musa sola
basta a secar del campo la verdura,
y al lirio y la viola,
do hay tanta hermosura,
estragar la color y la frescura.

(13–20; 26–30)

[fierce and spirited Mars, / gazing on you, has laughed to himself / to see you wander lost after Apollo. / Ay! for the captains / who inhabit the celestial gyres, / even if they are Germans, / if they have been entrusted to your muse / for their praise! / . . . / For your muse is enough / to dry up the green from the field, / and to strip from the lily and the violet, / where there is such beauty, / the color and the freshness.]

As a writer and as a subject of the new Spanish court, then, Acuña was a man who thought carefully about the various types of political significance that could be attached to form. This makes him worth attending to when he frames statements about the sonnet. In poems such as Sonnets 45, 30, and 94, the principle is clear: Sonnets *formally* interpellate courtly subjects. The structure of the sonnet itself shapes and disciplines utterance into abbreviated and self-reflexive confessions of dependency and circumscribed agency, above and beyond a poem's particular content. For this reason, sonneteering, in Acuña's view, might better be termed sonnetization. More than a witty conceit, this notion has a formal logic. In order to see it, we need to recall some aspects of the sonnet in its origins.

Little Songs

When Giacomo da Lentino and his circle in the thirteenth-century Sicilian court of Frederick II developed their new "little songs," they did so by superimposing the short and pointed *sirma* over the limitless Provençal canzone.[20] Their combination had the effect of abbreviating the long form into

---

20. Oppenheimer objects to the attribution of the word *sonnet* to a derivative of *song*, pointing out that the Latin word employed by Dante for the form was *sonitus* (179–83). However, if we follow the more general history of the rise to prominence of the *poemi brevi* tracked by María José

a single-stanza poem, and this act of curtailing in turn had an immediate impact on how the resulting poem would achieve its effects of meaning. Court poetry commonly had, up to this point, run for numerous stanzas, in forms such as the *arte mayor, quintillas, octavas,* or *terza rima,* all of which are identified by means of the patterns of recurrence (assonance, beat) inscribed through their fixed schemes of rhyme and meter. But sonnets are primarily *short:* their characteristic rectangular shape is their most recognizable feature. Thus the new poem that was the sonnet in the fourteenth through the sixteenth centuries was to one degree or another "about" the necessity of ending. We have already seen two examples of the inventiveness with which a good sonneteer could draw the fixed number of syllables allotted to the poem into the service of its capacities of signification. In Acuña's Sonnet 45, the word *sólo,* by virtue of its position at the poem's end, represents both the declaration of the sovereign subject and the exposure of the illusory nature of that sovereignty. In Sonnet 30, *desasosiego* similarly calls the constancy of the subject of reason into question. In other well-known poems from the Spanish sixteenth-century canon, the ruled closure of the form is deployed to achieve other sorts of ingenious effects. Consider the baroque statement of the total annihilation of the body in death in Luis de Góngora's famous "Mientras por competir con tu cabello" ("While, in competing with your hair"): "en tierra, en humo, en polvo, en sombra, en nada" (14) ("in dirt, in smoke, in dust, in shadow, in nothing").

Equally important, the sonnet was, and remains to the present day, about reflexivity. The form is derived from the forced intersection of two slightly unequal statements. The first eight lines are allowed to gain momentum through the unfolding of two complete units of its rhyme pattern before being cut off by the last six lines, and this structure establishes the rhetorical template for a poetic utterance that breaks and turns on itself.[21] As we saw

---

Vega ("Poética de la lírica"), the specifics of one writer's terminology matter less than the broader constellation of qualities that became associated with the "new poetry" over time. Both Sonnet 45 and Sonnet 30 by Acuña reveal a preoccupation with the relationship of sonnet to song. Furthermore, as we will see in Chapter 2, his view had an anchor in the terms through which Juan Boscán introduced the Italianate new poetry into Castilian letters. On the history and evolution of the early sonnet, see Spiller (*The Development of the Sonnet,* 1–27), and also the informative and nuanced essay on the sonnet as genre, "Some Species of the Sonnet as Genre," by Elías L. Rivers (*Muses and Masks,* 33–61). The argument here is indebted to each of these thoughtful discussions.

21. Historians of the genre tend to agree that da Lentino made the 8 + 6 stanza a complete poem, but that Guittone d'Arezzo (1235–1294) established the **ABBA ABBA** rhyme scheme of the quatrains (the scheme did not hold as consistently in the English tradition). As many readers are aware, the rhyme scheme of the tercets of a sonnet vary from the Petrarchan **CDE CDE** through the English tendency to finish with a couplet.

in Sonnet 30, this break and turn, volta, changes the poem's direction and/ or tone. Present in all sonnets, either at line 9 (i.e., after the quatrains and before the tercets) or, less frequently, at line 13 (if the sonnet is composed in terms of 12 + 2, instead of 8 + 6), the volta introduces a comment on what has come before, in the manner of proposition-conclusion or figure-gloss.[22] Because the volta is so central to the sonnet, Michael R. G. Spiller can summarize: "To announce a theme, to change it, and to close it: these features are essentially part of the sonnet and, though they can be rearranged, they cannot be eluded. So a tripartite structure of discourse—statement, development and conclusion—belonging to a speaker whose *eloquentia* is the outgrowth of wisdom begins to appear on top of the binary structure of the octave and sestet" (*The Development of the Sonnet*, 17). Paul Oppenheimer makes a similar point and adds an important observation, namely, that the reflexivity and the argumentative nature of the sonnet are framed within a conceit of the self, and that this feature distinguishes the new type of poem from conventional court songs. Unlike other forms of poetry that presented suffering, pleasure, contradiction, and doubt in extended narratives that did or did not, beyond simply ending, reach closure, the sonnet form trained lament to dialectics and hence produced a discourse in which emotions were resolved by logic:

> When we consider that a good deal more music for other types of poetry has survived from Giacomo's time we are forced to question

---

22. Romance writers tend to set it between lines 8 and 9 (although this is not what happens in Francisco de Aldana's Sonnet 30, read in the Introduction); English writers tend to "turn" between lines 12 and 13, although both Wyatt and Sidney wrote their sonnets in the Italian style and placed the volta between the quatrains and the tercets. Critics have offered a number of explanations for the asymmetrical nature of the sonnet stanza and for the ratio of 8 + 6 that was its most common rule in the premodern and early modern era. Most of them agree that da Lentino and his circle were influenced by the intellectual culture of the Sicilian court, in which the study and practice of the arts of logic, music, and mathematics were actively encouraged. Most also point to the legalistic bent of da Lentino's circle (Spiller, *The Development of the Sonnet*, 17–18). Spiller links the asymmetry of the sonnet to the musical harmonies that da Lentino and his fellows were trying to import into written language. The eight : six proportions of the form imitated the lyric units favored by medieval singers (15–16). Oppenheimer underscores the connection of the sonnet to the *Timaeus* and to recent discoveries in mathematics (*The Birth of the Modern Mind*, 171–90). In his *Manual de versificación española*, however, Baehr observes that to identify the precise origins of the sonnet form in Italy is less important to scholars of the Spanish sonnet, since the form was brought into Castilian poetry in the sixteenth century (or in the fifteenth, if we take the *versos fechos al itálico modo* of Santillana into account). What matters most is how Spanish writers themselves understood the form, and in the case of Acuña, we can see clearly that it is circumscribed, rationalized song. He is working with Italian notions and also with the ideals for the form set out by Juan Boscán, as I will detail in Chapter 2.

whether the earliest sonnets were ever intended for music or public performance . . . the sonnet, as it was originally conceived, may have been intended less for public displays (in the sense of performance) than for private encounters between reader and poem. . . . Giacomo's earliest sonnets, while revealing an enormous debt to certain troubadour attitudes toward love, break sharply from troubadour poetry in their insertion of a "turn" within a stanza; their dialectical resolution of emotional problems within a single stanza . . . their indifference to a mass audience, or even to an audience of more than one; their reduction of the two personae of troubadour love lyrics to one . . . herald . . . a departure from the tradition of lyrics as performed poems and introduces a new, introspective mode. (186–87)

Oppenheimer's identification of the fundamentally private nature of the sonnet form is helpful in understanding the early modern trope of sonnetization. However, we need to qualify it somewhat, since to identify the form with an introspective poetic persona and with intimate communications between poem and reader is not to remove it from the sphere of politics. On the contrary, the two sonnets we have read by Acuña are ruminative pieces about the modern subject's dependency on discourse, and most of the writers discussed in this book share similar insight into the structuring effects of language. Furthermore, as I noted earlier, one of the principal ingenious flashes of wit (*agudezas*) in Sonnet 45 is the exposure of the speaker's claim to solitude and self-sufficiency as false consciousness, a misrecognition of the status of his conventions of speech. Sonnet 30 turns on the tendency of rational discourse to confine "peoples" into gendered "subjects of knowledge": consider the lines "viniendo a más razón los hombres, / los que fueron más sabios y constantes" (9–10) ("when men came to more reason, / those who were the wisest and most constant"). Both poems foreground the courtly subject's interpellation by the discourse of the private individual, an interpellation that imposes an artificial, artful, and even "artlessly artful" regulating form over states of being variously associated with unsubjected and natural states.

The difference between the view that Oppenheimer seems to be positing and what we find in early modern Spanish poetry is perhaps best understood within a historical context. In the first half of the sixteenth century, the humanist investment in reason as the means by which men could master their passions and "civilize" themselves shifted the orientation of the sonnet from a medieval-scholastic mode to the modern system of thought that granted increasing power to the idea that the self could be mastered and contained by the operations of reason. While the form maintained a connection to scholastic argument, it also became associated with constraint. Thus, when Juan Boscán introduced his new poetry to Spanish readers, he praised it as capable of framing "any type of material whatsoever." A number of years later, Fernando de Herrera would expand on Boscán's words:

> Es el Soneto la más hermosa composición, de mayor artificio y gracia de cuantas tiene la poesía italiana y española. Sirve en lugar de los epigramas y odas griegas y latinas, y responde a las elegías antíguas en algún modo, pero es tan extendida y capaz de todo argumento, que recoge en sí sola todo lo que pueden abrazar estas partes de poesía, sin hacer violencia alguna a los preceptos y religión de la arte, porque resplandecen en ella con maravillosa claridad y lumbre de figuras y exornaciones poéticas la cultura y propiedad, la festividad y agudeza, la magnificenica y espíritu, la dulzura y jocundidad. (263)

> [The sonnet is the most beautiful composition, and of the greatest artifice and grace of all of those in Italian and Spanish poetry. It serves in place of epigrams and the Greek and Latin odes, and responds to the ancient elegies in a certain way, but it is so extensive and capable of any argument that it gathers into itself all that these other kinds of poetry can embrace, without doing a single violence to the precepts and the doctrine of the art, because in it shine forth with marvelous clarity and light of figures and poetic adornments, culture and propriety, festivity and wit, magnificence and spirit, sweetness and humor.][23]

As Gary J. Brown noted some time ago, the association between the epigram and the sonnet was particularly marked in Spain. We should bear in mind that while the Italianate new lyric was introduced into Spain in a manner similar to what took place in England and France—that is to say, in conjunction with Petrarchism, and with prescriptions for reformed practices of writing through scholarly research and imitatio—many Spanish writers

---

23. Quotations from the *Annotaciones* are taken from the Pepe and Reyes edition, although I have modernized the spelling.

did not engage with the sonnet as a building block in the construction of a Petrarchan lyric sequence, but rather foregrounded its formal tendencies toward regularization and its association with emergent discourses of reason. Thus early modern defenses such as the ones shown above claimed for the sonnet—and for the new lyric, or poemi brevi, generally—the status of a new poetic genre: a short poem whose excellence and suitability to adoption by the elite was based on its capacities to contain the principal elements of poetry within an abbreviated space.

This idea marked a significant shift from earlier arguments that had identified the nobility of a poetic form as residing in its capacities to represent the whole of poetic tradition. In *De vulgari eloquentia,* Dante had argued that of the vernacular forms, the canzone was the noblest, because

> in artificiatis illud est nobilissimum quod totam comprehendit artem; cum igitur ea que cantantur artificiata existant, et in solis cantionibus ars tota comprehendatur, cantiones nobilissime sunt, et sic modus earum nobilissimus aliorum. Quod autem tota comprehendatur in cantionibus ars cantandi poetice, in hoc palatur, quod quicquid artis reperitur in omnibus aliis, et in cantionibus reperitur; sed non convertitur hoc. Signum autem horum que dicimus promptum in conspectu habetur; nam quicquid de cacuminibus illustrium capitum poetantium profluxit ad labia, in solis cantionibus invenitur. (2.3.32–41)

> [among things made according to an art the most noble is that which embraces the whole art. Therefore, since things which are sung are made according to an art and since only in *canzoni* is the whole art embraced, *canzoni* are the noblest, and thus their form is the noblest of all. And that the whole art of singing in poetry is embraced in *canzoni* is evident from this, that whatever of art is found in all others is found also in *canzoni,* but not vice versa. And there is clear evidence before our eyes for these things which I say: for whatever from the pinnacle of illustrious poetizing minds has flowed to the lips, is to be found only in *canzoni.*] (Botterill, 97–99)

The difference between Dante's view and the words of Boscán and Herrera is marked. Dante's remarks address a poetry that is still conceived in terms of the plenitude and a sense of connectedness to origins, sources, and the whole art that is implicit in the idea of poiesis. Boscán and Herrera draw Spanish poetry over a threshold of modernity when they locate wholeness within a self-contained fragment and base poetic excellence on a given form's ability to *replace* originals with representations. Herrera's passage, especially, displays the double edge of fantasies of poetic containment.[24] The new poetry functions as a container in that it gathers in, but it is also a container that cuts the sonnet off from the processes encapsulated in the idea of poiesis: the new poem "serves in place of" (*sirve en lugar de*) other poetic genres, whereas Dante sought a poem form that could comprehensively include them.[25] This is a radical shift, albeit one that is admittedly harder to see from the perspective of our present-day culture, in which poetry occupies a less central place than it did in the sixteenth century. It entails, as Acuña has shown, the disavowal of an entire category (armígero son) and is tenable only within the greater social transformation in which displacement and representation, generally, are valued over nature. From the perspective of the new view, it is acceptable to displace the long tradition of native culture preserved and transmitted in "the whole art" of the illustrious poets (i.e., the heroic tradition) in favor of Herrera's graceful, festive, witty, spirited fragments. That is to say, the success of the sonnet as a poetic form was contingent on a wider cultural context of courtierization, as well as on a nobility that was willing to accept not only subordination within court hierarchies of dependency and service, but also the burden of disguising subjection in the continuous exercise of an effort to please (the discourse of sprezzatura). How suitable, then, that the principal source text for Herrera's passages on the sonnet form was penned by that early self-fashioned prince, Lorenzo de' Medici. In his *Comento de' miei sonetti* (1490?), Lorenzo openly declared himself to be resituating virtù from the domain of greatness to that of "difficulty." He thereby shifted the grounds upon which both poetry and men should be judged, clearing the way for future elaborations of the overlap between the sonnet and the courtier: "mi s'forzerò mostrare, tra gli altri modi delli stili vulgari

---

24. The contemporary critic and poet Juan Barja has written compellingly on the powers of the sonnet form to include, exclude, and generate. See "El destino de Sí: El soneto como forma material."

25. It is difficult to determine whether or not Boscán's swerve from Dante was intentional; however, Alicia Colombí-Monguió has argued convincingly that Boscán's knowledge of most Italian humanism was likely received secondhand, from friends such as Navagero and Castiglione ("Boscán frente a Navagero"). What can be said of Boscán's formulation and of the "Letter" overall is that he successfully positions the new lyric as the ideal poetic solution to modern Spanish courtiership, as it was governed intellectually by the discourses of sprezzatura and imitatio, and politically by the imperative to contain the power of the *diestro braço*.

e consueti per chi ha scritto in questa lingua, lo stile del sonetto non essere inferiore o al ternario o alla canzona o ad altra generazione di stile vulgare, arguendo dalla difficulta: perchè la virtù, secondo e filiosofi, consiste circa el difficile" (585) ("I will try to show that among the verse forms usually available to those who have written in Italian, the style of the sonnet is not inferior to terza rima, the canzone, or other vernacular genres. I will base my argument on the difficulty of composing the sonnet, for *virtù, according* to the philosophers, entails that which is difficult") (*A Commentary,* 112). Later in the same text he asserted that "il verso vulgare essere molto difficile, e, tra gli altri versi, lo stile del sonetto difficillimo, é per questo degno d'essere in prezzo quanto alcuno degli altri stili vulgari" (587) ("verse in the vernacular is difficult, and that among the other verse forms, the composition of the sonnet is the most difficult, and because of this, it is as worthy of being esteemed as any other genre in the vernacular") (ibid., 113).

Critics have discussed Lorenzo's counter to Dante as signaling a new and cosmopolitan attitude about classical rules of decorum as he elevates the virtues of complexity over those of expansive length ("new" in the sense that the sonnet, a form that did not exist in the time of the ancients, can assume pride of place within a hierarchy of poetry that is weighted significantly in favor of the lyric). What has not been pursued fully is the significance of shifting virtù from the domain of greatness to that of difficulty, but with this move Lorenzo was courtierizing poetry in a manner equivalent to the displacement of the hero by the complexified, interiorized courtly subject. The substitution is emphasized throughout Herrera's elaboration of Lorenzo's comments, however. For example, in the passage quoted above, Herrera elaborates on the festive and graceful characteristics of the sonnet in order to invite comparison with the qualities of the ideal courtier. But the passage in which he expands on Lorenzo's endorsement of the virtues of brevity is also telling:

> Y en ninguno otro género se requiere más pureza y cuidado de lengua, más templanza y decoro, donde es grande culpa cualquier error pequeño; y donde no se permite licencia alguna, ni se consiente algo, que ofenda las orejas, y por la brevedad suya no sufre, que sea ociosa, o vana una palabra sola. Y por esta causa su verdadero sujeto y materia debe ser principalmente alguna sentencia ingeniosa y aguda, o grave, y que merezca bien ocupar aquel lugar todo; descrita de suerte que parezca propia y nacida en aquella parte, huyendo de la oscuridad y dureza, mas de suerte que no

descienda a tanta facilidad, que pierda los números y la dignidad conveniente. (266)

[And in no other genre is there required more purity and caution of tongue, more moderation and decorum, where whatever small error is a great fault; and where no license whatsoever is permitted, nor is anything condoned that offends the ears, and for its brevity it does not suffer a single vain or idle word. And for this reason its true subject and material should be principally an ingenious and witty sentence, or a grave one, and let it well deserve to occupy its whole space; described in a manner that appears proper and born to that place, fleeing darkness and difficulty, but in a way that it does not descend to such facility that it loses the measures and dignity suitable to it.]

With the advent of modern systems of thought and of government in Spain, the gravitas, the authority, and the physical agency of the old-style nobleman—the knight—are displaced by new ideals of noble masculinity, ideals whose source is, overwhelmingly, the mind, with its capacities of nimble thought and rational self-subjection. The new virtues are gracefulness and judicious speech that cover over any persistent war-making desires that play beneath the courtier's civilized and contained surface. In this passage, and in other passages on the sonnet quoted earlier, Herrera describes the form as allegorizing not only the courtly subject, but also the *tension* between the two identities that the sonnet form emblematizes and calls into question, namely, the nobleman as abject hero and the nobleman as he is validated in his new festive and graceful form of the courtier.

As will be developed in Chapter 4, the complexity and the ambivalence with which Herrera viewed the sonnet form were informed by his view of the stakes of poetry in modern Spanish culture. A significant portion of his lyric and his writing on the lyric were aimed at testing the capacities of modern discourse to frame Castilian heroism in the new era that was celebrated in the wake of the so-called second Reconquest that was the victory at Lepanto (1571). It is also the case, however, that both Herrera's decision to use Lorenzo as a model and, it seems, the ways in which he enhanced his precursor's language were also informed by the juncture of historical and poetic circumstances with which the new lyric had been associated by Boscán. This context informed the ways that the poetry would be received and discussed through most of the century.

Caballeros and Cortesanos

Courtier, humanist, and admirer of Castiglione, Juan Boscán (1487–1542) introduced his new art of poetry as Spain was transforming itself from the newly minted and relatively insulated peninsular kingdom it had been under the Catholic kings to the seat of a trans-European and global empire. In a letter published posthumously in 1543—the famous "Carta a la duquesa de Soma," or "Letter to the Duchess of Soma"—Boscán claimed that the inspiration to compose a new style of poetry had come to him in 1526, during conversations held with a celebrated fellow courtier and humanist Andrea Navagero. Whether factual or not, his assertion positioned the new art on the threshold of old and new Spanish culture in two ways. The festivities held in Granada in 1526 marked a ceremonial endpoint to the struggles between the emperor and his Spanish subjects after a difficult period following his accession to the throne. Upon coming to power in Spain, the interventionist policies of Charles's Burgundian and Italian councilors had interfered with established networks of power and clientage on the peninsula. This infuriated members of some noble houses and the local ruling parliaments, the *cortes*. In addition to the clash of political cultures, the new monarch's eagerness to assume the positions of Spanish king *and* Holy Roman Emperor was viewed by many of his subjects as a sign of his relative disregard for Spain itself. These factors contributed to the rebellions of 1520–22, generally referred to as the *comuneros* revolts.[26] Open struggles and battles were followed by a period of alternating negotiation, repressions and placation, and the celebrations marking the emperor's 1526 marriage to Isabel of Portugal served as a useful ceremonial point of departure for a new era of peace between the ruler and his subjects: the bride had been chosen

---

26. On the revolts of the *comuneros* and the *germanías*, see Lynch, *Spain Under the Hapsburgs*. The insurrections of the nobility were probably also fostered by the loosening of crown control during the years preceding Charles's arrival in Spain. Between the death of Isabel the Catholic in 1504 and the coronation of her grandson, Charles V of Hapsburg and late of Mechlen (famously, on his arrival in Spain, he did not speak Castilian, although he later remedied this and made Spain his final home), warring factions of nobles promoted the causes of various rulers: the possibly "mad" Queen Juana of Castile (Charles's mother), Ferdinand of Aragon (who exercised intermittent powers as regent, both on Juana's behalf and on his own), and grandees such as the Duke of Nájera (Aram, *Juana the Mad*, 91–136). This patchwork of authority led to factionalization, but also to the strengthening overall of the local authority of the nobility, and the early years of Charles's rule were troubled by insurrections such as the revolts of the comuneros in Castile and of the germanías in Aragon. Aram's discussion of this period is detailed and especially useful.

by the *cortes*, which had stipulated as a condition of their pacification that they be permitted to choose their queen.[27]

As a point of reference, the wedding was useful to Boscán because it linked the new poetry to the spirit of new beginnings, more generally. Furthermore, since Boscán most likely composed the "Letter" in 1540 or 1541 (as he was preparing the text of the *Obras completas,* where the "Letter" appears in the preface to the Second Book), he was aware of the favorable view that his countrymen and peers now held of the emperor and his reign. It seems likely that Boscán hoped that his innovations in letters would be received with less suspicion if they were undertaken in a context of wider social and political change. But the *location* Boscán chose to assign to his inspiration was important as well. As a symbolic site, Granada was charged with a particular power. From the declaration of the successful Christian "Reconquest," in 1492, the city served as an icon of Spain and Spanishness. Boscán drew on Granada's historical significance as the linchpin of unified Christian Spain as he attempted to naturalize Italian poetics into Spanish culture. This rhetorical task was all the more important because of the mutual imbrication of poetry and identity in Castilian letters. From 1492, the Catholic kings had endorsed the view that Castilian political and military hegemony on the peninsula would receive important support from the establishment of a common language and a common culture of letters. Thus, famously, Isabella sponsored the first European vernacular grammar, Antonio de Nebrija's *Gramática de la lengua castellana* (1492), and an accompanying dictionary.[28] These projects reflected her ideals as a Christian humanist, but they also flowed into the gap torn into the cultural fabric of the peninsula with the expulsion of the Jews, the forced conversion of Spain's remaining Muslims, and the efforts to erase, wholesale, the vibrant poetic and linguistic traditions of multicultural Al-Andalus.[29] Indeed, the very term Reconquest indicates the importance of this ideological project to Spain's incipiently modern, postmedieval identity. While the victory of Christian forces over the remains of the Islamic empire in Granada in 1492 was indisputably a *conquest*—the final subjection of a culture that

---

27. Final pardons for the rebellions were issued in 1522 (Lynch, *Spain Under the Hapsburgs*), but the emperor and his councilors chose to capitalize on the ceremonial moment.

28. On Nebrija and notions of *translatio imperii* and *translatio studii,* see Navarrete, *Orphans of Petrarch,* 18–24.

29. On the ideological nature of post-1492 "Spain," see Resina, "The Role of Discontinuity." See also Fuchs, *Mimesis and Empire*. On the poetic repercussions of the expulsion of the Jews and the forced conversions of the peninsular Muslims, see Menocal, *Shards of Love,* 1–53.

had flourished on the Peninsula for more than seven hundred years—the term *Reconquest,* or *Reconquista,* served the patently ideological function of inscribing the new Castilian hegemony within the terms of a universalist Christian "always-already."[30] Epics and *romances,* or ballads, that recounted key events and battles from the centuries of struggle reinforced this new view of an essentially Christian and European Spanish identity, and Boscán himself participated in disseminating it in his remarks on the new poetic style. Comparing native Castilian forms to Petrarchan ones, he wrote: "Vi que este verso que usan los castellanos, si un poco asentadamente queremos mirar en ello, no hay quien sepa de dónde tuvo principio. Y si él fuese tan bueno que se pudiese aprovar de suyo, como los otros que hay buenos, no habría necesidad de escudriñar quiénes fueron los inventores dél" (*Obra completa,* 118–19) ("I saw that this verse that is employed by Castilians, if we want to sit down and look at it, there is no one who knows where it came from. And if it were so good that it could be approved on its own terms, as is the case with other ones that are good, there would be no necessity of scrutinizing who were its inventors"). In point of fact, the origins of Castilian verse were *not* hard to trace. In the *Diálogo de la lengua* (1533), Juan de Valdés engaged in an extended discussion of the origins of the Castilian language, touching on poetry and acknowledging the impact of Arabic on Castilian vocabulary.[31] But Boscán's statements are emblematic of the ambivalent process of acknowledgment and erasure by which

---

30. Resina has argued that Isabella and Ferdinand achieved the "integration of state and territory," but their military successes were made mythic by the discourse of Reconquest, which cast them as "giving second birth to a community legitimated by its alleged existence prior to the . . . scattering of national essence" ("The Role of Discontinuity," 284).

31. In 1575 Argote y Molina demonstrated little reservation about referencing the diverse cultures that informed the poetry of the present day. In his "Discurso sobre la poesía castellana" he invoked French, Catalan, Italian, Muslim, Morisco, and Turkish traditions of coplas and "great verse," as he discussed Castilian poetics. While his sense of license to do so was most likely influenced by the triumphalism that followed in the wake of the "Second Reconquest," the contrast between his representation of Castilian poetry and that presented by Boscán is notable. As one example of the *verso grande* (great, or long-lined, verse), he cites a Morisco lament over the fall of Granada: "desta cantidad son algunos cantares lastímeros que oímos a los Moriscos sobre la perdida de su tierra a manera de endechas, como son: Alhambra hanina gualcozor taphqui / alamayarali, ia Muley Vuabdeli") (229–34) ("from this group are some songs of lamentation that we have heard from the Moors about the loss of their land, written in the form of endechas, as in: Beloved and loving Alhambra, your fortresses weep, / O Muley Vuabdeli, they find themselves lost"). My translation of the lament is in fact a translation of the Castilian version of the poem provided by Argote ("Discurso sobre") in lines 249–50: "Alhambra amorosa, lloran tus castillos / O Muley Vuabdeli, que se ven perdidos." I discuss the impact of Lepanto on ideas about poetics in Chapter 4.

repressed histories are raised, aired, and subsumed into the foundational myths of a state.[32]

Yet while Boscán tapped into the fifteenth-century wellspring of Spanish identity in the "Letter," he also sought to use Granada and the ceremonial events of 1526 to legitimate new ideals for members of the Spanish nobility (and perhaps especially for Spanish noblemen) by setting the era of the Reconquest firmly in the past, and replacing old-style militaristic values with new codes of self-restraint and mental—as opposed to physical—prowess. A section in which Boscán describes the critics who attacked him for working in the new lyric style draws a distinction between garrulous Spanish knights and the men and women of his circle who enjoy a sophisticated and understated urbanity:

> poniendo las manos en esto, me topé con hombres que me cansaron. Y en cosa que toda ella consiste en ingenio y en juicio, no teniendo estas dos cosas más vida de cuanto tienen gusto, pues cansándome había de desgustarme, después de desgustado, no tenía donde pasar más adelante. Los unos se quejaban que en las trovas de esta arte los consonantes no andaban tan descubiertos ni sonaban tanto como en las castellanas; otros decían que este verso no sabían si era verso, o si era prosa, otros arguían diciendo que esto principalmente había de ser para mujeres y que ellas no curaban de cosas de sustancia sino del son de las palabras y de la dulzura del consonante . . . ¿quién ha de responder a hombres que no se mueven sino al son de los consonantes? ¿Y quién se ha de poner en pláticas con gente que no sabe qué cosa es verso, sino aquél que calzado y vestido con el consonante os entra de un golpe por el un oído y os sale por el otro? . . . Si a éstos mis obras les parecieren duras y tuvieren soledad de la multitud de los consonantes, ahí tienen un cancionero, que acordó de llamarse general para que todos ellos vivan y descansen con él generalmente. (116–17)

---

32. Notably, Charles V, Isabel, and their promoters also made use of the symbolic power of Granada. Royal biographers insisted that Philip II was conceived in the city, during the royal honeymoon. In addition, during the same stay, Charles ordered that the remains of his father, Philip the Fair of Burgundy, be removed from his mother's castle at Tordesillas for reburial by the tomb of Isabel and Ferdinand. His order reflected his desire to enhance his subjects' consciousness of his relationship to the Catholic kings, although in point of fact he was related to them through his still-living mother and not through his long-deceased father. On the politics of the reburial, see Aram, *Juana the Mad*, 97–101 and 132.

[setting my hands to this, I ran into men who tired me. And in a practice that depends entirely on wit and on judgment, neither of which have life apart from pleasure, once I became tired, I necessarily became displeased, and once displeased, I had no way of proceeding. Some complained that in the songs of this art the consonance did not proceed as openly, nor did it sound out in the manner of the Castilian songs; others said that they did not know if this verse was verse or prose, others argued, saying that this must be principally for women, who cared nothing for matters of substance but only for the sound of the words and the sweetness of the rhyme . . . who needs to respond to men who are not moved but by the soundings of consonance? And who needs to engage in conversation with people who do not know what verse is unless it be that which, shod and saddled with its consonantal rhyme, enters you with one blow to the ear, and departs with another? . . . If my works seem rough to these men, and they feel lonesome for a multitude of rhymes, they have a *cancionero* that kindly called itself "general" so that all men of that sort might live and take repose with it generally.][33]

The metaphor here relies on the fact that the copla forms favored by members of the nobility and contained in volumes such as the 1511 *Cancionero General* were composed in relatively short, accentual-syllabic lines that were governed by a close rhyme scheme. In contrast, the new Italianate poetry employed the more flexible rhyme schemes of the sonnet and the canzone. Furthermore, the hendecasyllabics in which they were composed were longer and did not rely on fixed rules of accent. On the one hand, Boscán's words frame a distaste for verse versus poetry that was shared by fellow humanists and writers throughout Europe. On the other, the trope maintains a specificity to its Spanish context. The galloping meters bring to mind *caballeros,* or old-style Castilian aristocrats: the highly

---

33. Translating this passage has posed a challenge, because of differences in English and Spanish vocabularies of rhyme and meter and also because questions of beat, rhyme, and measure were the subject of serious debate among sixteenth-century humanists. Navarrete has translated *consonantes* as "rhyme," but Spanish consonantal rhyme is based on whole syllables. This inscribes a rule of beat that is absent from the contemporary English understanding of the word. David Darst uses the rather awkward "consonantal rhyme" in his translation. I have decided to use the terms "consonance," "rhyme," and, in one case, when it is unavoidable, "consonantal rhyme," as I think they are indicated by the overall sense of Boscán's text.

regular, accentual-syllabic rhymed couplets and quatrains of the traditional Castilian coplas and *arte mayor* ride roughshod through the mind like warring knights; they strike the ear with blows (*golpes*) before slamming off and away. In this passage, the traditional poetry and its loutish defenders are bested by the tasteful, arch Boscán, by the duchess to whom he writes, and by their circle—a group whose identity is fashioned "entirely" of judgment and wit. But when this group pokes fun at the old verse and its champions, their motivation is not simply aesthetic. Rather, it is informed by the history of rebellions such as the *comuneros* revolts and the processes of subjection and courtierization of the traditional nobility that were ongoing during the sixteenth century.[34] Evidence for the importance of this context appears in a debate that was being carried on about the Italianate hendecasyllable and the traditional, twelve-syllable line of the great medieval Castilian verse, the arte mayor. The Castilian courtier and poet Cristobal de Castillejo (1480?–1550), for example, dismissed Boscán's claims that he was introducing a new poetry to Spain by asserting that Spain's traditional poets had been writing in this ostensibly new line form all along. In his *Reprensión contra los poetas que escriben en metro italiano* (Reproof Against Poets Who Write in Italian Meters), Castillejo imagines the famous poet Juan de Mena, author of the celebrated medieval poem *El laberinto de la fortuna* (The Labyrinth of Fortune), returning from the dead to turn up his nose at claims on behalf of the new art:

> Juan de Mena, como oyó
> la nueva trova polida,
> contentamiento se mostró,
> caso que se sonrió
> como de cosa sabida,
> y dijo: "Según la prueba,

---

34. Boscán's relationship to Castilian hegemony seems to have been ambivalent. A page in the court of Ferdinand of Aragon, he was a supporter of the emperor and a proponent of the Castilian language. His interest in social reform, however, seems to have been directed primarily at reinscribing the nobility as a humanist and cultured elite, as opposed to an elite whose membership derived from title and traditional rank. A subtler plane of reference in the "Letter" suggests some identification with his Aragonese heritage, however. Boscán writes of "nuestra España" at one point, and it seems likely that here he is suggesting that with the rise of modern culture in Spain, Castilian pride would give way to an idea of Spain that encompassed all the Christian kingdoms in a homogenous totality. Critics have also wondered if Boscán's praise of Ausiàs March was intended to remind his readers of the important role played by a subject of the Crown of Aragon in transmitting Provençal song into Spain.

once sílabas por pie
yo hallo causa por qué
se tenga por cosa nueva,
pues yo mismo las usé"

(157–65)

[Juan de Mena, when he heard / the new, polished song, / showed contentment, / such that he smiled, / as in recognition, / and said, "According to the example, / eleven syllables a foot / I find cause to wonder / why it is taken for a new thing, / for I myself used them"]

Actually, two features separate the arte mayor from the hendecasyllable. First, the arte mayor line has prescribed patterns of stress—classically, an emphasis on syllables five, eight, and eleven—whereas the new hendecasyllable was *suelto,* or free of those restrictions.[35] Second, defenders of vernacular lyric tradition linked the arte mayor to "heroic" Greek hexameter, whereas Boscán's aim for the new lyric was that it be, precisely, *not* heroic, but rather prudent and circumspect in the manner of the chastened Hapsburg courtier. Thus, unlike many of his contemporaries, Boscán did not defend his new line on the basis of its connections to hexameter, and he made only the vaguest and most general reference to the Greeks when he provided the conventional humanist genealogy of the worthy provenance of the new poetic forms. Rather, in the manner that would be picked up on

---

35. In his *Epístola Séptima,* López Pinciano has Fadrique praise the arte mayor as having more charm than the hendecasyllable because of its stress pattern: "hay un poco más primor, porque no sólo ha de tener sus sílabas, que son doce, mas ha de quebrar con el acento en ciertas partes y, no quebrando, no es metro" (289) ("it has more charm, because it does not only have to have its syllables, which are twelve, but must also break the accents in various parts, and with no break there is no meter"). "Torno, pues, al metro castellano de doce sílabas; a éstos diría yo verso o metro heróico de mejor gana, y con más justa razón, que no al italiano endecasílabo suelto, que se ha alzado con nombre de verso heroico. Entre los italianos que lo sea en hora buena, pues que ellos no tienen verso mayor y de más sonido; mas nosotros que (de más sonido y más correspondiente al exámetro) razón será que no quitemos a la nuestra el nombre de heroico, por le dar a la nación extranjera italiana, a la cual confieso mucho primor en todo y en la poética mucho estudio; mas no mayoridad en este género de poesía" (290) ("Now I turn to Castilian meter of twelve syllables; I would call those heroic verse or meter more willingly, and with more reason, than I would the free Italian hendecasyllable, which has been raised to the name of heroic verse. Among the Italians, may they benefit from that, since they do not have a greater verse with more sonority; but for us [there being more sonority and more correspondence with the hexameter], we should not take the name heroic away from our line, to give it to that foreign Italian nation, of whom I will confess much charm in everything and much study in their poetry; but not superiority in this kind of poetry").

by later writers (such as Acuña and Herrera, for example), Boscán presented the Italianate hendecasyllable as an appropriate, tasteful, and restrained substitute for the crude and boisterous heroic line. Implicitly, then, the difference between the new line and the old one was the difference between the warrior and the cosmopolitan, the stubborn knight and the flexible courtier. It was the difference between the "new" man and the caricature described in an anecdote offered by Ludovico in *The Book of the Courtier*:

> a worthy lady once remarked jokingly, in polite company, to a certain man . . . whom she honored by asking him to dance and who . . . refused . . . protesting that such frivolities were not his business. And when at length the lady asked what his business was, he answered with a scowl, "Fighting. . . . " "Well then," the lady retorted, "I should think that since you aren't at war at the moment and you are not engaged in fighting, it would be a good thing if you were to have yourself well-greased and stowed away in a cupboard with all your fighting equipment so that you avoid getting rustier than you are already." (58)

Not all sixteenth-century poets engaged with the nuances of the new poetics. Obviously, some were interested in the aesthetic possibilities presented by the Italian style, some participated in sonneteering as courtly social exchange, and some enjoyed the play of rhetoric and wit foregrounded in the new art. However, Boscán's arguments fixed the specificities of poetics into the ideological networks by which the nobleman and his psyche were being remapped in the early modern social imaginary, and the link he forged between the legitimation of a new poetry and the new Spanish subject met with remarkable success.

It bears underscoring, however, that this link was founded in *form*. Reading Spanish writers for what they reveal about the new lyric as form yields a significantly different picture from the one we gain when we read for discussions of content. Sánchez de Lima's *El arte poética en romance castellano* (The Art of Poetry in Vernacular Castilian) (c. 1580), opens with the skeptical Silviano addressing his friend Calidonio:

> SILVIANO: . . . sepamos (si se puede saber) en que veniades ahora imaginando: porque mirando en ello, de rato en rato os veíamos diferentes señales en el rostro, cuando de triste, y cuando de alegre: unas veces muy confiado, y otras como de hombre que quiere

desesperar: y pareciómе que veniades entre vos ruminando algunas palabras, que por estar lejos no pude entender.
CALIDONIO: venia trazando entre mi un soneto, aunque me parece que en octava cuadrada quedara mejor, por ser más breve.

(16–17)

[SILVIANO: . . . let us find out (if it is possible to know) what it was you came along just now imagining: because looking at you, from time to time we saw different signs in your face, now sad, now happy: a few times very confident, and others, in the manner of a desperate man; and it seemed to me that you came ruminating with some words to yourself, but because I was distant, I could not hear them.
CALIDONIO: I came sketching a sonnet to myself, although it seems to me that it would fit better within an octave, since that is shorter.]

Set pieces such as this one treat the sonnet as trivial, and often end with its dismissal: in the passage quoted above, Calidonio ponders setting his thoughts in *octavas cuadradas*. In another well-known example, Aretino, in *The Book of the Courtier*, suggests that he and his fellow courtiers spend the evening in sonneteering, but his idea is politely rejected in favor of a colloquy—"So then, everyone having applauded happily and praised Aretino's sonnet, after a moment's conversation signor Ottaviano Fregoso, whose turn it was to speak, began laughingly as follows" (49). The conversation moves off in a different direction. If the sonnet is not treated as frivolous, it is often associated with madness. In Sánchez de Lima's dialogue, after Calidonio tells Silviano that he has been thinking of a sonnet, Silviano replies, "Os tengo lastima a todos los Poetas: porque todo el día os andáis con mas sobra de locura que de dinero" (17) ("I pity all poets: because you wander all the day long with a greater surfeit of madness than of money").

When these statements are read alongside the poetry of Acuña and the remarks of Boscán, Lorenzo, and others, they allow us to grasp the two seemingly contradictory discourses that the sonnet form inspires. Earlier, we encountered a group of writers who focused on the form *as* a form and who observed, with a range of responses, its capacities to abbreviate and complexify song, effecting alterations in the nature and purpose of poetry and of men. In contrast, Castiglione, Sánchez de Lima, and like-minded writers dismissed the sonnet as so much distracting fluff.[36] Given the close association I have been tracking between the rise of the sonnet and the process of courtierization, it may come as little surprise that I propose that the discourses through which the form is deemed inconsequential themselves invite closer scrutiny. Sonnets 45 and 30 raise a question about whether the discourse that associates the sonnet form with shallow and frivolous content is not in part a sleight-of-hand that distracts from what is truly ideological and coercive about the new lyric. Using Acuña's perspective to guide our own, we can find evidence in Sánchez de Lima's dialogue, in particular, of the ideological nature of associations of the sonnet with the trivial and the frivolous. As the two interlocutors warm to their theme, Calidonio responds to Silviano's assertion that all poets are mad by distinguishing between old and new poets:

> Engañado vives en eso, porque antes no hay mayor delicadeza de ingenio, que es la de un Poeta, si es verdaderamente Poeta: que los que son de a quince en libra, no merecen este nombre, pues está claro que no le merece, sino él que ha rompido su lanza, y muchas lanzas en el campo, o campos de los buenos ingenios, que son las academias, y universidades: y también en otros tiempos lo solían ser los cortes de los Reyes, y Príncipes, y se tenía en tanto un hombre de buen juicio y claro entendimiento, como era razón: que se sabe del excelentissimo poeta Garcilaso de la Vega, don Jorge Manrique . . . y otros muchos grandes, que nunca por la pluma dejaron la lanza, ni por la lanza la pluma: antes lo uno con lo otro les adornaba tanto, que por esto y por la afabilidad con que trataban a los inferiores, fueron tan amados, queridos y acatados de todos, que no lo son tanto deste nuestro. Y es la causa, el desdeñarse hoy día los Príncipes, y grandes de las ciencias: porque han tomado en caso de honra, que un señor sea buen escribano, buen arithmético, buen músico, o tenga otra alguna gracia, las cuales querían que tuviesen sus criados. (18–19)

> [You are living deceived by this view, because there is no greater delicacy of mind than that of the poet, if he is truly a poet: for fifteen in a pound do not deserve this name, since it is clear that one does not deserve it if he has not broken his lance, and many

---

36. They were also thinking of the court lyrics of the jongleur. See note 17.

lances, on the battlefield, or on the battlefields of the great minds, which is to say, the academies and the universities; in other times, they were also the courts of the kings and princes, and a man of good judgment and clear understanding was much esteemed, as was right; this is known from the most excellent poet Garcilaso de la Vega, from don Jorge Manrique . . . and many others who never set down the lance for the pen, nor the pen for the lance; instead, they were so adorned first by one and then by the other, that for this and for the affability with which they treated their inferiors, they were so loved, desired, and welcomed by all, as those of our time are not. And the reason is that nowadays, the princes and the great men disdain the fields of knowledge; because they have made it a point of honor that a man who wishes a good writer, a good mathematician, a good musician, or another talent, wishes his servants to possess those talents.]

What stands out about these passages when we are reading for sonnetization is how this dialogue, which initially seems so dismissive of the sonnet—and of short and "mad" lyric forms more generally—manages to make a point very similar to the one made by Sonnet 45, that is, the embrace of sonneteering marks a watershed for the nobleman's inclusion in a modern social order at the expense of his virility and agency. The dialogue singles out the sonnet as the form that gives poetry its reputation for madness and foolishness and then presents a series of metaphors that are structured around the cultural eclipse of Spain's "real men," those who did their own fighting and writing, instead of outsourcing it to their servants, or social inferiors (the reference is to the lettered commoners, or the letrados who occupied increasingly important political positions with the rise of the modern and bureaucratized court). A principal effect of the dialogue, when it comes to the sonnet, at least, is the representation of the form as symbolic of the decadence and the laziness of the modern nobility. But we can make two points here. First, repeating the message about the uselessness and the lack of substance of the contemporary nobleman only reinforces the politicized discourse of a superfluous nobility, a discourse that will be elaborated in seventeenth-century drama, especially. Second, poems such as Acuña's Sonnet 45, as well as many of the other works we will encounter in this book, suggest that attributing the emasculating and enervating properties of the sonnet to its content is misleading, since what matters most about the form *is* its form, the fact that it elevates abbreviation and self-reflexivity not only to the status of art, but to the status of a noble art—even as, in order to take up the pen, Spain's sonneteers must momentarily set down their swords.

Its Italian origins in abbreviated song, its Spanish origins in the sixteenth-century culture of humanist Renaissance and Hapsburg courtierization, the Spanish sonnet developed an identity based on the victory of the civilizing forces of reason over archaic and traditional modes of being. This identity, in turn, became further elaborated as the policies and the mechanisms of Hapsburg absolutism were consolidated. Within the context of the new court, the war songs of old were no longer legible, but, rather, looked crude when compared to the gracious new lyric, which seemed to accommodate all the old forms within its abbreviated, constrained, but infinitely complex space. Because of this, and because of the complex codes of self-repression, dissembling, and the self-consciously artless postures of sprezzatura, the sonnet appears as an increasingly suitable allegory of the tension between the nobleman's double identity as a knight and as a subject.

The "Reproof"

Once we understand that politics structured not only the debate on the sonnet form, but, in a real way, the abbreviation of song into the sonnet itself, we can better place the vituperative attacks and the wry satires levied against the form. Such invectives inspired Baltasar de Alcázar (1530–1606) to pen his humorous poem (a sonnet) "contra un mal soneto" ("against a bad sonnet"), which begins with the rousing call:

> "Al soneto, vecinos, al malvado
> al sacrílego, al loco, al sedicioso,
> revolvedor de caldos, mentiroso,
> afrentoso al señor que lo ha criado"
>
> $(1-4)^{37}$

> ["After that sonnet, good neighbors, after that terrible / that sacrilegious, that mad, that seditious, / stirrer up of the cauldron, that deceitful, / offender of the man who created it"]

37. The poem is reproduced in *La poesía de la edad de oro*, vol. 1, 220.

Alcázar was lampooning the violent reactions that courtiers allowed themselves in their quarrels on poetry, responses along the lines of Acuña's lambasting of the "good knight and bad poet" we saw above, for example. The best known of these attacks is probably the courtier-poet Cristobal de Castillejo's midcentury "Represión contra los poetas que escriben en metro italiano" (Reproof Against Poets Who Write in Italian Meters), which we began to examine above. Composed with a decided emphasis on content, as opposed to form, the poem is useful to this discussion, not only because Castillejo dismisses the distinction between Italian hendecasyllables and heroic meter, but also because of the relationship he figures between the new poetry and the new Spanish nobleman. The "Reproof" is in many ways the companion piece to Boscán's "Letter."

Written probably around the same time as the "Letter" and Acuña's "sonnetizing" sonnets, the "Reproof" is a long poem composed in native quintilla stanzas punctuated by three fourteen-line poems that are ostensibly sonnets. The piece is a comical but pointed invective against poets who betray their native poetry and take up the new art. Its flavor can be gleaned from its opening lines, in which the poem's speaker calls down the Inquisition on the two poets whom he refers to as poetic Anabaptists:

> Pues la sancta Inquisición
> suele ser tan diligente
> en castigar con razón
> cualquier secta y opinión
> levantada nuevamente,
> resucítese Lucero,
> a corregir en España
> una tan nueva y extraña,
> como aquella de Lutero.
>
> (1–9)

[Since the sainted Inquisition / is accustomed to being so diligent / in punishing, rightly, / whatever sect and opinion / that is newly risen up, / let Lucero be revived, / to correct in Spain / one as new and strange, / as that of Luther.]

Castillejo calls the infamous Cordoban inquisitor Diego Rodriguez Lucero to rise from the dead in order to take on the poetic heresy of poets who are Lutherans, or even Anabaptists: "pues por ley particular / se tornan a bautizar /

y se llaman petrarquistas" (13–15) ("since by their own law / they turn and baptize themselves / and call themselves Petrarchans"). The conceit is both ingenious and unintentionally telling, since a subtext of the poem overall is anxiety about the invisibility of the transformations affecting "gentiles españoles caballeros" (Spain's gentle knights).[38] These transformations divide them into two groups, one traditional and one traitorously, heretically modern.[39] Castillejo expands his conceit of a poetic inquisition by summoning the famous poets of Castile to comment on Boscán and Garcilaso's folly:

> aquella musa cristiana
> del famoso Juan de Mena,
> sintiendo desto gran pena,
> por infieles los acusa
> y de aleves los condena.
> "Recuerde el alma dormida"
> dice don Jorge Manrique;
> muéstrase muy sentida
> de cosa tan atrevida,
> Garci-Sánchez respondió . . .
>
> (26–36)

[the Christian muse / of the famous Juan de Mena, / greatly pained by this, / accuses them as infidels / and condemns them as fickle. / "Recall the slumbering soul"[40] / says don Jorge Manrique; / he shows himself quite affected / by something so outrageous, / Garci-Sánchez responded . . .[41]]

---

38. Along these lines, this poem is also topical, as Castillejo spent much of his mature career in the Viennese court, during the period in which Ferdinand, king of the Romans, and the emperor, his brother, were working to maintain a mutual tolerance between Catholics and Protestants in the region. See Reyes Cano, *Estudios sobre Cristóbal de Castillejo*.

39. Castillejo probably did not consider how beginning his poem in the vein of religion, faith, and the Inquisition establishes a medieval religious worldview that is overcome, as the poem proceeds, by the politics that constitute the interiority of a modern man. The poem accidentally reproduces the phenomenon that is troubling it.

40. The first line of Jorge Manrique's most famous poem, the "Coplas por la muerte de su padre" (Verses on the Death of His Father), a poem composed around 1476.

41. Juan de Mena and Jorge Manrique (1440–1479), composer of the equally famous "Coplas por la muerte de su padre," written in the seven- and five-syllable "broken foot" or *pie quebrado* form, may be the best known of the poets Castillejo lists here. Garcí Sánchez de Bajadoz (1460–1526?) was a poet well-known for his cancionero poetry.

Throughout the poem, these writers, accompanied by Bartolomé Torres Naharro (1450–1520?) and Alfonso de Cartagena (1386–1456) will submit the new lyric to scrutiny for national and poetic (although not religious) heresy.

The "Reproof" is primarily composed in a traditional Castilian form, but three apparent sonnets are intercalated in the work. The first is the best known; it stages an encounter between Boscán, Garcilaso, and the distinguished poets of Castilian tradition:

> Garcilaso y Boscán, siendo llegados
> al lugar donde están los trovadores
> que en esta nuestra lengua y sus primores
> fueron en este siglo señalados,
> los unos a los otros alterados
> se miran, con mudanza de colores,
> temiéndose que fuesen corredores
> espías o enemigos desmandados;
> y juzgando primero por el traje,
> pareciéronles ser, como debía,
> gentiles españoles caballeros;
> y oyéndoles hablar nuevo lenguaje
> mezclado de extranjera poesía,
> con ojos los miraban de extranjeros.
>
> (61–74)

> [Garcilaso and Boscán, having arrived / at that place where the troubadours are found / who in this our language and its charms / were distinguished in this age, / each group gazes upon the other, shocked, / coloring, / fearing that they might be scouts, / spies, or lawless enemies; / and judging first by their outfits, / they seemed to be, as they should be, / gentle Spanish knights; / and listening to them speak a new language / mixed with strange poetry, / they looked at them with the eyes of strangers.]

If above I referred to Castillejo's "apparent" sonnets, it is because both this poem and the later ones that appear in lines 135–48, "Si las penas que dais son verdaderas" (If the Pains You Give Are Real)—a weak imitation of a sonnet by Boscán—and lines 217–30, "Musas italianas y Latinas" (Italian and Latin Muses), are fourteen-line, hendecasyllabic lyrics that follow the conventional rhyme scheme of ABBA, ABBA, CDE, CDE. Beyond that, however, they show little of the internal logic or the art of the sonnet form. In "Garcilaso y Boscán, siendo llegados," for example, the volta is signaled with a semicolon at the end of line 8, but there is no marked "turn" of thought or point of view, and there is only the weakest shift in the action as the parties move from staring ("miran") to judging and listening ("juzgan," "oyéndoles"). Whether or not he could do better with the form, the jocular tone of the work overall, added to the fact that he had studied under Erasmus, the author of the satirical *In Praise of Folly* (1511), suggests that this flat-footedness was pointed and meant to exaggerate the vapidity of the new art.[42]

Castillejo's "sonnet" presents a different perspective on the phenomenon we have been tracking in this chapter, the suspicions and fears about the implication of poetry in the changes that were taking place among the ranks of gentle Spanish knights. Like Acuña (and like Lorenzo), Castillejo assumes an implicit alliance between sonnet form and the complexified and cosmopolitan existence that yields the subject. Once again, we encounter the pairing of new poetry, and new man, the latter endowed with an interiority that is both hidden from view and subject to hidden operations of meaning deriving from the political, ideological world. The dilution of the ranks of the aristocracy at court by the increased numbers of the letrados, and the suddenly expanded, heterogeneous amalgamation of kingdoms, duchies, cities, and hemispheres that constituted the holdings of Charles V and of Spain during Castillejo's lifetime—changes such as these meant that even men such as Castillejo, Boscán, and Garcilaso, all noblemen, all courtiers from esteemed houses, all lifelong members of the highest circles of the court, found themselves divided and routed into factions, alliances, and even distant territories in which they became alien, or "hard to read," to one

---

42. Erasmus was the tutor of Charles V's brother Ferdinand from 1518. Building on their connection, Rogelio Reyes Cano, one of Castillejo's most thoughtful readers, has suggested that the true target of the "Reproof" was not Italianate lyric, specifically, but bad poetry of all types, inasmuch as it dishonored the Castilian tongue (17–19 and 85–105). This reading helps to undermine the problematic critical opposition Boscán-Castillejo, and it also fits better with the portrait of the urbane and Europeanized figure that Castillejo seems to have been. Bearing in mind the cosmopolitan makeup of the Viennese court during Castillejo's residence there, Reyes's interpretation carries weight. Attacks on bad Petrarchans were common in the writings of the courtly and the lettered elites, throughout Europe (see Reyes Cano, *Estudios sobre Cristóbal de Castillejo*).

another.[43] It was thus impossible to trust contemporary Spanish courtiers because of the radical differences that might mark them beneath the surface, "under their garments," according to the words of the poem, "juzgando primero por el traje / pareciéronles ser como debía" (70), but also on their "insides," where their language was formed and where internalized attitudes and ideologies shape their speech: "oyéndoles hablar nuevo lenguaje . . . con ojos los miraban de extranjeros" (73–75). But whereas Acuña understood the production of his lyric subject to take place through the twinned operations of the rational mind and the sonnet form, as each was enhanced and reinforced by the workings of the other, Castillejo was unable to engage or was uninterested in engaging with the structuring effects of poetry on identity and attributed the difference in the two types of courtiers to what Cascardi has referred to as the "the authority of taste" (*Ideologies*, 12).

The Ideology of Form

The introduction and the defense of the sonnet in the sixteenth century coincided with the rise of a new way of thinking about poetry. The nature and purpose of poetic discourse were transformed from the creation and the imitation of greatness to the containment of the voice within the human (and humanist) contours of a new kind of self. We might understand this watershed as the lyricization of poetry; but it took place as the aristocrat adopted the persona of the courtierized nobleman and acceded to the demand that he alternate his grasp of two implements, the sword and the pen, instead of the one great *ardiente espada*. Along with this embrace of subjection came a renewed emphasis on what we would now term the subjective. As the modern courtier internalized contemporary political ideologies of circumscribed agency, he elaborated on them in lyrics shaped by the particular inflections of his personal voice.

---

43. Castillejo's own biographical situation was notable in this regard. Castillejo and Boscán had both been pages in the court of Ferdinand the Catholic before Castillejo was attached to the household of Prince Ferdinand and Boscán entered into service of the Dukes of Alba. Castillejo witnessed at close hand the rough and tumble of the transition from the political culture under the regencies of Cisneros and King Ferdinand and the new Burgundian-style order that was imposed during the early years of Charles's reign. When Prince Ferdinand was dispatched to the Low Countries and then to Vienna, Castillejo stayed behind; however, it has been suggested that he was associated with the losing side of the *comuneros* revolts and that this was one of the reasons that it was deemed expedient to eventually send him to Vienna to rejoin his Prince (Reyes Cano, 17–21).

Another element that we have observed here is that the sonnet is more than a neutral vehicle for content in the sixteenth century. It is not trivial as a form. Nor, to take on another dismissive convention, is it the kind of poem one writes when one is not of sufficient caliber and talent to write an epic. Or, rather, the sonnet *is* what one writes when one is unable to compose an epic; however, we need to understand that the epic and its close relative, the traditional Castilian song, could not achieve their traditional sorts of meaning in the sixteenth century, not because a given poet was insufficient to the task, but rather because the cultural framework that supported this poetry had been eclipsed.[44] There will be more to say on this matter in Chapter 4. For the present, it is sufficient to observe how the poems of Acuña that treat the phenomenon of sonnetization foreground the form's poetic mandate to summon and frame its subjects. Moreover, the readings offered above have shown that close-reading practices and reading lyric texts *as lyric*—as poetry, specifically—are worthwhile tasks. The evidence for this view will only mount over the course of the remaining chapters.

---

44. Such are the social and political conditions "fatal to epic," according to David Quint, quoting Joseph Schumpeter in *Epic and Empire* (10).

2

OTRO TIEMPO LLORÉ Y AHORA CANTO:
JUAN BOSCÁN COURTIERIZES SONG

ONE OF THE RECURRING THEMES ENCOUNTERED in the last chapter was the deliberate conflation of notions regarding kinds of poetry and kinds of men. The new lyric became consolidated and rose to privilege within the context of an ideological break with the culture of the so-called Reconquest. This break was undertaken to reconstitute Spain both politically and within the social imagination as a unified and cosmopolitan seat of the Hapsburg Empire, and key elements of Spanish identity were appropriated in the service of that shift. Chief among them was the ideal of the Spanish nobleman, who in previous eras had been central to the constitution of the national myth. But neither the regional associations of figures such as the Cid nor his association with heroic acts of violence and daring that were carried out to the eventual benefit of the realm, but performed first and foremost to the credit of his own honor (the constellation of features collected within the trope of the *diestro braço*), reflected the ideals of the nascent modern state. The state, after all, coalesces through the suppression of internal boundaries and the substitution of loyalties to the home region and the *patria chica* with identification with "nuestra España," the country as a whole.

Chapter 1 focused on the ways in which the sonnet form lent itself to the redescription of the noble Spanish masculine ideal. In this chapter, I will be exploring the peculiar set of cultural and subjective meanings that became attached to "song" in the poems and the criticism discussed there. If we think back to Sonnet 45 or Sonnet 30, by Acuña, or when we think about the distaste Boscán expresses for consonance in the "Letter," we find that the "previous songs," the "older songs," the *canción* that precedes the "present" of the poem are figured as wielding a kind of power that must be mastered and contained if modern civilization is to progress. Both armígero son (Acuña) and the "caballero consonance" that gallops through the mind in Boscán's "Letter" attribute a suspect force to poems themselves, and not simply to the men who compose and enjoy those poems. Part of the reason for this resistance lies in a shift in the function assigned to poetry between nonmodern and modern contexts. This shift is often referred to in terms of "Homer and Horace," a distinction that connotes the difference between the memorializing role played by epic and ballad—in which poetic discourse is assumed to play an important role in the conservation and the transmission of culture—and a lyric-based poetics that critics from the time of Horace forward have associated with urbane and sophisticated humanism that celebrates the self. In this chapter, I address Boscán's poetry, focusing on the First and Second Books in order to show how they supported and extended Boscán's project of accommodating Spain's noblemen to the social and cultural circumstances of the modern Spanish state. The First and Second Books of Boscán's text represent a trajectory of song, first, as an initial account of irrational, uncontainable and maddening consonance is mediated and rationalized through its remodeling into the forms and conventions of Petrarchan discourse, and, second, as this Petrarchan lyric is refashioned into a poetic discourse appropriate to the modern Spanish courtier. At the end of the Second Book, Boscán's new lyric emerges as a poetry that is neither traditional to Castile nor to Petrarchism, but which represents instead the utterance of the man who understands the stakes of both languages and who selects a middle path. Thus, in Poem 115, near the end of the sequence, Boscán's lyric speaker will crow that "su cantar del nuestro es diferente" (8) ("their song is different from ours"). He is referring to the fact that in distinction to other courtly lyrics, his poems now assimilate Castilian logic, Italian models and the native *Spanish* (though not Castilian) lyrics of the Valencian troubadour Ausiàs March, and thus that lyric has been reconstituted as the poetry of "nuestra España." But he is also pleased with the wider implications of this type of song: his songs are the product of satisfied, moderate love that is both lived and sung in terms of neo-Stoic values that accord with the Horatian golden mean.

Las obras de Juan Boscán y algunas de Garcilaso de la Vega repartidas en cuatro libros

We tend to read Boscán's Italianate poetry on its own, focusing on the "Letter" to the Duchess of Soma and the Petrarchan sequence that constitute the Second Book of the *Obras completas*. But as we begin to look beyond Boscán's Petrarchism and into his larger aim of reforming Castilian song, it is helpful to consider the relationships between the First and the Second Books. As Margherita Morreale and Navarrete have each shown, the "Letter" and Boscán's translation of *The Book of the Courtier* work in tandem to frame and disseminate a discourse of modern Spanish courtiership.[1] The First and Second Books of the *Obras* work in a similar way, and the *Obras* as a whole thereby provides a systematic critique of the past and present of Spanish poetry. In the First Book, Boscán reviews the fifteenth-century Spanish lyric tradition. In the Second Book, he criticizes and reforms this tradition, politicizing it by linking it to the new political culture of Hapsburg Spain by means of the "Letter" to the Duchess of Soma.[2] In the Third and Fourth Books he provides additional models of the new art, including the poetry of Garcilaso. The First and Second Books concern us most here, since they link the courtierization of the Spanish knight to the mediation and the constraint of his song.

1. See Navarrete, *Orphans of Petrarch*, 39–57, as well as Morreale, *Castiglione y Boscán*.
2. Armisén has argued that while the Second Book is complete as a Petrarchan sequence and can be read on its own, it was in fact intended to be read with the First Book, that is, with the collection of Castilian verse that precedes it, a dedicatory proem, followed by twenty-six lyrics composed in the traditional Castilian forms: six short songs (canciones), nineteen coplas, and two *villancicos* (the forms are intercalated). He bases this argument on the structure of fifteenth-century Neopolitan *canzonieri* and on a detailed discussion of the various manuscripts in which Boscán compiled his Castilian verse before settling on the ordered series presented in the Book. He concludes that Boscán selected and arranged the Castilian poetry of the 1543 text deliberately, with the purpose of creating a book suggestive of a literary "apprenticeship" that would appear to precede his 1526 "conversion" to Italian forms (*Estudios sobre la lengua*, 354–55). What joins the two books most overtly is their prefatory material. Both are dedicated to the Duchess of Soma, in texts that were probably written at roughly the same time, which is to say in about 1541, when Boscán was preparing his manuscript. The First Book opens with a twenty-nine-line proem, which, unlike the rest of the poetry in the book, is written in hendecasyllabics and begins: "A quién daré mis amorosos versos, / que pretenden amor, con virtud junto, / y desean también mostrars'hermosos? / A ti, señora en quien todo esto cabe, / a ti se den, por cuanto si carecen / destas cosas que digo que pretienden, / en ti las hallarán cumplidamente. Recógelos con blanda mansedumbre / si vieres que son blandos, y si no, / recógelos como ellos merecieren" (1–10) ("To whom will I give my verses of love, / which seek to express love, joined with virtue, / and desire also to show themselves beautiful? / To you, my lady, in whom all of these are contained, / to you they are given, so that if they lack / these things that I say they seek to effect, / those things will find themselves fulfilled in you. / Gather them with gentle tenderness / if you see that they are gentle, and if not, / gather them as they deserve"). The fact that it is written in hendecasyllabics associates the proem with the period after 1526. In addition, critics have also noted the similarity between these lines and Epigram 1 by Catullus: "Quoi dono lepidum novum libellum / arida modo pumice expolitum? / Corneli, tibi" (1–3) ("To whom do I give this charming little book / newly polished, as with dry pumice? / Cornelius, to you"); Armisén credits Caro Lynn with the discovery; see also Arnold Reichenberger, "Boscán and the Classics," *Comparative Literature* 3, no. 2 (1951): 97–118. Boscán mentions Catullus in the *Epístola*, line 274. Armisén argues that the allusion, coming at the head of the first dedication, links the proem to the "Letter" through the idea of "new poetry" (343). Since Catullus was a member of a group of Latin poets (the *neoteroi*) who introduced Greek alexandrines into Latin poetics, it seems likely that Boscán was making a connection between his introduction of the

The First Book

The First Book does not inscribe the unities and the multiple links between the individual poems and the greater whole that are necessary to the crafting of a full lyric sequence; however, it is clear that the poems included in it were selected with some care, presumably by Boscán, and that they are designated to function as a type of prehistory to the speaker who begins his hendecasyllabic laments in the Second Book.³ In various short and highly musical poetic forms they recount his descent into suffering. Poem 2 is a charming *villancico* that frames the medieval idea that the image of the beloved enters a lover through his eyes and fixes itself inside him:

> Si no os hubiera mirado
>   no penara
> pero tampoco os mirara.
> Veros harto mal à sido,
> mas no veros peor fuera;
> no quedara tan perdido
> pero mucho más perdiera.
> ¿Qué viera aquél que no os viera?
> ¿Cuál quedara
> señora, si no os mirara?
>
>   (1–10)

[If I had not gazed upon you / I would not suffer, / but then neither would I have gazed upon you. / To have seen you has caused sorrow enough, / but not seeing you would be worse; / I would

---

hendecasyllable and the acts of a formidable ancient precursor. Certainly, Boscán has expressed his anxiety about that perilous early modern activity, linguistic innovation, in the "Letter" ("no querría que me tuviesen por tan amigo de cosas nuevas . . . Antes quiero que sepan que ni yo jamás he hecho profesión de escrivir esto ni otra cosa ni, aunque la hiziera, me pusiera en trabajo de provar nuevas invenciones" [117] ["I did not want them to take me for such a friend to new things. . . . First I want them to know that I never made a profession of writing this, nor any other thing, nor, while I have done so, did I put myself to work trying new inventions"]). The model of Catullus would have lent prestige and legitimacy to his efforts, protecting him from the charge of "novelar."

3. David Darst reviews Crawford's argument that the First Book follows a trajectory that parallels the Second Book, from absorption in love to "alguna extravagancia lúdica social" ("a degree of social, ludic extravagance") (Darst's discussion is treated in Armisén, *Estudios sobre la lengua*, 354). The tone of many of the poems in the Book would seem to inscribe the context of court and its ludic nature. For example, one recurring theme is the regretful valediction at the close of an affair. See Poems 11 and 17.

not find myself so lost / but I would have lost much more. / What would he see at all, he who had not seen you? / What would remain, / my lady, if I did not gaze upon you?]

In the next poem, which is composed in coplas in the *pie quebrado* form, the speaker describes the effects of love on his mind, where it stimulates vain fantasies, "dicen que mi fantasía / no se guía / sino toda contra mí" (3.11–13) ("they say that my fantasy / is not aimed / anywhere but fully against myself"), and on his soul, which is suffering, but whose salvation he ignores by refusing to repent: "Mi alma se favorece / si padece / y toma por mejoría / que crezca la pena mía . . . Yo la siento / mas della no m'arrepiento" (21–24, 26–27) ("My soul is privileged / if it suffers / and takes it as a boon / my pain grows . . . I feel the pain / but I do not repent"). In poems such as numbers 15 and 16, Boscán recounts his experience as a prisoner of love ("Amor, que'n mi pensamiento / rige, manda, suelta y prende"; 15.1–2 ["Love, which, in my thoughts, / reigns, rules, sets free and seizes hold"]) and his sufferings over time ("¡O fin de mis alegrías, / comienzo de mis tristezas! / Alcancen ya mis porfías / que s'acaben las cruezas / que s'acaben ya mis días"; 16.1–5 ["Oh end to my happiness, / beginning of my sorrows! / My struggles now reach the point where / they put an end to these cruelties / which now end my days"]).

The early poems also join the two themes that serve as structuring preoccupations in the Second Book: the perils of fantasy, and the moral and social implications of contained and uncontained speech. The perils of fantasy begin to be presented in poems such as 11 and 21. In Poem 11, the speaker admits that his daydreaming leads him astray: "Yo conozco que mi pena / toda fue por culpa mía, / pues siempre tuve porfía / de dejar la parte buena / por seguir la fantasía" (6–10) ("I know that my suffering / was all my fault, / for I always dared / to leave behind the better part / to follow my imaginings"). In Poem 21, he describes his daydreams as "más vivas que pintadas / hallaréis mis fantasias" (3–4) ("more live than painted / you will find my fantasies"). The trouble with fantasy, as the speaker frames it in these poems and as Boscán will maintain over the course of the First and the Second Books, is that it isolates men from "la parte buena," drawing them further into a state I referred to in the last chapter as monadic and enthralled.[4] This emphasis on the isolation of the obsessive lover establishes a crucial distinction between Boscán's text and both medieval lyrics

---

4. See the discussion of Acuña's Sonnet 45 above, in Chapter 1.

that frame the conventions of *loco amor* and Petrarch's *Canzoniere*. Each of these kinds of poetry represents erotic desire as idolatrous.[5] In contrast to such metaphysical views, Boscán foregrounds the radically *antisocial* nature of medieval courtly love, repeating the message, across numerous poems, that in order to persist in their illusions (*engaño, fantasía*), obsessive lovers erroneously shun the company of their fellows, turning inward not only to seek pleasure in their imaginings, but also to avoid correction from the surrounding society. Therefore, immoderate lovers not only serve as shameful examples of error to surrounding onlookers (*escarmiento*), they are potentially destructive, since they do not attend to the internal and external regulations that assure the smooth functioning of a civil society. In the First Book, Boscán links these characterological problems to poetic ones by representing the self-indulgent and self-destructive obsessions of the lover in poetic forms that foreground sound over sense. As the First Book progresses, the speaker will complain to his lady, lament his pain, and continue along the path of the fifteenth-century victim of mad love. But while these poems bemoan the misery, the confusion, and the experience of being buffeted about by the whims of a fickle woman and a more fickle universe, their tone is lightened by the relatively short lines and the close rhymes of the copla forms, both of which lend a playfulness to the speaker's voice, even when it is describing suffering, as it does in Poem 8 ("Señora, pues que no'spero") or Poem 12, which begins:

> Tristeza, pues yo soy tuyo
> tú no dejes de ser mía;
> mira bien que me destruyo
> sólo en ver que'l alegría
> presume d'hazerme suyo.

---

5. Over the course of the *Canzoniere,* Petrarch's poetic speaker, "Petrarch," elaborates the image of himself over and against the figure of the laurel tree, in an overt imitation of Augustine's self-fashioning in terms of the fig tree in the *Confessions*. Critics such as Freccero ("The Fig Tree and the Laurel") and Durling (*Petrarch's Lyric Poems,* 1–33) point to this feature of his work as a sign of idolatry: "Petrarch makes no claim to reality or to moral witness. Instead, he uses Augustinian principles in order to create a totally autonomous portrait of the artist, devoid of any ontological claim" (Freccero, 21). Furthermore, the intertextuality with the *Confessions* and the fragmented narrative permit Petrarch to appropriate not only language, but the Word—i.e., "the silence that subtends the system" grounding both desire and language (23)—to the aim of fashioning an eternal poetic self: "The moral struggle and the spiritual torment described in the *Canzoniere* are . . . part of a poetic strategy. When the spiritual struggle is demystified, its poetic mechanism is revealed: the petrified idolatrous love is an immutable monument to Petrarch" (21).

¡O tristeza!
que apartarme de contigo
es la más alta crueza
que puedes usar conmigo.

No huyas, ni seas tal
que m'apartes de tu pena.
Soy tu tierra natal

(1–12)

[Sadness, because I am yours / you never cease to be mine; / look well on how I am destroyed / just by seeing that happiness / presumes to make me its own. / O sadness! / To part from you / is the greatest cruelty / that you can do me. / Do not flee, nor make it so that / I am exiled from your grief. / I am your native land]

The consonance of poems such as this one masks the darker aspects of the scenarios the speaker describes. It also leads poets and lovers astray by encouraging them to elaborate and expand on their laments and vain hopes in lines that "like a river from a mountain rushing down, which the rains have swollen above its wonted banks . . . seethe, and, brooking no restraint, rush on with deep-toned voice."[6] The lines are from Horace. According to the Roman writer, the power of poetic song is dangerous when it is unleashed by any but the most skilled and self-knowing of poets, and Boscán aligns himself with humanists such as Castiglione when he represents the speaker of the First Book as not up to the task of subduing the forces of song through an equal force of mind.[7] Thus, Poem 19 is a long song composed in octosyllabics, and it broaches the theme that undisciplined song leads men to peril:

Ya puedo soltar mi llanto
pues para llorar me hallo;
é callado, y más me'spanto
de'star tal y ver que callo,
que de ver que peno tanto.
Que tenga ya libertad
mi lengua, yo lo consiento;

---

6. "Monte currens velut amnis, imbres / quem super notas aluere ripas, fervet immensusque ruit profundo / . . . ore"; Song 4.2, quoted in Greene, *The Light in Troy,* 68.

7. See Thomas M. Greene's reading of Horace on the Pindaric ode (ibid., 66–68).

hasta'quí fue sufrimiento,
ahora ya es poquedad
callar el dolor que siento.

Mi vida, para pasarla
téngola de publicar

(1–12)

[Now can I let loose my lament / for I find myself ready to weep; / I have been silent, and it has frightened me more / to be in that state and to find myself silent / than to find that I suffer so. / Let my tongue now have its liberty, / I consent that; / up to now, all has been suffering, / now it is miserly / to silence the pain that I feel. / In order to live my life / I must publish it]

Poem 19 assigns a moral character to the Castilian octosyllables. The speaker states that he is unleashing an utterance of pure passion—the song as the sob, or lament (*llanto*)—in order to relieve his suffering. But as the song rolls forward, propelled by its short lines and its rhyme, the momentum *increases* the speaker's passion and his sorrow: "Mi dolor, cuando sosiega, / es para mayor cuidado; / revuelve en tan alto grado / que a poco rato se entrega / del tiempo que se ha tardado" (211–15) ("When my pain is calmed / it only causes further worry; / it returns to such a great degree / that in a short while it regains / the time it has lost"). Neither the 230 lines of this song nor the 300 lines of one that follows it assuage the speaker's suffering or contain his voice, a fact which indicates that a life experienced in terms of simple "publishing" (*publicar,* line 12), unmediated by reason and unrestrained by prudence, is as vain and empty as the consonance whose inertia speeds it forward. Poem 19 thus sets up a theme that will return as a structuring preoccupation of both Books, namely, that the speaker's suffering is his own fault because he has allowed himself to unleash his tongue and loose a song comprised of pure emotion and no reason.

As I have suggested, this is a Horatian view.[8] In the *Letter to the Pisos,* Horace writes that "a good and prudent man will censure lifeless lines . . .

---

8. As Reichenberger observed in his essay on Boscán's "Epístola a Mendoza," Boscán's writing reflected a Horatian-Epicurean sensibility that was clearly filtered through the *Book of the Courtier.* Colombí-Monguió also reminds us that Boscán's humanism was most likely the result of his conversations and his study with Castiglione and Navagero ("Boscán frente a Navagero"). For a comprehensive reading of Boscán's imitative strategies, see Cruz (*Imitación y transformación*) as well as Navarrete (*Orphans of Petrarch*). For a discussion of the various manuscript versions of the Book, see Armisén, *Estudios sobre la lengua,* 379–411.

he will cut away pretentious ornament. . . . He will not say, 'Why should I give offense to a friend about trifles?' These trifles will bring that friend into serious trouble." This trouble manifests itself in both poetry and life. Horace's advice consistently conflates the two. Just as he is suspicious of unbridled song, he cautions men to seek the counsel and restraint of their fellows, "my view and the public's are the same."[9] At the end of the Second, courtierizing, Book, Boscán's speaker will accept this view; in Poem 130, the final song of the Book, he casts a look back over his former condition:

> mi alma'staba por Amor contenta;
> y aunque'ra el contentarse desvarío,
>
> . . . .
>
> yo andábame'ntre mí sin mostrar nada;
> queriendo'star doblado,
> con gente que traer pensé engañada,
> conmigo estaba ya tan confiado,
> que holgaba de fingirme mal tratado
>
> . . . .
>
> Si algún prudente amigo me decía
> "estos bienes d'Amor no permanecen,"
> por pesada sentencia la juzgaba.
> Ninguna forma de desdicha hallaba
> que'mbarazar pudiese mis venturas
>
> (19–20; 26–30; 34–38)

[my soul was contented in Love; / although this contentment was folly / . . . / I wandered about caught up in myself, showing nothing; / I was two-faced / among people I thought I deceived, / I had such confidence in myself, / that I took pleasure in pretending that I was mistreated. / . . . / If a prudent friend said to me, / "those pleasures of Love do not last," / I judged that to be a tiresome opinion. / No form of misfortune did I find / that could thwart my plans]

But in order to achieve this position of thoughtful contemplation, he must be led out of his fantasy world and into identification with the society of prudent friends and their advice.

---

9. "Vir bonus et prudens versus reprehended inertis . . . ambitiosa recidet ornamenta . . . nec dicet: 'cur go amicum / offendam in nugis?' hae nugae seria ducent in mala" (Horace, *Satires, Epistles, and Ars Poetica*, 445–51); I have modified the translations.

The Second Book

This awakening will not happen for some time. Throughout the First Book and through the start of the Second, Boscán's speaker assumes a natural right to sovereign and uncontained speech, in the manner of Horace's "freeborn knight," who frames verses "that fall to the bottom" because he is convinced that his birthright is to "stand clear from every blemish."[10] Another way of describing the speaker's attitude is that it is arrogant in the manner of the Castilian caballeros. In the First Book his undisciplined llanto leads to no great consequences. He suffers, but the credibility of his laments is lessened by the lilting sounds in which they are framed. Coplas are, after all, in a description Boscán attributes to Diego Hurtado de Mendoza, "roly-polys" (*redondillas*), child's verse and of no great consequence (*Obra completa*, 115). In the Second Book, unrestrained speech and the generation of pleasurable, empty sounds inscribe the speaker within a far more disorienting form of madness by which he becomes unable to position himself in time and space. Boscán will narrate the gradual recovery of his speaker and his song over the course of the Book. They will be transformed within a Petrarchan sequence that Boscán modifies to suit his specific aims of courtierization: unlike in the *Canzoniere,* the destination of the sequence is not medieval transcendence, but a modern ideal based on the *Book of the Courtier,* and especially on the final speech of Bembo that celebrates middle-aged contentment and moderate love. But if the subjectivity of the speaker is transformed, his poetics and especially his relationship to song change as well. Boscán modifies the forms of the songs, from coplas to canciones based on Italian models, most often eleven- and seven-syllable lines with an unstructured rhyme scheme. As presaged in the "Letter," this formal shift mediates the propulsive energies of the lyrics, slowing their progress from a gallop to a more meditative progress. The first result is alienation, as the speaker recognizes that his old mode of thinking and speaking is radically unsuited to the

---

10. "Mediocribus esse poetis / non hominess, non di, non concessere columnae . . . sic animis natum inventumque poema iuvandis, / si paulum summam decessit, vergit ad imum. Ludere qui nescit, campestribus abstinet armis . . . qui nescit versus tamen audet fingere. Quidni? / liber et inenuus, praesertim census questrem / summam nummorum vitioque remotus ab omni" ("that poets be of middling rank, neither men nor gods . . . ever brooked . . . so a poem, whose birth and creation are for the soul's delight, if aught it falls short of the top, sinks to the bottom. He who cannot play a game, shuns the weapons. . . . Yet the man who knows not how dares to frame verses. Why not? He is free, even freeborn, nay, is rated at the fortune of a knight, and stands clear from every blemish"); Horace, *Satires, Epistles, and Ars Poetica,* 480–81.

narration of his plight. As he becomes accommodated to the courtly society around him, he begins to temper his speech with reason and achieves his final, successful song.

Courtierizing Song

The first song of the Second Book, Poem 47, represents the speaker in a far more serious condition than what has been portrayed in the First Book:

> Quiero hablar un poco
> mas teme el corazón de fatigarse
> porque si hablo sé que será tanto
> que'l seso à de alterarse
> y a su culpa no es bien tornarse loco
> . . . .
> Pero pasar este peligro es fuerza,
> y escójolo por menos peligroso;
> de suerte que si oso
> es ya por el aprieto que me fuerza,
> y el alma ha de probar
> su seso y su poder, y así se esfuerza.
> Con esto tales cosas he de hablar,
> que aún ahora estoy pensando de callar.
>
> Callaré, si pudiere;
> mas no podré, que ha mucho que no puedo;
> hablaré, por no estarme como estoy
>
> (1–5; 8–18)

> [I want to speak a little / but my heart is afraid it will grow weary / for if I speak, I know it will be at such great length / that my brain will be shocked / and it is not a good thing to go mad on my heart's account. / . . . / But I must pass through this danger, / and I choose it as the less perilous path; / for if I dare to try / it is because my condition makes me do so, / and my soul must test / brain and brawn, and make the attempt. / Having said this, I have such things to tell, / that even now I think of silencing them. / I will be silent if I am able; / but I will not be able to do so, for

I have been unable to speak for a long time; / I will speak so as not to remain as I am]

Whereas in Poem 19 the consequences of unleashing llanto are mild, in Poem 47, they are grave. The speaker is completely disoriented by the racing processes of his thought, which is so disorganized that he is not even able to sing out his lament. Self-absorption is no longer pleasurable in this poem, and it will rarely be represented as pleasurable in the Second Book. Instead, it leads to agony, frustration, and alienation. The reason for this displeasure is that the speaker has crossed over from the naive and childlike world of the First Book and into the courtly world of the Second. The most material effect of the threshold is the alteration of the musical register of the song. The long lines and the loosened rhyme scheme place a new burden on the lyric to proceed intelligibly at the level of content. When it does not do so, the speaker takes notice and begins to doubt himself. But the Second Book is also preceded by the "Letter," with its loosely veiled social threat about the political fate that awaits those who maintain loyalty to the old poetry. So the moral narrative is subtended by the local politics of the new Spanish state.

The difference between "song" as it is represented in the First Book and at the start of the Second Book, then, is that in Poem 47, the speaker is illegible, politically, aesthetically, morally, and grammatically.[11] The following lines are representative of the tenor of the song, in which, by line 46, the speaker is still trying to commence his tale:

> Faltará la memoria
> para poder decir lo que'n mi siento.
> Mas, aunque ataja el mal, también se despierta
> y pone tal aliento,
> que m'atrevo a contar tan gran historia,
>
> . . . .
>
> Olvidando el comienzo, el fin no hallo;
> mal concierto tendrá cuento tan largo
>
> . . . .
>
> Trabajan mis sentidos

---

11. Navarrete has also discussed the problematic narration in the early songs. See his useful analysis in *Orphans of Petrarch*, 77–81.

en buscar lo que siento, por echallo.
Oyo llamar de lejos mis gemidos,
y he lástima de ver que van perdidos.
¡O mis crudos dolores,
dadme un poco d'alivio porque pueda
probar a ver si diré lo que digo!

(46–50; 53–54; 57–63)

[My memory will falter / in managing to say what I feel inside. / But although my sorrow binds me, it also awakens me / and infuses me with such spirit, / that I dare to recount this long history / ... / Forgetful of the beginning, I cannot find the end; / a tale this long will be discordant / ... / My senses labor / searching for what I feel, to let it forth. / I hear my own groans from far away, / and I pity to see them out wandering lost. / Oh, crude suffering, / give me a bit of relief / that I might test myself to see if I can say what I have to say!]

We can list the elements that lead the speaker astray here: his song is driven by emotion and not by the desire to frame rational utterances. In line 30, he says that his reason is completely overwhelmed by madness ("el seso y la razón es ya locura" ["my mind and reason are now mad"]), while in lines 25–26 he muses whether it is wrong to sing when he is in such pain ("quizá es desvarío ... llanto que en tal dolor tan tarde viene" ["perhaps it is an error, this lament that comes so late in my suffering"]). In the envoi, he defends his prolixity as justified (as in Poem 19 of the First Book) by his suffering: "Canción: si de muy larga te culparen, / respóndeles que sufran con paciencia; que un gran dolor de todo da licencia" ("Song: if they fault you for being too long, / respond that they should suffer with patience; / for a great pain licenses all") (451–53). It is also the case that throughout the poem his processes of thought, such as they are, are led astray by consonance. I have said that the tendency of the Second Book is to mediate music, and Poem 47 does not rhyme regularly. But Boscán inscribes internal rhymes, such as the *é,* and the speaker pursues the sound, leading himself off course. In a similar way, the rhyme *desventura / locura,* in lines 29–30, is significant.

Poem 47 is ingeniously structured to link cancionero poetry and the types of speakers it represents with the scrambled (*alterado*) brain and the tiresome discourse of "tiresome" men. It thereby reinforces the portrait of the recalcitrant Castilians presented in the "Letter." The reference to uncontrolled speech is placed at the head of the first Italian-style song—that is, at the head of the first poem in the Book that is not constrained by the rules of the sonnet form. It thus signals that part of the work of the sequence will be to civilize and circumscribe the speaker and his voice so that he will be able to speak just a little ("un poco") when he wishes to do so, and subsequent songs in the sequence do not reproduce the baffling disorganization of Poem 47. However, progress toward reason is slow. Boscán inscribes advances in the speaker's capacity to organize and narrate his experience thematically and grammatically late in the sequence, in songs such as Poem 103, "Gran tiempo ha que amor me dize 'scrive'" ("For a long time love has said to me, 'write'"; a poem based on Petrarch 93, "Più volte Amor m'avea già detto: 'Scrivi'"). Such poems represent halting steps toward sanity. In Poem 104, the speaker reflects: "Bien pensé yo pasar mi triste vida / del arte que otro tiempo la pasaba, / concertándome en mí con mis tormentos; / pero engañéme en lo que pensaba" (1–4) ("I well thought to pass my sad life / by the same art by which I had passed it before, / making peace within myself with my torments; / but I was deceived in what I thought"). The process begins to reach its fulfillment with Poems 114 and 115, both sonnets, in which the speaker celebrates his mastery over the various traditions of song and also of his passions. Thus in Poem 115, he states that the songs of lyric tradition—the songs of Petrarch, of March, of the cancionero—"del nuestro es diferente . . . yo de ver quien me ama y a quien amo, / en mi cantar terné gozo contino" (8; 13–14) ("are different from ours . . . I, gazing upon she who loves me, she whom I love in return / will take continuous joy in my song"). In a manner that parallels the process recounted in Acuña's sonnets 45 and 30, then, the lyric sequence of Boscán's Second Book maps the interpellation of the old-style lover into the discourses and practices of modern courtiership, by means of regulating and restructuring his song, "civilizing" it such that it becomes capable of legible narration. A principal mechanism for effecting this transformation is the Petrarchan sequence.

Boscán and Petrarch

The 102-poem lyric sequence in the Second Book (92 sonnets and 10 songs) begins after the "Letter" and unfolds in a succession of series. It opens with a lover wretched in the manner of the fifteenth-century lovers of the cancionero and the *cants* of Ausiàs March.[12] A slave to his passions, he cannot exercise the rational self-mastery that will help him stave off the accidents of fortune and passion. Instead, he retreats into a fantasy world in which pleasurable imaginings about receiving favors from his beloved compete with "torments" of jealousy (Boscán plays on the word *tormenta,* which means storm, as well as suffering). These fantasies receive some support in the excessive behavior of the lady herself, whose erratic cruelties add to the speaker's suffering and tax his brain (*seso*). Finally, exhausted, he comes to a crisis in Poem 66. Subsequently, he is transformed in a manner that resembles the Petrarchan conversion and the Dantean vita nuova. However, in Poems 71, 78, 79, and 80, it becomes apparent that what Boscán's speaker has actually undergone is a courtly resocialization more than it is a divine conversion: he has shifted from identifying with the internal fantasy world of the asocial lover to adopting Horace's "public view." This new outlook is represented in two registers. First, the speaker achieves an increasingly rational, legible narration in both his sonnets and his songs as he adopts a mode of speaking that is structured by Renaissance humanist imitatio, as opposed to naive, pleasurable telling. Second, he embraces two important Renaissance discourses: chaste love and perfect friendship. It is under the influence of these two forces that the speaker celebrates his new and "different" song in Poem 115.

As this overview suggests, Petrarch's *Canzoniere* serves as a crucial structuring model for Boscán's lyric sequence. The Spanish text is organized in the manner of the *rime sparse,* with series of sonnets punctuated and commented on by longer songs that summarize the story thus far (to the extent they are able, given the speaker's troubles with narration) and introduce new themes. But as I have already indicated, Boscán's narrative is oriented toward the conversion of the self-absorbed lover to the worldly

---

12. I am emphasizing the sequence's intertextuality with Petrarch, Horace, and Castiglione, but the Second Book also draws liberally on Ausiàs March and on poems from the cancionero and *cantiga* traditions, which were native to Castile. March is the most evident of these Iberian sources. Clavería notes ten poems that contain direct imitations (Poems 29, 32, 43, 46, 105, 106, 107, 108, 109, and 112); but the mode of love that the speaker experiences with the first lady is closely modeled on the sufferings, the melancholia, and the obsessive self-display of the speaker in the lyrics of Ausiàs March. Especially important, perhaps, are the poems to the "Lily among Thorns" (*llir entre cards*), one of which, Cant 19, "Oïu, oïu, tots los qui bé amats," would seem to provide the opening line to Boscán's poem 46 (14), "Oíd, oíd, los hombres y las gentes." For comprehensive studies of the influence of March on Boscán, see McNerney, *The Influence of Ausiàs March;* Armisén, *Estudios sobre la lengua;* and the excellent notes to the Clavería edition of Boscán's *Obra completa.* On March in Boscán, see Cruz, *Imitación y transformación.*

culture of the modern Spanish courtier's life, whereas the *Canzoniere* works in the direction of a man's transcendence of the earthly world into exalted registers of poetry and of divine revelation. The two texts therefore maintain a crucial difference, and the distinction is evident from the opening poems of Boscán's sequence.

Poem 29 is the first poem of the Second Book.[13] It opens in a manner that announces its affiliation to Petrarch 1, "Voi ch'ascoltate." Petrarch's poem represents his speaker calling on those who listen to his "scattered rhymes" to pity him for his sufferings.[14] Boscán invokes both Petrarch's language and his narrative in the tercets of his own sonnet:

> ¡O vosotros que andáis tras mis escritos
> gustando de leer tormentos tristes,
> según que por amar son infinitos!,
> mis versos son deciros, "¡O benditos
> los que de Dios tan gran merced huvistes
> que del poder d'Amor fuésedes quitos!"
>
> (9–14)

[Oh you who follow my writings / taking pleasure in reading these sad torments, / which, in love, are infinite!, / my verses say to you, "O blessed / are those who received that great mercy from God / so that they were saved from the power of Love!"]

From that point, however, the texts diverge. In Poems 2, 3, 4, and 5 of the *Canzoniere,* Petrarch turns to the systematic development of the classical

---

13. The poems of the First and Second Books are numbered continuously, which provides further evidence that they should be read together.

14. "Voi ch'ascoltate in rime sparse il suono / di quei sospiri ond'io nudriva'l core / in sul mio primo giovenile errore, / quand'era in parte altr'uom da quel ch'i sono: / del vario stile in ch'io piango et ragiono / fra le vane speranze e'l van dolore, / ove sia chi per prova intenda amore / spero trovar pieta, non che perdono. / Ma ben veggio or sì come al popol tutto / favola fui gran tempo, onde sovente / di me medesmo meco mi vergogno; / et del mio vaneggiar vergogna è'l frutto, /e'l pentersi, e'l conoscer chiaramente / che quanto piace al mondo è breve sogno" ("You who hear in scattered rhymes the sound of those signs with which I nourished my heart during my first youthful error, when I was in part another man from what I am now; for the varied style in which I weep and speak between vain hopes and vain sorrow, where there is anyone who understands love through experience, I hope to find pity, not only pardon. But now I see well how for a long time I was the talk of the crowd, for which often I am ashamed of myself within; and of my raving, shame is the fruit, and repentance, and the clear knowledge that whatever pleases in the world is a brief dream"); *Petrarch's Lyric Poems,* 36–37.

and the Christian universes and to the universe of letters, which the lady Laura will mediate over the course of the text to come. Boscán, while imitating the Petrarchan structure by employing his first five poems to establish the speaker's universe, initiates a different theme: the folly and also the vulnerability of the man who is isolated from the stabilizing forces of "la buena parte," the anchoring institutions and practices of the daily world. In a manner that prepares the way for the disastrous Poem 47, Boscán represents his speaker's error as misunderstanding the terms of public speech. In Poem 30, the speaker requires his wounds to tell the tale of his suffering:

Poem 30

Las llagas que, d'Amor, son invisibles,
quiero como visibles se presenten,
porque aquellos que umanamente sienten
s'espanten d'acidentes tan terribles.
Los casos de justicia más horribles
en público han de ser, porqu'escarmienten
con ver su fealdad, y a'admedrienten
hasta los corazones invencibles.
Yo traigo aquí la historia de mis males,
donde hazañas d'amor han concurrido,
tan fuertes, que no sé cómo contallas.
Yo solo en tantas guerras fui herido,
y son de mis heridas las señales
tan feas, que é verguenza de mostrallas.

[I want those wounds of Love that are invisible / to present themselves as visible, / so that those with human feeling / are frightened by such terrible misfortune. / The most horrible trials / should be held in public, so that they warn off / by means of their ugliness, and instill fear / in even the most invincible hearts. / I bring here the history of my sorrows, / in which love wrought so many deeds, / with such strength, that I do not know how to recount them. / It was I alone who was wounded in these many wars, / and the signs of my wounds are / so ugly that I am ashamed to display them.]

The folly here is requiring wounds to talk. The image is as deliberately risible as Horace's "human head on a horse's neck ... a melding of limbs covered everywhere with multicolored plumage."[15] Other sonnets in the opening section of the sequence go on to pave the way for Poem 47. They start, stop, turn back on themselves and present an image of narrative confusion that is paired with glimpses into the chaos of the speaker's isolated, inward world. In Poem 31, Boscán writes: "cada vez que bien me arrepentiere, / gran logro llevaré de mis tristuras; / de esta cura saldrán otras mil curas / para mí y para quien verme quisiere" (5–8) ("each time I repent well, / I gain greatly from my sorrows; / from this cure flow forth another thousand cares / toward me and toward they who wish to look on me"). On one level, Boscán is playing an arch courtly game with the notion of thousands of poems that are produced by the speaker's sorrows.[16] On the other, he is establishing his speaker's powerlessness in the face of his fate, a theme he expands on in Poem 33:

> Aún bien no fui salido de la cuna,
> ni de la ama la leche hube dejado,
> cuando el amor me tuvo condenado
> a ser de los que siguen su fortuna.
> Diome luego miserias de una en una
> por hacerme costumbre en su cuidado
> . . . .
> ¡O corazón que siempre has padecido!
> dime: tan fuerte mal, ¿cómo es tan largo?
> Y mal tan largo—di—¿cómo es tan fuerte?
>
> (1–6; 12–14)

[I was not yet well out of the cradle, / nor had I left behind my nurse's milk, / when Love condemned me / to be one of those who follow his fortunes. / Thereafter he fed me miseries, one by

---

15. "Humano capiti cervicem pictor equinam / iungere si velit, et varias inducere plumas / undique collatis membris . . . risum tenatis, amici?" ("If a painter chose to join a human head to the neck of a horse, and to spread feathers of many a hue over limbs picked up now here now there . . . could you, my friends . . . refrain from laughing?"); Horace, *Satires, Epistles, and Ars Poetica*, 450–51.

16. Navarrete observes the textuality of Boscán's sequence: whereas Petrarch speaks to his listeners, Boscán invokes readers (*Orphans of Petrarch*, 75–76).

one / so that I became accustomed to woe / ... / Oh heart, which has always suffered! / tell me: a suffering so strong, how can it be so lengthy? / And to my suffering, so lengthy, tell me—how can you be so strong?]

Having studied the speaker's problems as they are framed in the songs, we can answer these questions for him: his trouble is less love than it is his isolation and his persistence in the monadic universe of the Castilian singer. The transformation of that state of being will provide the narrative arc of the sequence. For this reason, the lyrics that introduce the lady, Poems 36 and 38, appear after the initial, establishing poems.[17] Furthermore, when she does appear, there is not very much to say about her. She is unnamed, and she is fickle and disdainful in the manner of the desired lady in the poetry of *fin amours* and Ausiàs March. Her role is principally that of contrasting with the second beloved, who extends to the speaker the prospect of chaste love, or *casto amor*.

Taken together, the contents of the first part of Boscán's sequence indicate that whereas the "ravings" (*vaneggiar*) of the speaker in Petrarch's *Canzoniere* are the fruits of a shame whose roots lie in idolatry, the "wounds" and "sorrows" that speak (however haltingly) for Boscán's speaker derive from his isolation from the regulatory supervision of his fellows. Imprisoned in his self-absorbed, fantastic universe, in which small cares can flood over themselves on their own musical momentum and create effects of alienation and dislocation that far exceed what is merited, he is in need of rescue. A series of poems that begins with Poem 53 and ends with Poem 66 portrays the stumbling end of his twin follies of wrong loving and wrong singing.

The Crisis of Llanto

The opening stanza of Poem 53 and the envoi of Poem 66 create a frame around a group of poems that take up the principal themes elaborated over the course of the first half of the sequence. They develop a vision of a life

---

17. Boscán provides a form of closure to his introductory series at Poem 35: "Solo y pensoso en páramos desiertos" ("Alone and brooding in black deserts") imitates Petrarch's Poem 35, "Solo et pensoso i più deserti campi." The correspondence between the two texts at this juncture serves to punctuate Boscán's sequence before he introduces the element of the lady.

that has been up to this point not only badly narrated, but lived in error. Following are the first thirteen lines of Poem 53:

> Yo ya viví, y anduve ya entre vivos.
> bien sé que'engañaba por vivir,
> pero, en fin, como quiera yo vivía.
> Sentía el mal, sabíale sufrir;
> mis sentidos andaban harto'squivos,
> mas quedaba algún gusto todavía.
> El alma parecía
> que a lo menos podía sostenerme;
> yo quería valerme
> con alguna esperanza, mala o buena.
> No estaba tan agena
> de todo mi juicio mi razón
> que un rato no acudiese al corazón.
>
> (1–13)

[I lived, and I wandered among the living. / I know well that my life was an illusion, / but, in the end, however I did it, I lived. / I felt the sickness, I knew how to suffer it; / my senses wandered in complete folly, / and yet there remained some pleasure still. / My soul seemed / to give me some support me, at least; / I wanted to redeem myself / with some type of hope, bad or good. / My reason was not so foreign / to all of my judgment / that it did not sometimes enter my heart.]

The poem continues on to recount a mode of living dominated by the illusions produced by the confused internal state brought on by the speaker's isolation from the surrounding society. He wanders about lost in a series of poems that elaborate on the theme. In Poem 57, he recognizes the folly of protecting his false happiness from the corrective gaze proffered by his fellow courtiers;[18] and in Poem 58, he reflects on how difficult it is to think clearly when one is prey to the accidents of experience.[19] Finally, in

---

18. "Anda conmigo, falsa, mi alegría; / yo la entiendo, más cúmpleme su maña. / Apártome de quien me desengaña / por no verme'stragar la fantasía" (57.1–4) ("My false happiness wanders with me; / I understand this, but it achieves its object, maddening me. / I distance myself from those who might disenchant me / so that I will not see my fantasy destroyed").

19. "Sueños de amor me traen en gran duda; / y no estoy ya para sufrir rebatos. / Pudiera el seso andar en estos tratos / si fuera mi fortuna menos cruda" (58.1–4) ("Dreams of love keep me uncertain; / and I can no longer suffer their attacks. / My brain might continue on in these affairs / were my fortune less harsh").

Poem 66, he reaches a crisis and declares his defeat before the onslaught of the forces that have been assailing him, forces that are summarized in the first and eighth stanzas of the song:

Stanza 1

Llévame el desvarío
del pensamiento a diferentes partes,
y a mi pesar, tras todas ellas guío.
Son por dondequiera muchos los embargos.
Yo, para tantas cargos,
digo al seso: "Porqué no te repartes?
Nuevos casos requieren nuevas artes;
pues trae'l mal tan grandes diferencias,
conviene al alma que ande diferente,
y, según la moviere'l acidente,
que busque en sí conformes esperiencias."
D'aquí son mis sentencias,
las unas de las otras tan contrarias,
que no son voluntarias.
¡O revolver del cielo, que dispuso
acá, en el mundo, un hombre tan confuso!

(3–18)

Stanza 8

Faltan ya mis movimientos,
los buenos y los malos igualmente;
también, por consiguiente,
yo é de faltar a mí y a todo el mundo.
No digo más sino que'estoy ausente
y'stán perdiendo ya sus fundamentos
todos mis pensamientos.
De'este milagro nace otro segundo:
que al alma tiene un sueño tan profundo
que no puede'l tormento despertalla,
y duermo yo a do todos me lloran.
Los sentidos que'n mi corazón moran,
huyen en ver sospecha de batalla.
Todo mi bando calla.

> Yo no oso decir esta pena es mía,
> ni sé qué's alegría,
> ni puedo solamente imaginalla,
> del dolor que me da nunca alcanzalla.
>
> (127–44)

[Stanza 1: My straying thought leads me / to different places, / and I follow each thought to my peril. / Obstacles are many and everywhere. / Because of all of these burdens, / I say to my brain: "How do you not split in two? / New situations require new arts; / and as sorrow brings so many, and such vastly different things, / it is fitting that the soul becomes different, / and that having been moved by an accident of fortune / it moves differently." / Hence are my sentences, / quite contrary to one another, / they are not governed by will. / Oh revolutions of the heavens, who placed / here in the world so confused a man!

Stanza 8: I err in my movements, / in both the right and the wrong ones, equally; / as a consequence / I am lost to myself and all the world. / I will not say more beyond that I am absent, / and that all of my thoughts / now lose their foundation. / From this miracle another is born: / my soul is wrapped in a sleep so profound / that torment cannot waken it, / and I sleep through that which others mourn on my behalf. / The senses that reside in my heart / flee, suspecting battle. / All of my band falls silent. / I do not dare to say that woe is mine, / nor do I know what joy is, / nor can I even imagine it, / for pain does not let me grasp it.]

The speaker holds to the present tense here, in an acceptable, if somewhat unsophisticated, mode of narration. He has made gains in shaping his voice for the public view, and he has also adopted that view to the extent that he reflects on the errors of his past, criticizing his old ways of loving and thinking as based on misguided thoughts. In keeping with what we have seen expressed elsewhere in the sequence, these errors are linked to his having been "absent" in fantasy. He describes how, self-exiled from the anchoring presence of rational company, he has drifted further and further into confusion and daydreams, where, burdened by passion and suffering, he perceived confused "new" things ("nuevos casos," line 9). As in other Renaissance traditions, we need to read this newfangledness as suspect. It taxes the brain ("seso," line 8), leading to doom (lines 141–44). The song's envoi is a statement of complete defeat:

> Canción: yo quedo muy peor que digo:
> sin corazón para mandarte nada.
> Tu vete ya, o queda, si quisieres;
> no cures de mí más, si bien me quieres,
> que ya mi cuenta queda rematada
> y hecha mi jornada.
>
> (199–204)

> [Song: I am much worse off than I say: / without heart to send you off with anything. / Go now, or stay, if you wish; / do not mind me anymore if you love me well, / for now my fate is sealed / and my journey is done.]

Poem 66 marks the point at which the speaker ends his old love and begins to experience the new. The route to his salvation is structured in terms of the two principal discourses of the Second Book, the Petrarchan and Horatian views, filtered through Castiglione, that formed Boscán's particular variety of Stoicism. In the wake of Poem 66, the speaker turns to a new beloved who will serve as a mediating figure on the order of the lady in Dante, Petrarch, or Bembo. However, unlike a true Petrarchan, he turns to this new woman gradually, in a series of poems that turn on the verb *mudarse,* or "change." In Poem 67, the speaker refers to having liberated himself from the prison of his former love, although he fears that he may become entrapped in a new one.[20] The clearest sign that the new experience will be different, and good, is that the speaker's heart is changing in accordance with a natural process:

> Todo es amor en quien de verdad ama,
> hasta el mudar que haze es más firmeza.
> Si mudare, pensá que's de tristeza,
> que'l mal le haze aver de mudar cama.

---

20. "Confesaré, si dizen que é mudado, / que mudó el acidente algún pedazo, / no la raíz del mal acostumbrado. / Un mudar fue d'un corazón cansado, / como es mudar en el izquierdo brazo / el peso del derecho atormentado" (67.9–14) ("I will confess, if they say that I have changed, / that the symptoms changed a little, / but not the root of my accustomed sorrow. / It was the change of a weary heart, / as one shifts to the left arm / a burden that torments the right one").

> Así me hizo a mi mi vieja llama
> que sosegar no pude en su crueza,
> y el alma ahora a nuevo amor s'aveza;
> mas no podrá, que'l otro amor la llama.
>
> (Poem 68; 1–8)

> [All is love in he who loves truly, / even change makes one all the more constant. / If I should change, consider it to be one sorrow exchanged for another, / for suffering causes me to take a new bed. / Thus it was with me, / I could not bear the cruelty of my old flame / and my soul now seeks a new love; / but it cannot go further, for the other love calls to it.]

For late Medieval and Renaissance writers, *mudanza* often referred to change associated with natural processes and cosmic harmonies.[21] But as we have seen elsewhere—in Acuña's Sonnet 45, for example—in the new lyric, natural shifts are often *naturalized* ones, changes adopted in response to social opinions and codes that a speaker internalizes as his own as he accepts his interpellation into a particular social regime. In this section of the sequence, the discourse of a natural metamorphosis is complicated by the fact that in Poem 64 the speaker has begun to identify his suffering with extremes that should be addressed by seeking the golden mean: "Mientras más voy, más lejos voy del *medio;* / con esto é de parar, y el mal reparto / en sufrir, en llorar y en lastimarme (12–14, my emphasis) ("As I go further I stray further from the middle ground; / I should stop here, / I will share out my grief / in suffering, in weeping and in self-pity"). Discourse thus competes with nature as the source to which the speaker's transformation should be attributed, and discourse wins the day, since from Poem 68 forward the new love is modeled on the moderated Neo-Platonism elaborated in *The Book of the Courtier*, in which love for the right lady leads to balance, happiness, and a Stoic sense of invulnerability to the contingencies of love and fate.[22]

---

21. For example, in his Sonnet 23, Garcilaso de la Vega will remind his lady, "Marchitará la rosa el viento helado, / todo lo mudará la edad ligera, / por no hacer mudanza en su costumbre" (12–14) ("The icy wind will wither the rose, / fleet age will change everything, / to avoid change in its own custom"). On the natural course of mudanza in this poem, see Friedman, "Creative Space," 53.

22. In Poem 101, the speaker declares that the second love provides him with the means to understand the mudanzas, which can also mean "contingencies," of human experience: "A mi gran mal, gran esperanza crece / por las mundanzas que del mundo entiendo. / Con este pensamiento

The Second Lady

The speaker accepts the second lady in a cluster of poems between 78 and 80. As Poem 78 is among the most beautiful poems in the sequence, I reproduce it in full:

Poem 78

Mueve'l querer las alas con gran fuerza
tras el loor de aquella que yo canto.
Al comenzar, levántase un espanto
tal que's peor del seso si s'esfuerza.
Por otra parte, la razón m'esfuerza:
yo hablo y callo, y'stóyme entre tanto;
esfuerzo alguna vez, y otras me'spanto;
en fin, la gana de'scrivir refuerza.
Del mundo, bien; de nuestros tiempos, gloria,

me defendo, / o a lo menos así me lo parece. / Si en su dolor el alma se'ntristece, / con ira o blandamente la reprendo; / ella entre sí mi voz está siguiendo, / y así también se'nsaña o se'nternece. / Pues si es así, y es d'ambos la caída, / ¿cuál dará a cuál, al levantar, la mano, / si nadie pasa que ayudarnos quiera? / Veo venir de lejos por lo llano / quien tiene fin a descansar mi vida, / y en alta boz me dize: 'Espera, espera'" ("Towards my great sorrow, a great hope grows up / because of the changes I perceive in the world. / This thought is my defense, / or at least it seems this way to me. / If the soul is saddened in its suffering, / I reprove it with anger or gently; / she herself is following my voice, / and she, too, grows angry or tender. / But if it is thus, and if both of us are falling, / which of us will extend to which the hand by which to rise up / if no one passes by who desires to help us? / I see approaching from afar on the plain / someone whose aim is to provide rest to my life, / and in a great voice the person calls to me, 'Hope, wait'"). *Esperar*, in Spanish, means both "to hope" and "to wait." Both meanings are engaged in this sonnet. The poem suggests that because the speaker can hope, he can be patient, and because he is patient, he is on his way to achieving the Stoicism that will protect him from the vulnerabilities that plagued him in the early poems of the sequence and in the First Book. Lines 1-4 of the sonnet thus express a version of an idea that Boscán describes more completely in the "Epístola a Mendoza," in which he describes the amusement of the Stoic when he contemplates the mad dance of the passions: "Así el sabio que vive descansando, / sin nunca oír el son de las pasiones, / que nos hazen andar como bailando, / sabrá burlar de nuestras turbaciones, / y reírs'á d'aquellos movimientos" (63-67) ("Thus the wise man who lives in repose, / never hearing the sound of the passions, / that make us wander as if dancing, / takes amusement at our turbulation, / and laughs at our movements"). Boscán describes himself as having achieved that attitude through having made the right marriage: "Y así yo, por seguir aquesta vía, / héme casado con una mujer ... Ésta m'á dado un nuevo ser ... Ésta me haze ver que'lla conviene / a mí y las otras no me convenían ... En mí las otras iban y venían" (127-36) ("And thus I, in order to follow this path, / have married with a woman.... This lady has given me new life.... This lady makes me see that she suits / me and that the others did not suit me.... The others came and went in me").

fue nacer ésta por la cual yo vivo:
enmienda fue de cuanto aquí se yerra.
Fue declarar lo natural más vivo,
fue de virtud hacer perfeta historia,
y fue juntar el cielo con la tierra.

[Desire moves its wings with great force / in praise of she whom I sing. / At the start, a fear rises up / that if it strives, my brain will suffer. / For its part, reason forces me: / I speak and I am silent, and I am caught between the two; / I strive at times, and at others I am frightened; / in the end, the desire to write gives me new strength. / A joy to the world; a glory for our times, / was the birth of that lady for whom I live: / it was the repair of all that here goes astray. / Her birth showed nature at its most vivid, / it brought completion to the history of virtue, / her birth joined heaven to earth.]

In a sequence that contains notably few memorable examples of figurative speech, Boscán borrows from Tansillo to forge an image of the speaker's desire to write praise of his new love as a great bird beating the air with strokes of its powerful wings.[23] The metaphor reflects Renaissance wit (agudeza) in the implicit pun between the quills of a pen and the feathers of wings, which, as the first quatrain moves along, may be those of Phaeton (a conventional mythological reference in poems about fearing and daring to write is to Phaeton, the son of Helios, who dared to try to drive the chariot of the sun). It also provides a powerful visual counterpart to the rhythmic propulsion of the dactyl and trochees that dominate in the first line. In addition, the poem, drawing on Petrarch, introduces the message of Christian salvation in its tercets, as the new lady brings perfect virtue, the union of heaven and earth, to the world. Poem 79 expands, triumphantly, on the divine theme:

Poem 79

La tierra, el cielo y más los elementos
han puesto su arte, hizieron a porfía
ésta, cuyo nombre es señora mía,
so cuya mano'stan mis sentimientos.

---

23. The source was identified by Armisén, *Estudios sobre la lengua*.

Quedaron los maestros muy contentos
de su labor, y vieron que acudía
la mano al punto de la fantasía;
y en paz fueron allí sus movimientos.
Dichoso el día, dichosa la hora,
también la tierra donde nacer quiso
ésta del mundo general señora.
Dichosa edad, que tanto se mejora,
Pues entre sí ya tienen paraíso
Los que infierno tuvieron hasta'gora.

[The earth, the sky, and also all the elements / have worked all their art, have prided themselves in making / this woman whose name is my lady, / all my sentiments are held beneath her hand. / These masters were quite contented / with their labor, as they saw all their dreams gathered up in her hand, / and that she came in peace. / Fortunate is the day, fortunate the hour, / and also the ground where she chose to be born / this great lady in our world. / Fortunate the age, which is much improved, / for they now have paradise / those who up to now had hell.]

This sonnet is followed by Poem 80, which begins with a close paraphrase of the opening line of Petrarch 159: "¿En cuál parte de cielo, en cuál planeta / guardado fue tan grande nacimiento?" ("In what part of heaven, by which planet / was so great a birth hidden?"). In the tercets, Boscán's speaker gives the answer:

Diónosla Dios, mas no porque la diese,
que fuera enagenar de su corona:
prestada fue para mostrar su obra.
Y según es el ser de su persona,
porque más tiempo en ella él se viese,
tarda quizas, que presto no la cobra.

(9–14)

[God gave her to us, but He did not, in giving her, / exile her from her crown: / she was lent in order to show His work. / And such is her being, / that He may tarry, / so that He may see Himself in her and not recall her soon.]

What the open and extended allusions to Petrarch are asking us to see here is that this group of poems, plus Poem 71, invoke Petrarch's Poems 55–65, a series in which Petrarch's speaker undergoes a crisis in his love for Laura as he experiences his passion to be waning and willfully renews its force. Thomas Roche has discussed the Petrarchan series (*Petrarch and the English Sonnet Sequences*, 47–49). He observes that Petrarch 55 represents a crossroads for Petrarch's lyric speaker, who is at the midpoint of his love for Laura *in vita*: Poem 62 refers to eleven years of love ("Or volge, Signor mio, l'undecimo anno"; 62.9 ["Now turns, my Lord, the eleventh year"]; Petrarca, *Petrarch's Lyric Poems*, 140–41), and the speaker loves Laura for twenty-one years before her death. Petrarch 55 begins, "Quel foco ch'i pensai che fosse spento" ("That fire which I thought had gone out"), but continues, "dal freddo tempo et da l'età men fresca, / fiamma et martír ne l'anima rinfresca. / Non fur mai tutte spente, a quell ch'i'veggio, / ma ricoperte alquanto le faville, / et temo no'l secondo error sia peggio" (1–5) ("because of the cold season and my age no longer fresh, now renews flames and suffering in my soul. They were never entirely extinguished, as I see, those embers, but somewhat covered over; and I am afraid that my second error will be worse") (ibid., 132–33). Roche argues that the renewal of the speaker's passionate love presents a grave danger. In lines 1–13 and 17, he "makes the wrong reply" when offered salvation:

> Perché quel che mi trasse ad amar prima,
> altrui colpa mi toglia,
> del mio dermo voler già non mi svoglia
> . . . .
> non vó che da tal nodo Amor mi scioglia.
>
> (59; 1–3, 17)

[Although the fault of another takes away from me what drew me first to love, it by no means dissuades me from my firm desire . . . I do not wish Love to loose me from such a knot]
(translated by Durling, cited in Roche, *Petrarch and the English Sonnet Sequences*, 49)

Rejecting grace redoubles his sin, as Roche explains: "With this willful desire Petrarch can go on in 60 to praise 'l'arbor gentil che forte amai molt'anni' (the noble tree that greatly I have loved for many years) and to wonder about the effects of 'le mie nove rime,' but this concern does not prevent his launching into a blasphemous litany of all that ties him to his love" (49). The blasphemous poem in question is Petrarch 61, "Benedetto sia'l giorno, e 'l mese, et l'anno," the source text for the tercets of Boscán's Poem 70, quoted above, "Dichoso el día."

Schooled by Roche's reading of Petrarch, we find the point of Boscán's Poems 71, 78, 79, and 80. In the *Canzoniere,* the speaker has rejected the opportunity for salvation, and the lines of benediction therefore read as titillating *errore,* blasphemous statements of the speaker's perverse commitment to idolatry. Boscán draws the Petrarchan crisis into his own text in order to foreground the contrasting, moderate stance that *his* speaker adopts toward love. In this way, Boscán frames another statement of the liberation that modern, courtierized self-restraint provides its subjects: in the modern Spanish world that is described in the Second Book, desire is authorized as long as it is contained; and the second lady will lead Boscán to his self-containment. For this reason, Boscán's speaker utters nearly the same lines that have condemned Petrarch's speaker, but the words read as beautifully worked statements of praise directed toward the lady who has saved him from peril.

Socializing Petrarch

The speaker experiences doubts, reversals, and hesitations with the second lady; however, when the sequence begins to resolve itself it does so rather abruptly, as Navarrete has observed (*Orphans of Petrarch,* 87–90). Between Poems 100 and 112, the speaker continues to refer to suffering and doubt, but from Poem 112, he finds himself in the "clear afternoon" of repose, reflecting that "como después del tempestuoso día / la tarde clara suele ser sabrosa" (1–2) ("just as, after a stormy day / the clear afternoon is delicious"), so he can now enjoy "reposar d'un hombre que camina, / que a la sombra descansa un breve rato" (12–13) ("the repose of a man who, walking, / rests in the shade a brief while"). From here, the sequence rushes towards it end. Poem 119 employs the same anaphoric structure, and the same key word (*dulce*) that appeared in Poem 95, and directly counters the pleasures enumerated in the earlier poem, resolving the error of taking joy in self-deception by substituting the more appropriate leisurely activity of sweet, but disciplined, repose:

> Dulce reposo de mi entendimiento;
> dulce plazer fundado sobre bueno;
> . . . .

> Dulce pensar que'stoy en paraíso;
> sino que, 'n fin, m'acuerdo que soy hombre
> y en las cosas del mundo tomo aviso
>
> (1–2; 12–14)

[Sweet repose of my understanding / sweet pleasure founded on the good; / ... / Sweet thought that I am in paradise; / but in the end, I remember that I am a man, / and that I take my counsel from things of this world.]

In contrast to his earlier habit of wishful thinking, the speaker corrects himself, pulling back from his fanciful allusion to paradise to recommit himself to reality: not paradise, but the regular world, not someone specially marked out by fortune, but a regular man.

What brings about this rapid enlightenment? Unlike Petrarch's text or the sixteenth-century sequences of writers such as Sidney or Spenser, there is no clear formal or numerological pattern that sets it up. It is possible to say that Boscán is following Dante and Petrarch in representing salvation as a sudden flash of insight brought about, as he says in Poem 116, "strangely" ("El milagro fue hecho 'strañamente, / porque resucitando el mortal velo, / resucitó también la immortal alma"; 9–11 ["The miracle was performed strangely, / for as the mortal veil was resurrected, / so was the immortal soul resurrected as well"]). *Extraño/a* can refer to the miraculous, and an element of divine intervention is obviously at work in the speaker's salvation, particularly here, when he compares it to resurrection. But once again we need to recognize the worldly orientation of this text, in which love is not transcended; in fact it is realized when he is joined with his lady in *casto amor*:[24]

Poem 127

> D'una mortal y triste perlesía
> en su cama tendida mi alm'estaba,
> y como el mal los nervios l'ocupaba,
> ni de pies ni de manos se valía.
> El casto Amor, que Dios del cielo envía,

---

24. Darst cites Crawford on the idea that Boscán's speaker has married his lady by the end of the sequence (*Juan Boscán*, 50–51).

le dijo en ver la pena que pasaba:
"Suelta tus pies, tus manos te destraba,
toma tu lecho a cuestas y haz tu vía!"
Volví luego a mirarme y vime sano
y caminé sin rastro de dolencia
por las cuestas así como en lo llano.
¡O poder eternal y soberano!
¿Quién sanará con propia diligencia
si la salud no da tu larga mano?

[With a mortal and sad paralysis / my soul lay in her bed, / and since the sickness had penetrated down to her very sinews, / she could employ neither feet nor hands. / Chaste Love, whom God sent from the heavens, / said to her, seeing the sorrow in which she passed her hours, / "Loosen your feet, your hands are freed, / leave your bed behind and make your way!" / I turned then to see myself and I found myself healed / and I walked without a trace of pain / through rough places and smooth. / Oh eternal and sovereign power! / Who can truly be healed / if their health is not given by your great hand?]

The reference to the Gospel of John in line 8 ("Jesus said to him: 'Stand up, take your mat and walk'"; 5.8) appears to cast the speaker's salvation in the terms of a divine intervention; however, since it is "casto amor" and not God or Christ who frees the soul and commands her to walk, and since "casto amor" refers to Church-sanctioned, married love, Boscán has once again mediated Petrarchan metaphysics with his more pragmatic and socially oriented spiritual views. In Poem 127 as in Poem 119, it is possible to be saved through the wise and moderate enjoyment of the worldly pleasures that have been provided by God to man. We can identify this view not only with Horace and the ancients but with Boscán's particular pre-Tridentine humanist moment in Spain, in which Epicureanism and Christianity come together. The Christianity that inflects the close of the sequence will not survive the Counter-Reformation. But in Boscán's sequence, the miracle is the world.[25]

---

25. Boscán's clearest statement of these ideas appears in his "Epístola a Mendoza." On the representation of God in Boscán's writings, see Lorenzo, "Displacing Petrarch."

Canto

Among the poems Boscán uses to draw the sequence to a close, Poems 114, 120, and 126 stand out for special mention since they systematically correct the *errore* I have been stressing are central to the sequence, and to the First and Second Books taken together—namely, the perils of fantasy and of uncontained song. In Poem 114, the speaker begins to reflect on his previous and his present state, framing the difference as the one between llanto and canción: "Otro tiempo lloré y ahora canto, / canto d'amor mis bienes sosegados; / d'amor lloré mis males tan penados, / que por necesidad era mi llanto" (1–4) ("Another time I lamented and now I sing, / I sing of the leisurely pleasures of love; / I lamented my grievous sufferings, / and my lament was of necessity"). The poem indicates the moral and the poetic distance that the speaker has traveled between poems such as Poem 19 and Poem 47, in which he judged bad song to be, precisely, "necessity," the unavoidable, and the justifiable, outcome of suffering. The tercets of Poem 114 attribute the emendation of his song, his writing, and his speech to reason, thus reinforcing the message set forth in the "Letter," that the means to appropriate and satisfying poetry is the exercise of rational judgment:

> Razón juntó l'onesto y deleitable,
> y de'stos dos nació lo provechoso,
> mostrando bien de do engendrado fue.
> ¡O concierto d'Amor grande y gozoso!,
> sino que de contento no terné
> qué cante, ni que'scriba, ni qué hable.
>
> (9–14)

[Reason united the honest and the pleasing, / and from those two was betterment born, / well illustrating from where it was conceived. / Oh great and pleasurable harmony of Love![26] / without whose contentment there can be nothing / to sing, write, or speak about]

---

26. The word *concierto* here makes a nice pun, which is also available, though less common, in English, namely, "concert" as harmony and "concert" as concord, or agreement. This helps make sense of the next line: the mutual agreement and concord of happy lovers is what distinguishes the new love and allows the speaker to sing, write, speak.

We can associate "reason" as it is used here more completely with the speaker's successful courtierization when we think about this self-correcting gesture. It appears in Poem 119, as we have seen; it appears in these lines; and it reflects the self-policing of the man who has turned himself over to the gaze of his peers for their correction, internalizing their prudent counsel and voicing it himself, as his own belief.

The problem of the talking wounds is resolved in Poem 120, as the speaker describes with the self-consciousness of an educated narrator how "tristes años y largos fui cuitado, / en tormentos d'Amor tan afligido" (1–2) ("sad, long years I was troubled, / afflicted by torments of love"), but that now "mi guerra convertió en tanta vitoria, / que ahora vencedor estoy triumphando, / dejando'scrita en todos larga historia" (12–14) ("my war was changed to such a victory, / that I am now the triumphant champion, / leaving my long story written in all [things]"). The "things" upon which he finds his story written are not wounds but rocks, plants, and animals ("Contemplaba la piedra sin cuidado, / la planta . . . / y el animal"; 4–6 ["I contemplated the rock, carefree, / the plant . . . / and the animal"]). This is one reason he can write about them in lines that are so clearly narrative of a past state. Now that he has become integrated into the society around him, the speaker can assume an appropriate subject position within its grammar. Indeed, one significant element of this poem is his facility with the imperfect tense.

In a similar fashion, Poem 126 closes the theme of naive versus prudent modes of speech, as the speaker describes his earlier mode of publishing his woes: "hablilla fui" (4) ("I was a chatterbox"). The word *hablilla,* with its lilting sound and suggestions of the diminutive or the infantile, echoes *redondilla,* the word Boscán uses to describe his earlier poetry when he refers to it in the "Letter," and it reminds us that euphony is one of the characteristics attributed to unreasonable poetic speech in the Second Book. The quatrain continues to fill out the theme: "que'n mi se componía / de lástima y dolor y de tormento, / y entre lenguas se mejoraba el cuento / que a su plazer cad'una le dezía" (5–8) ("for I was made up / of grief and pain and torment, / and as tongues wagged, the story got better / for each one told it in the way that pleased them") in a repetition of the earlier idea that the momentum of loose speech has the capacity to enhance emotion, as well as error.

Of course, to be corrected, the speaker must be rendered socially and culturally visible, which, in the world of the lyric sequence means "legible" to his fellows. And in this sequence, as we have already seen, this means that he must be capable of a self-narration that is more polished and considered than the uncontained, metonymic "publication" we saw earlier (*publicar,* Poem 19). Hence with the same insistence that earlier poems in the sequence drift between present, past, and a timeless space of daydream, Boscán fills the final poems with references to then and now and has his speaker deliver a clear-eyed assessment of the causes of his follies in loving and in speech. Poems 123, 124, and 127 all inscribe clear references to present and past; the final song, Poem 130, combines good narration with references to the other principal themes of the sequence: the self-absorbed lover, prisoner of Amor, the notion of error, the poetry of llanto:

> Gran tiempo Amor me tuvo de su mano,
> el bien con el dolor en mí templando,
> traiéndome con gusto y con tormento;
> conmigo mismo entonces fui pasando,
> embuelto en mis dolencias como sano,
> pues que todo paraba en ser contento
> . . . .
> Duraron largo tiempo estos errores,
> y ¡ojalá, pues tan grande fue'l errarse,
> no comenzaran o no duraran tanto!
> No había mi alma tanto de'ngañarse
> (por más que'n mí pudiesen los amores)
> que tan gran bien parase en tan gran llanto.
> De lo que fui, por lo que soy, me'spanto

(1–6; 46–52)

[For a long time Love held me in his hand, / moderating joy with pain within me, / leading me along by means of pleasure and torment; / then I spent my time with myself alone, / wrapped up in my sufferings, appearing like a healthy man, / for my sole aim was happiness. / . . . / These errors lasted a long time, / and would that it were, since the error was so great, / that they had not begun, or lasted so long! / My soul did not have enough to deceive itself with / (despite of what loves were capable of working in me) / that such great happiness did not end in great lament. / Of what I was, because of what I am now, I am frightened]

Earlier in this chapter, I quoted lines from this poem in which the speaker refers to his rejection of the counsel of his prudent friends. Returning to the poem at this juncture, we see the different kinds of salvation that are represented in the *Canzoniere* and in Boscán's own text. The two part on the matter of the world: Petrarch's speaker turns to the Virgin in poem 366 of the *Canzoniere,* in a textual and spiritual rejection of the terrestrial. In contrast, Boscán invokes Christ in his aspect of carnal man to inscribe earthly redemption. Beginning at line 61, the speaker celebrates "nuestro Dios a quien tanto costamos, / que derramó su sangre por nosotros" (61–62) ("our God, whom we cost so much, / who shed his blood for us"), and the balance of the poem is directed to "Aquel que ha perdonado / ser muerto y tormentado / injurias padeciendo cara a cara" (84–86) ("He who forgave / being killed and tormented / suffering wounds face to face"). He fills out the repercussions of these references in lines 106–20 (lines that make use of the future tense, as well as the past and the present):

> Mis errores veré, mas ya los veo
> y entiendo bien el vano fundamento
> sobre'l cual levantaba mi cuidado
>
> . . . .
>
> El mundo m'ha vengado con su lanza
> con crueldad tamaña
> que he dolor ya de tanta destemplanza.
> Nunca pidió la rabia de mi saña
> ser vengada con furia tan estraña.
>
> [I will see my errors, but I already see them / and I understand well the vain foundation / upon which I built up my cares / . . . / The world has avenged me with its lance / with a cruelty of such dimensions / that I now am pained by its lack of moderation. / The rage of my anger never asked / to be avenged with such strange fury.]

The divinely sanctioned vengeance unleashed in the modern world on resistant subjects is their consignment to continued suffering. Devoid of sheltering Stoic distance from the accidents of experience, they are condemned to experience the world as a series of continual shocks, outrages, and causes for lament. But the clearest statement of Boscán's speaker's rebirth from undisciplined singer to the modern and circumspect Spanish courtier is Poem 115.

Poem 115

Antes tendré que cante blandamente,
pues amo blandamente y soy amado;
sé que'n Amor no es término forzado
sólo escribir aquel que dolor siente.
Desabafase quien está doliente,
y canta en la prisión el desdichado,
con hierros y cadenas fatigado,
mas su cantar, del nuestro es diferente.
Yo cantaré conforme a la avecilla
que canta así la sombra d'algún ramo,
que'l caminante olvida su camino,
quedando transportado por oílla.
Así yo de ver quien me ama y a quien amo,
en mi cantar tendré gozo contino.

[Now I maintain that I will sing gently, / for I love gently and I am loved; / I know that in Love it is not a forced rule / that only he who feels pain should write. / He who is suffering unburdens himself, / and the wretched man sings in his prison, / fatigued by his irons and chains, / but their song is different from ours. / I will sing in keeping with the little bird / who sings in the shade of some branch, in such a way / that the wanderer forgets his path, / standing still, he is transported, in hearing it. / Thus I, gazing upon the one who loves me and who I love in return, / will take continuous joy in my song.]

As I have indicated at various points in this chapter, this poem declares the speaker's triumph over old ways of loving and singing and his emergence as the new, self-contained, and self-contented author of a new type of courtly song. He rejects the conventions of courtly love as so much antiquated "*término* forzado" and sings his sweet new tune from "some" (*algún*) branch, neither the highest nor the lowest on the tree. The image of the shady branches that invite the wanderer to stray from his path, and the song that fixes him beneath their canopy transported in continuous joy, are evocative of Petrarch 142, "A la dolce ombre delle belle frondi." Poem 116 confirms that it is the Petrarchan laurel, as the speaker proclaims, "Celebrado seré en toda la gente, / llevando en mi triumpho para'l cielo, /

con el verde laurel la palma blanca" (12–14) ("I will be celebrated amongst all the people, / carrying to heaven, in my triumph, / the green laurel and the white palm"). But the laurel joined with the palm serves as the figure for a Petrarchism that is mediated and moderated by peace. This peace is gained through daily intercourse with a society of which the speaker forms a part. In contrast to his former habit of fleeing from his peers, he exists among them: "Celebrado seré *en* toda la gente" (12; my emphasis) ("I am celebrated among all the people").

Garcilaso

Poems 115 and 116 frame the completion of the speaker's journey from isolated Castilian to cosmopolitan courtier, and the few remaining sonnets that follow elaborate on the speaker's contentment and demonstrate his newfound ability to narrate his past. He speaks in short, comprehensible statements that stand in contrast to his paralysis in Poem 47. Poems 128 and 129, however, seem to disrupt the closing moves of the sequence. The first is a sonnet written in praise of Garcilaso, "El hijo de Peleo, que celebrado" ("The son of Peleus, celebrated") The second, "Garcilaso, que al bien siempre aspiraste" ("Garcilaso, you who always aspired to the good"), is also a sonnet and laments the fact that Garcilaso did not take Boscán with him when he died. After this poem, the sequence is completed with the long summary song of Poem 130, "Gran tiempo Amor me tuvo de su mano" ("For a long time Love held me in his hand").

Ana Girón, Boscán's wife, asserted that she followed his instructions in preparing the text of the *Obras* (the text was published in 1543, with an introductory comment lamenting that Boscán was unable to complete work before his death in 1542). So it seems likely that Boscán requested that the two sonnets to his friend be included in the sequence. Whether or not he did so, their impact on the text is to inscribe another significant social discourse into the Second Book, that of Renaissance friendship. Ullrich Langer has discussed how Renaissance writers, following the model of the ancients, privileged the discourse of friendship, distinguishing *"philia . . . from desire, concupiscence, or erotic love (eros) and from simple good will (eunoia)* or, later on, Christian charity and the love of God *(agape)*" (*Perfect Friendship,* 20). Theorized as more perfect than heteroerotic desire because it was (ostensibly) desexualized, true friendship was spoken of as a rare and beautiful phenomenon, one that was capable of transforming its participants in a manner similar to Neo-Platonic love. Garcilaso represented his friendship with Boscán as exemplary of this kind of friendship in his "Epístola a Boscán," describing the "strange" (*extraño*) effect of his bond with "vos, del amistad ejemplo" (31) ("you, the exemplar of friendship"), that "ninguna cosa en mayor precio estimo . . . tanto como el amor de parte mía" ("I deem nothing more precious . . . than the love I bear you").[27] The theme of perfect friendship is also present in Boscán's Poem 129, "Garcilaso, que al bien siempre aspiraste" ("Garcilaso, you who always aspired to the good"), since Boscán is lamenting his having been left behind when his friend ascended to Heaven, the word *bien*, or "good" is employed in the Neo-Platonic sense. We have already seen a socializing role attributed to masculine friendship in Acuña's Sonnet 45. In the Second Book, the poems to Garcilaso ascribe perfect friendship a role in accommodating men to their position as subjects in a courtly—but also a courtierized—society.

But while Boscán assigned friendship an important regulatory function within the shaping of the Hapsburg courtier, a number of poems by Garcilaso demonstrate an alternate use for the discourse. Elegy 2 and Sonnet 33 deploy the discourse of friendship to fashion a conceit of the private self who appears to *elude* the powers of the Hapsburg regime, as well as its principal mechanisms of institutional and discursive interpellation. The private voice that Renaissance writers and readers associated with the confidences of friendship enabled Garcilaso to play some arch games with the figure of the

---

27. "Iba pensando y discurriendo un día / a cuántos bienes alargó la mano / él que del amistad mostró el camino, / y luego vos, del amistad ejemplo, / os me ofrecéis en estos pensamientos / y con vos a los menos me acontece / una gran cosa, al parecer estraña, / y porque lo sepáis en pocos versos, / es que, considerando los provechos, / las honras y los gustos que me vienen / desta vuestra amistad, que en tanto tengo, / ninguna cosa en mayor precio estimo / ni me hace gustar del dulce estado / tanto como el amor de parte mía / . . . / amistad y la estrecheza nuestra / con solo aquéste el alma se enternece; / y sé que otramente me aprovecha / el deleite, que suele ser propuesto / a las útiles cosas y a las graves / . . . / hallo que'l provecho, el ornamento, / el gusto y el placer que se me sigue / del vínculo d'amor, que nuestro genio / enredó sobre nuestros corazones / son cosas que de mí no salen fuera, / y en mí el provecho solo se convierte" ("Epístola a Boscán," 28–41; 44–48; 51–56) ("I was thinking and pondering one day / about how many good things he held forth, / he who showed the path to friendship, / and then you, the exemplar of friendship, / came into my thoughts / and with you, in the slightest occasion / strange as it seems, a great thing happens to me, / and that you may know it in few verses, / it is this: considering the advantages, / the honors, and the pleasures that come to me / from our friendship, there being many, / I do not esteem anything more precious, / nor do I take more pleasure from that sweet state / than I do in the love that I bring from my side / . . . / friendship and our closeness / with only these is the soul made tender; / and I know that I am also improved / by the delight, that is often attributed / to useful and grave things / . . . / I find that the benefit, the ornament, / the enjoyment and the pleasure that come to me / from the bond of love, that our intelligence / wound around our hearts / are things that do not depart from within me, / and which convert themselves only in my gain").

imperial subject. In a widely discussed section of Elegy 2, for example, he describes to Boscán how,

> debajo de la seña esclarecida
> de César africano nos hallamos
> la vencedora gente recogida:
> diversos en estudio, que unos vamos
> muriendo por coger de la fatiga
> el fruto que con el sudor sembramos;
> otros (que hacen de la virtud amiga
> y premio de sus obras y así quieren
> que la gente lo piense y que lo diga)
> destros en lo público difieren,
> y en lo secreto sabe Dios en cuánto
> se contradicen en los que profieren
> . . . .
> Más, ¿dónde me llevó la pluma mía?,
> que a sátira me voy mi paso a paso
> y aquesta que os escrivo es elegía.
> Yo enderezo, señor, en fin mi paso
> por donde vos sabéis que su proceso
> siempre ha llevado Garcilaso
>
> (4–15; 22–27)

[under the shining standard / of the African Caesar we find ourselves, / the victors, gathered: / we are diverse in our studies, for some among us go on / half-dead, to seize from fatigue / that fruit we sowed with our sweat; / and others (who make virtue their friend and / the prize of their efforts, and desire / that people think precisely that, and speak of it) / those others dissemble in public, / and in secret God knows by how much / they contradict their oaths / . . . / But, where did my pen lead me? / for step by step I head toward satire / and what I write you is an elegy. / I will adjust, sir, my step at last / toward where you know its progress / has always led Garcilaso]

These lines reveal the hidden side of the modern man of arms and letters. Garcilaso describes his actions and those of his fellow imperial fighters in the aftermath of the battle for the fort of La Goleta in 1535. The Spanish victory is sometimes represented as the pinnacle of the emperor's career.

However, in this telling the scene and its players are portrayed decidedly ingloriously. No longer worthy knights who receive honor and privilege by birthright, Garcilaso's fellow fighters in the elegy struggle to gain a share of the spoils of their victory and expose their ignobility when no one is looking. Their moderation and sprezzatura are thus revealed as performances that men enact and let slip.[28] Even Garcilaso himself, a knight of Santiago, allows his pen to stray in the confidence of friendship and sends his elegy toward satire.

But this straying is obviously intentional. Garcilaso's sally into erroneous writing and undisciplined speaking—a swerve we might read as "publishing" or "telling" along the lines of the naive speaker of Boscán's First and Second Books—creates the effect of a gap between Garcilaso de la Vega, famed courtier of arms and letters, and a more "authentic" self who writes rapidly and unguardedly to his bosom friend.[29] The slip into satire thus creates the effect of a brief assertion of agency within a scene of profound subjection. The depths to which the proud Spanish members of the imperial forces felt they had sunk during the Tunisian campaign is illustrated by the historical record and by some of its more jaded chroniclers. Indeed, in an unfortunate historical coincidence, an account of Garcilaso's death provides a striking counterpart to the elegy. In his account of the event, the Cordoban don Martín de Cereceda relates:

> Aquí en esta torre había catorce personas, que eran doce hombres y dos muchachos . . . el Emperador quiso ver qué gente era y a qué estaba allí, y así mandó con el artillería que con el avanguardia era arrivada se diese batería a la torre y así se dió y se hizo un pequeño portillo . . . don Jerónimo de Urrea, caballero español, con una mala escala arremetió a la torre y entró por el portillo . . . quiso subir el capitán Maldonado y el maese de campo Garcilaso de la Vega, entre los cuales hubo alguna diferencia por la subida. A la hora llega don Guillén de Moncada, hijo de don Hugo de Moncada, diciendo: "Señores, suplicoos, pues vuestras Mercedes tenéis tanta honra, que me dejéis ganar a mí una poca honra." A la hora le respondió el capitán Maldonado diciendo: "Para tan

---

28. On the threat of the "slip" as constitutive of the figure of the courtier, see Berger, *The Absence of Grace*, chapter 1.

29. Paul Julian Smith was an early innovator in analyzing the rhetorical aspects of Garcilaso's intimate voice. See *Writing in the Margin*, 43–56. On the "sincerity debates," see Heiple, *Garcilaso de la Vega*.

valeroso caballero poca honra es esta; suba vuestra merced." Así fue la segunda persona don Guillén de Moncada. Subiendo Garcilaso de la Vega y el capitán Maldonado, los que en la torre estaban dejan caer una gran gruesa piedra y da en la escalera y la rompe, y así cayó el maese de campo y capitán, y fue muy mal descalabrado el maese de campo en la cabeza, de la cual murió a muy pocos días.[30]

[Here in this tower there were fourteen people, twelve men and two boys . . . the emperor wanted to see what people they were and what purpose they had being there, and thus he commanded that a battery be launched against the tower by means of the artillery with which the vanguard had arrived and so it was launched, and this made a small breach . . . don Jeronimo de Urrea, a Spanish gentleman, leaned a bad ladder against the tower and entered through the breach . . . the Captain Maldonado and the Fieldmaster Garcilaso de la Vega wished to climb, and there was a disagreement between them about climbing. Just then, don Guillén de Moncada, son of don Hugo de Moncada, arrived, saying, "Sirs, I beseech you, since your graces have so much honor, let me win a little bit of honor for myself." Then Captain Maldonado responded, saying: "For a valiant knight this is little honor; climb, your grace." Thus the second person was don Guillen de Moncada. While Garcilaso de la Vega and the Captain Maldonado were climbing, those who were in the tower let fall a great, thick rock which hit the ladder and broke it, and thus the fieldmaster and the captain fell, and the fieldmaster was badly injured in the head, from which he died in a very few days.]

The narrative reflects the erosion of the historical and material supports for the ideal of the *diestro braço* in the imperial wars. Cereceda describes a moment of transition, in which honor retains sufficient value to provoke

---

30. *Tratado de las campañas y otros acontecimientos de los ejércitos del emperador Carlos V en Italia, Francia, Berbería y Grecia desde 1521 a 1545 por don Martín de Cereceda, cordobés, soldado en aquellos ejércitos* (Account of the Campaigns and of the Other Occurrences Within the Armies of the Emperor Charles V in Italy, France, Barbary and Greece from 1521 to 1545 by don Martin de Cereceda, Cordoban, Soldier in Those Armies). The account is discussed by Aurora Hermida Ruiz, in an unpublished dissertation that should be considered required reading for students and critics in the field of sixteenth-century studies ("Historiografía literaria," 41–43). Hermida points out that the story tarnishes the legendary heroic death of the great paragon of Spanish arms and letters and that it is therefore not surprising, perhaps, that it is overlooked in most accounts of Garcilaso's life and death (43).

the assembled noblemen to arguments regarding which one has greatest need of the very little share there is to go around. In the context of this significant cultural shift, Garcilaso's wanderings between elegy and satire come into sharper focus, illustrating his sensitivity to the entirely discursive nature of the modern forms of identity that were being conferred upon Spanish subjects in his age. Anticipating late twentieth-century formulations presented by critics such as Judith Butler, perhaps, Garcilaso recognized that the "identity" of the subject is multiple, overdetermined, and in need of constant assertion and restaging. In keeping with Butler's ideas about resistance and "camp," he also observed that the necessity of this restaging establishes the conditions for witty reversals.[31] A more elaborately worked (and, in fact, camp) example of discursive resistance is Garcilaso's Sonnet 33, another poem devoted to the ambivalent representation of the victory at Tunis. This sonnet has inspired a fair amount of comment in recent years. Indeed, Elegy 2 and Sonnet 33 are often read together for their implicit critiques of early Hapsburg triumphalism in the wake of the Spanish victory at Tunis.[32] The poem serves as a fitting capstone to this chapter, since it testifies to some unexpected consequences of Boscán's project of courtierizing song. Garcilaso mobilizes two important poetic devices privileged in the new art, allusion and rhythm, to stage a scene of the radical undoing of the imperial subject.

Sonnet 33

Boscán, las armas y el furor de Marte,
que con su propia fuerza el africano
suelo regando, hazen que el romano
imperio reverdezca en esta parte,
han reduzido a la memoria el arte
y el antiguo valor italïano,
por cuya fuerza y valerosa mano

---

31. Butler has argued that "when power shifts from its status as a condition of agency to the subject's 'own' agency," the stage is set for discursive resistance through forms of parody and camp (*The Psychic Life of Power,* 12). As Garcilaso's death rather graphically illustrated, however, neither he nor Butler's individual subject "wields the power to rework or rearticulate the terms of discursive demand.... To thwart the injunction to produce a docile body is not the same as dismantling the injunction or changing the terms of subject constitution" (ibid., 88).

32. See Cruz, "Self-Fashioning in Spain"; Graf, "From Scipio to Nero"; and Helgerson, *A Sonnet from Carthage.*

África se aterró de parte a parte.
Aquí donde el romano encendimiento,
dond'el fuego y la llama licenciosa
solo el nombre dejaron a Cartago,
vuelve y revuelve al amor mi pensamiento,
hiere y enciend'el alma temerosa,
y en llanto y en ceniza me deshago.

[Boscán, the arms and fury of Mars, / which, irrigating the African / ground with its own force, cause the Roman / empire to flourish again in these parts, / have relegated to memory that art / and that ancient Italian valor, / by whose strength and worthy hand / Africa was rent, part from part. / Here, where the Roman torch, / where the fire and the licentious flame / left only the name of Carthage, / my thoughts turn and return to love, / my fearful soul wounds and burns, / and in weeping and ashes I am undone.]³³

The first line of the poem sets up the expectation that it is a celebratory piece commemorating the triumph of imperial forces in Africa. But the triumphalist imperial message is complicated by the fact that the Spanish do not receive mention in the poem. The arms and fury in line 1 are linked to Mars, not to Charles; and it is the ancient Roman power that serves as the exemplar of "valor" (lines 6 and 7) and the point of origin of the very idea of noble war. The resulting ambiguity casts the imperial victory in an ambivalent light. This ambivalence arguably prepares us to question whether a parodic register is inscribed in the poem through its structure of allusions. Garcilaso opens the sonnet in the key of hyperbolic masculine violence, with "the furor of Mars" and his sword streaming blood across the African plain. He concludes it with an imperial fighter adopting the posture of vanquished Dido, the Carthaginian queen who was undone, not by warfare but by passion. The dissonance between these two images is not entirely resolved by the heroic status that was assigned to Dido by Italian and Spanish humanists. Male and female worthies were rarely combined in a single exemplum. Rather, Garcilaso's use of the classical reference calls the nature of the contemporary African conquest into question: have the emperor and his troops superseded the ancient triumphs, or have they spent

---

33. Literally, "I undo myself."

their force vainly on an unequal foe? Is Garcilaso's courtly lyric speaker a man of Mars, or have modern circumstances transformed him into a beautiful but helpless figure who is ravaged by emotion, as opposed to action? The tercets of the sonnet extend this ambiguity by drawing on the constraining and disciplining pressures that we have already observed as inherent to the form's poetics. Whereas writers such as Acuña and Boscán mobilized those poetics to represent ideological and linguistic pressures that bind the subject, Garcilaso uses them to initiate a centrifugal motion. The shift is a function of both form and content, a combination of the rising sensation created by the syntax of lines 9 through 11 ("Aquí donde . . . / donde . . . ") and the repetitions in those lines and in lines 12 and 13 ("vuelve y revuelve . . . hiere y enciende"). The pattern of sound underscores the gyration of the speaker's thoughts in a neat feat of consonance that is entirely licit within the protocols of the Italianate new art. Its legitimacy does not prevent it from subverting the stability of the sonnet-subject, however. Insistent elisions and assonances propel lines 9 to 14 forward: "don-*de el*-ro-MA-*no en*-cen-di-MIEN-to" (line 9); "don-*de el*-FUE-*go y*-la-LLA-ma" (line 10); "VUEL-*ve y*-re-VUELVE-a-MOR" (line 12). The final effect is an inscription of centrifugal force whose release in line 14—"*y en*-LLAN-to- *y-en*-cen-I-za-me-des-HA-go"—underscores the final word, a form of *deshacerse*.[34]

Garcilaso and Boscán both understood that the new lyric was a poetry of subjects. For Boscán, the ultimate object of the new art was to guide courtly subjects into moderation and restraint. But after having focused in this chapter and in Chapter 1 on the ways in which the new lyric served as a tool through which to inculcate Spain's noblemen with doctrines of subjection and self-restraint, it is important to point out that Boscán's friend and fellow collaborator provided equally deft examples of its potential to subvert the self-contained figure of the Hapsburg courtier. I will return to this aspect of Garcilaso in Chapter 4. First, however, I will examine a less ambivalent subject of empire, Gutierre de Cetina, who also attempted to work Italianate lyric into forms that would better represent his imperial subjectivity.

---

34. We might contrast the tercets of Garcilaso's Sonnet 33 to those of Acuña's Sonnet 30, discussed in Chapter 1. In Acuña's poem, the volta functions to contain the chaos of song, bending the frenzies it inspires to the will of reason. In Sonnet 33, the compression created by the volta becomes the impetus for a spiral of movement that undoes containment.

3

IMPERIAL PASTORAL:
GUTIERRE DE CETINA WRITES THE HOME EMPIRE

Un modo diverso me hallé . . .

THE LESSON OF CHAPTER 2 MIGHT BEST be summarized: song enables, even as it constrains. However, most of the chapter represented Boscán's attempts to condition the *Canzoniere* to the culture of modern life. Boscán's poetics, as we saw, involved the subordination of consonance to the dictates of reason, an intervention directed toward curbing what he perceived as the excesses of traditional Castilian poetry to Horatian ideals of self-constraint. He enacted this formally through the substitution of Italian hendecasyllables for both the twelve-syllable arte mayor and the shorter line forms of the Castilian coplas. At the level of content, Boscán's lyric sequence represented the interpellation of the autonomous Petrarchan universe into the norms and regimes of the contemporary social world. The ideal outcome of the subjective and poetic transformations recounted over the course of the sequence was the innovation of a type of lyric that corresponded to neither the laurel nor the palm, but rather to a middlebrow tree from which the modern Castilian version of the Petrarchan sparrow could sing his different song (*nuestro cantar es diferente*).

Judging from what we can piece together of the biography of the Sevillian fighter, adventurer, and poet Gutierre de Cetina (1514?–1557), and based on the 296 poems that have been attributed to him, this was a man who differed significantly from Boscán, both as a poet and as a courtier. And yet the two can be linked, because Cetina, born more than a generation after Boscán, in many ways represented his Catalan elder's ideals for the modern Spanish nobleman.[1] A member of the minor nobility in Seville, Cetina was born into

---

1. The most comprehensive discussion of Cetina's life and work is the monograph by Begoña López Bueno *Gutierre de Cetina, poeta del renacimiento español*. Her resume of the poems, grouped by

a family that took advantage of the new financial and social opportunities extended them by the culture of the empire. According to Begoña López Bueno, Cetina's principal biographer, the Cetina family's income was derived in great part from New World commerce, while *juros* (bonds for loans issued to the Crown) and rents from holdings in Spain also contributed to their fortune. Uncles and cousins lived in the New World, and Cetina himself traveled there at least twice, dying there in his early forties from wounds suffered in a cloak-and-dagger episode in New Spain in 1557. But primarily, Cetina earned his living as a captain and a courtier in Spain's European domains. Recognized by Charles V and familiar with members of important circles in the courts of Valladolid and Toledo, as well as in Seville, he seems to have received his principal patronage from Fernando de Gonzaga (1507–1557), viceroy of Sicily and a trusted commander of the emperor's forces. Gonzaga apparently respected Cetina's abilities, and the two fought together frequently, against the Turks in 1538–1539 and also against the French in the fourth installment of the Hapsburg-Valois wars.[2] During the 1530s and 1540s Cetina was based principally, it seems, in Italy (although not in 1541, when López Bueno speculates that he may have participated in the battle for Tunis, or in 1546, when he traveled to the New World). His sonnets also make reference to periods spent in Germany during his short and peripatetic life.

Cetina's life and career, divided between commerce and fighting, and marked by European and transatlantic travel, were representative of the trends that were taking hold among members of the new nobility in the first half of the sixteenth century. Furthermore, there is ample evidence to find that his poetic tastes were similarly modern. After his death he would be praised by Fernando de Herrera as one of Spain's best sonneteers, despite a tendency to be too "soft," in the manner of Italian writers:

> En Cetina, cuanto a los sonetos particularmente, se conoce la hermosura y gracia de Italia . . . ninguno le negará lugar con los primeros . . . fáltale el espíritu y vigor, que tan importante es a la poesía . . . aunque . . . o sea causa la imitación o otra cualquiera, es tan generoso y lleno que casi no cabe en sí.

---

form, appears on page 119. Her summary of the sources of each of the Italiante poems appears on page 120. For a briefer biographical sketch of Cetina, see the introduction to López Bueno's edition of the *Sonetos y madrigales completos*. On Cetina in the New World, see González Echevarría, "Colonial Lyric," in the *Cambridge History of Latin American Literature* (198–99). For Cetina's influence on the New World writer Diego Dávalos, see Colombí-Monguió, *Petrarquismo Peruano*.

2. López Bueno, *Gutierre de Cetina*, 48–54.

[In Cetina, one recognizes the beauty and the grace of Italy ... no one will deny him a place among the best ... he lacks spirit and vigor, which is so important to poetry ... although ... whether the cause is imitation or another one, he is so generous and full that he nearly exceeds his own capacity.][3]

Judging from what was learned of Herrera's criteria for excellence in composition in the sonnet form in Chapter 1, we see why he might have held his fellow Andalusian in high regard.[4] Cetina understood Italian aesthetics, and often foregrounded sensual imagery and the representation of emotional states over the argumentative structure favored by Boscán.[5] Furthermore, unlike Boscán, Cetina chose single poems and compendia such as the *Rime diverse di molti eccellentissimi authori nuovamente raccolte* (1545) over the sequences of Bembo and Petrarch as textual models for his lyrics.[6] His collected works are comprised almost entirely of loose poetry: songs, sonnets, madrigals, and epistles, many of them recognizable imitations of Italian poets such as Ariosto, Tansillo, and Sannazaro, and some of them modeled on Spanish poems by Boscán, by Hurtado de Mendoza, by Garcilaso, and by Ausiàs March. More significantly, perhaps, Cetina, like Herrera, understood the potential for correspondence between the sonnet and the modern courtly subject.[7] The predominant persona in Cetina's lyric is that of the urbane dissembler whose utterance reveals a split between his graceful and pleasing exterior and a complex interiority. Cetina enhanced the conceit of this subjective interiority by manipulating the spaces internal

---

3. *Annotations,* 280–81. In the vein of practical influence, this success was demonstrated by Cetina's prominence in compendia such as the 1577 *Flores de varia poesía.* For New World poets, as for peninsular ones, he served as an important authority and model for lyrics composed in the Italianate style.

4. Regional loyalties may also have influenced Herrera's praise, since the north/south intellectual rivalry that pitted Salamanca against Sevilla was sparked into a fury by *Annotations.* See Montero, *La controversia.*

5. Actually, Herrera criticized Cetina on that point, observing that he had mastered the sweet style, but that his poetry lacked the appropriate Spanish vigor: "si acompañara la erudición y destreza de l'arte al ingenio y trabajo y pusiera intención en la fuerza como en la suavidad y pureza, ninguno le fuera aventajado" ("had he accompanied the erudition and finesse of his art with the ingenuity and the work and had he placed intention in force as he did in the suavity and purity, none would have bested him"); *Annotations,* 281.

6. López Bueno, *Gutierre de Cetina,* 88.

7. "Resplandecen en ella con maravillosa claridad y lumbre de figuras y exornaciones poéticas la cultura y propriedad, la festividad y agudeza, la magnificencia y espíritu, la dulcura y jocundidad, l'aspereza y vehemencia, la comiseración y afectos, y la eficacia y representación de todas.... y la brevedad suya no sufre que sea ociosa o vana una palabra sola" ("In it shine forth with marvelous clarity

to the sonnet and playing on the rules that govern the form. As I discussed in Chapter 1, and as we will find again in Chapter 4, writers from Lorenzo to Herrera judged the successful deployment of this figure as the sign of a sonneteer's success.[8]

More recently, Cetina's reputation as a poet has declined. For example, Antonio Prieto has asserted that the absence of a consistent object of desire in Cetina's work bars its formal and semantic diversities from cohering into a consistent poetic voice.[9] This criticism is representative of twentieth-century evaluations of Cetina and his lyrics. But in this chapter, I will argue that the characteristics that have been perceived as inconsistencies in his poetry in fact indicate its sophistication. The poems that relate the loves of the shepherd Vandalio, in particular, show that Cetina had mastered the Italian style and was exploring ways to adapt it to better represent *Spanish* lyric speakers, specifically, as they negotiated the divided loyalties they experienced as subjects in imperial Hapsburg Spain. In this series of works, Vandalio journeys from a self-contained lover's universe, a personal golden age in which he enjoys the pleasures of *Dórida* ("the golden lady") on the banks of the river Betis, to participation in the cosmopolitan life of the imperial court, as he takes up with *Amarílida* (Amaryllis, but also "the yellow lady"), by the shores of the Pisuerga. *Vandalio* means "the man from Andalucía," and the river Pisuerga was associated with Valladolid, an important city for the Hapsburgs, both symbolically and bureaucratically: it was the birthplace of Phillip II and the de facto seat of government until the construction of the Escorial.[10] Furthermore, since the name "Amarílida" alludes to Amaryllis,

---

and illumination through figures and poetic adornments the culture and propriety, the festivity and wit, the magnificence and spirit, the sweetness and jocularity, the bitterness and the vehemence, the sympathy and the affects, and the efficacious representation of all . . . and its brevity does not suffer one single frivolous or vain word"); *Annotations,* 267. See my discussion of this passage in Chapter 1.

8. As discussed in Chapter 1, Lorenzo's *Comento de' miei sonetti* (1490?) served as an important model for Herrera as he composed the *Annotations.*

9. "Ninguno de esos amores creó en el poeta un lenguaje própio, personal, que lo definiera" ("not one of these loves created for the poet a personal language of his own which would define him"); A. Prieto, *La poesía española del siglo XVI,* 121. The point of view is echoed in scholarship as recent as the critical guide to Cetina's work prepared by Víctor Montolí Bernadas (*Introducción,* 1993), which quotes Prieto and endorses his opinion (69.) See similar discussions in R. Lapesa, "La poesía de Gutierre de Cetina," and in López Bueno, *Gutierre de Cetina,* 33–45. In addition to mentions in González Echevarría ("Colonial Lyric") and Colombí Monguió (*Petrarquismo Peruano*), Cetina's work is included in Roland Greene's discussion of love poetry in the New World. See *Unrequited Conquests,* 135–70.

10. Kamen mentions the importance of Valladolid (*Spain 1469–1714,* 90). Among the privileges granted the city, the archive at Simancas was established on its outskirts in 1543.

the second love of the shepherd Tityrus in Vergil's overtly political First Eclogue, her introduction as the second beloved in the Vandalio poems establishes a subtext of empire for his story. Thus, despite the incomplete nature of the Vandalio poems, and despite the fact that Cetina's contemporaries did not describe him as having worked on an extended poetic text, there is evidence to read the poetry of Vandalio, Dórida, and Amarílida as a rudimentary, perhaps abandoned, sequence. Indeed, Cetina may have been experimenting with the important emergent sixteenth-century genre of the pastoral, perhaps with reference to the 1503 *Arcadia* of Jacopo Sannazaro (1458–1530). Sannazaro exercised tremendous influence on Spanish writers, and the *Arcadia* inspired the interest of Cetina's peers, most notably Jorge de Montemayor, with whom Cetina maintained a poetic correspondence in the 1540s.[11] Sannazaro's *Arcadia,* a text comprised of alternating sections of poetry and prose that draws contemporary politics into the bucolic locus amoenus inhabited by a group of courtly shepherds, may well have served as an inspiration to Cetina, who recounted the loves of Vandalio in a combination of lyrics and epistolary poems, and who linked the transformation of the shepherd's desire to the awakening of a provincial Andalusian to the cosmopolitan attractions of the life of an imperial courtier.

The Vandalio poems are consistent with Cetina's single lyrics, as they represent the complex and overdetermined lyric speakers he fashioned in many of his sonnets moving through an imperial landscape that extends across Europe. For this reason, before embarking on a reading of the Vandalio poems, we will first examine how Cetina fashioned a version of Petrarchan discourse in which desire is conditioned by history and politics. In the second part of the chapter, I will demonstrate how the Vandalio poems address the limitations of the new lyric as a discourse adopted to represent the subjectivity of the imperial Spanish courtier who desired political, as well as amorous, success.[12]

---

11. Montemayor's 1559 *La Diana* was both the first pastoral written in Spain and a tremendous success, maintaining an avid public from the time of its publication well through the seventeenth century.

12. In her 1990 edition of the complete sonnets and madrigals, López Bueno argued for a canzoniere-style sequence in Cetina's work, one again based on Vandalio, but organized as a trajectory from a bucolic innocence modeled on Italian lyrics to a violent, fearful experience of love that is keyed to the imagery of Ausiàs March. As I have argued elsewhere ("En Arcadia Betis," 2001), presenting the text in this way leaves out a good deal of relevant poetry that does not correspond to Petrarchan models, in particular, the epistolary poems that supply additional details of Vandalio's story. Equally problematic is the fact that emphasis on a Petrarchan sequence causes López Bueno to overlook a crucial aspect of Cetina's pastoral plot, namely, the link it fashions to Vergil's First Eclogue. My reading

Conditioning Desire

Cetina stands out among his fellow sixteenth-century poets for the consistency of his embrace of the identity of the modern imperial courtier. His poetry does not contain bitter and ingenious statements of resistance on the order of Garcilaso's Sonnet 33 or Francisco de Aldana's Sonnet 45, although there are several poems structured through the topos of the vanity of life at court. Rather, Sonnet 27 is representative of Cetina's most typical lyric subject. The poem is also an example of his dexterity with the sonnet form.

Sonnet 27

> Entre armas, guerra, fuego, ira y furores,
> que al soberbio francés tienen opreso,
> cuando el aire es más turbio y más espeso,
> allí me aprieta el fiero ardor de amores.
> Miro el cielo, los árboles, las flores,
> y en ellos hallo mi dolor expreso,
> que en el tiempo más frío y más avieso
> nacen y reverdecen mis temores.
> Digo llorando: "¡Oh dulce primavera,
> cuándo será que a mi esperanza vea
> ver de prestar al alma algún sosiego!"
> Mas temo que mi fin mi suerte fiera
> tan lejos de mi bien quiere que sea
> entre guerra y furor, ira, armas y fuego.[13]

[Amid arms, war, fire, rage, and fury, / which have oppressed the proud Frenchman, / where the air is most churning and at its thickest, / there the fierce ardor of love presses me. / I gaze at the sky, the trees, the flowers, / and in them I find my pain expressed, / such that in the coldest, most contrary time / my fears are born and

---

here draws on the lyrics and the epistles, based on my sense that the Vandalio poetry constitutes neither a sequence nor a proper pastoral, but rather represents Cetina's experimentation with the different modes of poetry through which he could best represent the subjectivity of the imperial courtier.

13. For the text and numeration of Cetina's Sonnet 27, I have followed the order established by López Bueno, *Sonetos y madrigales completos*. Her edition modifies the order established by Hazañas in his edition of the *Obras*. See note 21.

renewed. / I say, weeping: "O, sweet spring, / when will it be that I finally see my hope / lend solace to my soul!" / But I fear that my fierce fortune desires that my end / take place far from my joy / amid war and fury, rage, arms, and fire.]

This sonnet opens with the image of a battle in spring. In lines 1 through 3, the speaker recounts the chaos and smoke of battle. In line 5, the air clears and falls still as he turns inward and to a Petrarchan landscape of sky, trees, and flowers. In similarly conventional fashion, this landscape overtakes the external scene, remaking it as the image of the speaker's longing for his beloved, and from line 7 the poem speaks to both types of rigor, war and desire, until the end of the poem, where the possibility of violent death is deflected into a mood—call it elegant woe. The speaker's view of his indefinite future is phrased in the subjunctive: "temo que mi fin mi suerte fiera . . . sea" ("sea" in line 13 is the subjunctive form of the verb *ser* or "to be"). The shift into a bucolic Petrarchan register has displaced the historical scene into an aesthetic one. The substitution of the internal lover's landscape for the battlefield permits the resolution of a real world problem (the threat of death in war) through the inflections of tone that are drawn in by the shift into pastoralism and by the formal operations of the sonnet's mandate of closure.

As a second point, however, Cetina's aesthetic resolution depends on an ingenious manipulation of poetic discourse. This manipulation creates a conceit of internal subjective process: by placing the bucolic Petrarchan landscape at the physical center of the poem, Cetina enhances its association with a private interiority. The conceit is strengthened by his use of the word *expreso* in line 6, since the word suggests that the speaker's feelings are emerging from some hidden interior zone of his self. But the internal zone in fact serves a pragmatic purpose by overwriting the speaker's experience as it is initially presented, which is as chaotic and frightening, as is signaled by the jumbled list with which the poem begins, "entre armas, guerra, fuego, ira y furores." By line 14, these elements have been organized "internally" by the speaker, such that they reappear as elegant hemistichs: "entre guerra y furor, ira, armas y fuego" (because *y* is read as a vowel when it appears next to a vowel, line 14 breaks into two halves: *en / tre / guer / ra-y / fu / ror // i–ra-ar / mas / y / fue / go*). This transformation of the experience of war from a disorderly and dangerous field of action to a phenomenon that corresponds to the dictates of moderate courtly presentation reveals the ideological aspect of Boscán's assimilatory vision, the new lyric's "disposición muy capaz para recibir cualquier materia" ("disposition capable of receiving any material whatsoever") (*Obra completa,* 119). In this case, the "materia" received is the historical reality of contemporary warfare (a battle with the French, line 2), an event that is transferred, via its integration with the poem's form (the sonnet), and its accommodation to the Petrarchan tropes and utterances conventional to this form, into something quite different, namely, the enabling pretext for a lament about amorous longing.

In this way, the conceit of interiority crafted in Sonnet 27 inscribes a version of the phenomenon John Beverley has referred to as the "ideology of the lyrical," the tendency of lyric poetry to create the appearance of private experience "distinct from but not in contradiction with the public sphere and public identity of the subject as a social agent" (*Against Literature,* 38). The conceit of private subjectivity crafted in Sonnet 27 certainly appears to consist of an ideologically neutral bucolic fantasy, one whose relationship to more obviously coercive types of discourse is further disguised by the triteness of the convention of the internal landscape of the unrequited lover. However, what we see after engaging in even a brief analysis of the poem is that it actually serves an ideological purpose by making light of the possibility of death by war. Cetina's poem is therefore consistent with the broader cultural shift that was taking place within the social imaginary of early modern Spain: the lightening, even trivializing, of the figure of the aristocratic Castilian fighter, discussed in Chapter 1. However, whereas poets such as Hernando de Acuña associated the sonnet, specifically, with processes of courtierization and the interpellation of the modern Spanish subject, Cetina established something slightly different, associating Petrarchan discourse with the interiority of the new imperial man. This is important to notice because it bears on Cetina's treatment of Petrarchan desire in his pastoral text, but before moving into that discussion, it is worthwhile to spend a bit more time with Sonnet 27. Both its ingenuity and its rhetorical complexity come into relief when we compare it to Sonnet 20 by Diego Hurtado de Mendoza:

Sonnet 20

Vuelve el cielo y el tiempo huye y calla
y callando despierta tu tardanza;
crece el deseo y mengua la esperanza
y tanto cuanto más lejos te halla.
Mi alma es hecha campo de batalla,
combátenla recelo y confianza;

asegura la fe toda mudanza,
aunque sospechas anden por trocalla.
Yo sufro y callo y dígote, "Señora,
¿cuándo será aquel día que estaré
libre de esta contienda en tu presencia?"
Respóndeme tu saña matadora:
"Si juzgas que ha de ser por lo que fue,
menores son tus males en ausencia."

[The sky revolves and the time flees and is silent / and, in its silence it awakens your delay; / my desire grows and my hope diminishes / and all the more so the further off you are found. / My soul is made a battlefield, / dread and confidence battle there; / my faith assures against all change, / although suspicions wander forth to turn it. / I suffer and am silent and I say to you, "My lady, / when will that day come that I am / free of this struggle in your presence?" / Your deathly anger answers me: / "If you judge what is to be by what was, / your woes are fewer in my absence."][14]

Here the theme actually *is* "love is a battlefield." In lines 5 and 6, the speaker refers to war in order to illustrate the painful struggle between himself and the lady who has withdrawn her favors from him. But while love and war are drawn together at the level of the theme, the two are not subsequently elaborated in a way that figures the complex interiority that emerges within Sonnet 27. Therefore, despite the considerable artistry that has gone into the composition of Sonnet 20 (artistry evident, for example, in the elegant composition of lines such as 1 and 2, which bring the lover's vigil to life through their combinations of repetition and pause, "huye y calla . . . callando," or in the neat opposition crece/mengua, line 3), it does not work the complex imbrication of discourses that produce the effect of interiority in Cetina's poem. Perhaps the best way to frame the difference between the two is that in Sonnet 27, Petrarchism serves a purpose: the detour through the amorous landscape serves as a sort of furlough from which the fighter is delivered back to the battlefield, his courtly posture restored and fortified. Sonnet 20 is less complex. Despite the ostensibly topical nature of the battlefield metaphor, the poem emphasizes the familiar and ahistorical scene

---

14. Hurtado de Mendoza, *Poesía*, 275.

of the Petrarchan lover eternally turning, world without end, under the shadow of his lady. In fact, it more closely resembles Petrarch's Poem 30 than it does Cetina's Sonnet 27:

> . . . vola il tempo et fuggon gli anni
> sì ch'a la morte in un punto s'arriva
> o colle brune o colle bianche chiome,
> seguirò l'ombra de quel dolce lauro
> per lo più ardente sole et per la neve,
> fin che l'ultimo dì chiuda quest'occhi.
> Non fur giamai veduti sì begli occhi
> o ne la nostra etade o ne' prim'anni
> che mi struggon così come'l sol neve
> onde procede lagrimosa riva
> ch'Amor conduce a pie' del duro lauro
>
> (Petrarch 30, 13–23)

[. . . time flies and the years flee / and one arrives quickly at death / either with dark or with white locks, / I shall follow the shadow of that sweet laurel / in the most ardent sun or through the snow, / until the last day closes these eyes. / There never have been seen such lovely eyes, / either in our age or in the first years; / they melt me as the sun does the snow: / whence there comes forth a river of tears / that Love leads to the foot of the harsh laurel][15]

Readers of Petrarch have demonstrated that the Tuscan's principal legacy to poetics is the construction of a lyric speaker who coalesces as a subject through the sequence of "dimensionless lyric moments" (Freccero, "The Fig Tree and the Laurel," 20–21). As Freccero and Durling, among others, have observed, Petrarchan subjectivity is animated, not by Christian doctrine, but by engaging the reader in the work of constituting the poetic speaker's identity.[16] Hurtado de Mendoza participates in the spirit of the *Canzoniere* as he strands his speaker in the isolated, atemporal cycle of longing in Sonnet 20. In contrast, Cetina's Sonnet 27 draws on Petrarchan timelessness to achieve worldly and, it can be argued, imperial ends by

---

15. Original and translation appear in Durling, *Petrarch's Lyric Poems*, 86–87.
16. On Petrarchan fragmented subjectivity, see ibid., 1–33, as well as Freccero.

mobilizing Petrarchism to distract attention from the historical reality that wars kill. By creating an equivalence between love and the power of arms to injure and destroy (an equivalence whose way was prepared, obviously, by a long tradition of poetry composed before this lyric), Cetina recasts warmaking as highly suitable courtly activity, another area in which to exercise sprezzatura. His skills in courtierizing the martial situation are on display in the genteel and balanced phrasing of the poem's last line, whose elegance belies its message of despair.[17]

The Pastoral Love Plot: Vandalio, Dórida, Amarílida

Sonnet 27 is a skillful representation of a modern man's desire. The poem's speaker responds to the promptings of a private, interior world that comes into being through the operations of his own wishes and fears, as these wishes and fears are reorganized and transformed by the political and social forces around him. These forces require his participation in wars that are just as deadly as epic medieval struggles; however, modern warfare extended the promise of far less honor or individual glory. The sonnet form lent itself to the representation of the complex, dissembling, and self-reflexive persona that the empire required Spain's noblemen, especially, to inhabit, but its scope of representation was necessarily brief. For this reason, Spain's principal poets of the first half of the sixteenth century conducted experiments with various emergent genres as vehicles for the representation of the imperial courtier as he made his way out across the expanded terrains of the Spanish map.[18] Among these experiments were innovations in the pastoral. Sannazaro's *Arcadia* was opening the way for writers across Europe to create highly erudite and cultivated textual hybrids, poetry and prose drawn together in the service of elaborating complex narratives set in an

---

17. It is interesting to compare this poem to Sonnet 45, the poetic anamorphosis constructed by Francisco de Aldana. Like that poem, which was studied earlier in these pages (see Introduction), but which was most likely composed later, chronologically, than Sonnet 27, the present lyric unfolds within the two terrains conventional to courtly poetry, the battlefield and the locus amoenus. But whereas in Aldana's poem these two spheres represent warring discourses that cannot be contained within a single interpretive field, with the result that Petrarchan discourse is figured as an agent of violent exclusion, Cetina's Sonnet 27 represents the capacities of the new lyric to accommodate modern courtiers to the dangers and contingencies of battle.

18. On the discourse of the map in early modern Spanish literature, see Padrón, *The Spacious Word*.

alternate universe from the modern political world, notably by substituting the natural temporal cycle of night and day for the sophisticated and artificial patterns of activity at court. As "literary fiction grounded in historical fact," the pastoral maintained an ambiguous and mobile relationship to poetry.[19] It appealed to Cetina as a poetic discourse suitable to the cosmopolitan courtier of the most important nation on the global stage. In the text I am arguing for as an incomplete pastoral centered on the figure of Vandalio, a shepherd who leaves behind his beloved lady and his beloved Betis river to pursue his fortunes as an agent of empire in the Spanish domains in Italy and Germany, we find traces of Sannazaro's formal innovations, as well as a recasting of the notion that even the shepherd desires the political and politicized world.

The plot is based on two love affairs. The first is a "golden" idyll in which the shepherd Vandalio is immersed in his passion for the lady Dórida. This part of the story takes place on the banks of the Sevillian river Betis, and is dominated by the complete absorption of the lovers in an intensely dyadic experience of one another, to the exclusion of all else. This story is interrupted at its climax by a series of poems that represent the triangulation of the two lovers' desire by the intrusion of the classical love god Amor. His arrival brings a register of literary self-consciousness into their interaction, and thus awakens Vandalio's desires for the world beyond the bower. As Vandalio prepares to abandon the Betis for the imperial courtly world represented by the river Pisuerga, he and Dórida find themselves endowed with new knowledge of literary and historical contexts. These make it impossible for their affair to proceed, and Vandalio finds that his desire has been transformed and that he now loves Amarílida. Like her Latin model, Vergil's Amaryllis, Amarílida represents a compromise: Vandalio loves her in a manner similar to the way in which Titryus loves his second shepherdess in the First Eclogue. She fits into the pattern of his life as it is carried on under the aegis of an empire that wields the ultimate power of deciding how and

---

19. Quint, *Origin and Originality*, 45. In his discussion of the *Arcadia* in *Origin and Originality*, Quint observes the relationship of the pastoral space to the historical and political world: "From the vantage point of the bower, history is an external force beyond the pastoralist's control or understanding. The outside political world may be the guarantor of the contentment and security of a shepherd like Tityrus in Vergil's First Eclogue . . . But the very powerlessness of the shepherd—of the unlucky Meliboeus who in the same eclogue is driven out of his home in Arcady—generally darkens his view of history, whether it is seen as a capricious political order or, in larger terms, as the plague of time and death, the charnel house of Florence from whose contagion the young people of the *Decameron* retreat to Fiesole. To these ills the pastoral offers no solution but evasion and absorption into its bucolic routine. The pastoralist is too busy setting his own house in order to ponder the dissolution of history or his own mortality" (46).

where its subjects will graze their flocks. Far from distracting her lover from his worldly obligations, Amarílida helps accommodate him to them. However, in contrast to Vergil's text, the final resolution of the Spanish love is a compromise. After an initial rupture, Vandalio continues on in his love for Dórida, albeit in a manner that does not disrupt his contentment with Amarílida. In this way, the sequence elaborates on the virtues of internal complexity in a manner that resembles Sonnet 27. As I will demonstrate momentarily, the heart that contains two loves is Cetina's figure for the divided loyalties of the imperial Spanish courtier.

In sifting the pastoral from the larger body of Cetina's work, I have chosen to be conservative. I have included only poems that make reference to one or more of the main characters or to the pastoral loci of the Betis and Pisuerga. Reading for references to Vandalio, to the ladies Dórida and Amarílida, to pastoral treatments of the Betis, the Pisuerga, the Ticino, the Po, and the Rhine, or for pastoral details such as flocks and the rustic lyre, we can assemble five songs, thirty-six sonnets, and a number of loose poems in various meters including a sestina and four epistles that recount Vandalio's story. These groups can in turn be separated into an introductory poem (an imitation of Giraldi Cinthio's closing lyrics to the pastoral *Egle*),[20] followed by five groups of poems that narrate the movement of the plot. In cases where it is possible to establish a degree of narrative order, I have done so; however, because of the incomplete nature of the text, this ordering is necessarily approximate.[21]

The Dórida Relation (Sonnets 37, 38, 76, 85, 132, 105, 27, 28, 7 [LB], 71, 99, 101, 162, 173, 200, the Sestina, Anacretonic Song 6)

The poems to Dórida are tender, sweet, and suffused with the youthful erotic enthusiasm of two innocents entirely absorbed in their passion. They are marked by Petrarchan conventions such as poems to golden locks, "De tus rubios cabellos, / Dórida, ingrata mía, / hizo el amor la cuerda / para el arco homicida" (Song, 1–4) ("From your blond locks, / Dórida, my

---

20. On Sonnet 105, see H. Iventosch, "The Renaissance Pastoral and the Golden Age."
21. I use two sources for the poems discussed below. Generally, my numbering follows the Hazañas edition of all of Cetina's known works to 1895. Sonnets 7, 9, and 10 were identified by Lapesa in 1939, as discussed by López Bueno in her introduction to the *Sonetos y madrigales completos*. When discussing those poems I refer to the *Sonetos y madrigales completos* and place (LB) after the poem number.

ungrateful lady, / love made the string / for the murderous bow"; *Dórida, tus rubios cabellos*) and to eyes, "Ojos, cuya beldad entre mortales / hace inmortal la hermosura mía" (162.5–6) ("Eyes, whose beauty / makes my own beauty immortal among mortals"). The most important characteristics of the series for this argument are the continuous association of Dórida with the Betis and the situation of the idyll in a supremely idealized pastoral *locus amoenus*. The poetry is rife with mentions of shepherds, flocks, green fields, and cool shade, for example, Song 6:

> Guardando su ganado
> cerca el Bético río,
> Vandalio al pié de un álamo sombroso,
> en la yerba sentado,
> que llena de rocío
> mostraba el verde prado más hermoso
>
> (1–6)

[Guarding his flock / by the Betis river / was Vandalio, at the foot of a shady elm, / seated in the grass, / which, full of dew / showed the green field at its most beautiful]

The rich pastoral imagery of the series establishes the valley of the Betis as a space apart from the social and political world, a timeless, ahistorical bower in which the lovers perceive each other and the landscape that surrounds them in terms of sensual contact unmediated by rational perspective. In a similar fashion, the bucolic innocence of loves enjoyed on the Betis is figured in terms of erotic sensation that engulfs the world, subsuming all notions of difference between bodies, between the moments and hours of passing time, between subjects and objects of desire. A limited number of poems in this series inscribe a distance between lover and beloved; some treat unrequited love. Sonnet 173, for example, depicts Vandalio inquiring of a nightingale, "¿Qué haremos los dos, pues que, llorando, / nuestro triste cantar tan poco agrada? / ¿Qué—dijo el ruiseñor—Morir amando" (12–14) ("What will we do, the two of us, since, for weeping, / our sad song gives such little pleasure? / What, said the nightingale, but die weeping"). But the dominant perceptual framework in these poems is the lover's dyad as it is enjoyed in a bower that exists apart from the most basic codes by which social existence is organized: time and history, the difference between selves, the difference between desiring subjects and their passive objects. In Sonnet 162 Dórida assumes the position of the desiring shepherd, in order to gaze upon herself and see what her suitors see:

Sonnet 162

> Para ver si sus ojos eran cuales
> la fama entre pastores extendía,
> en una fuente los miraba un día
> Dórida, y dice así, viéndolos tales:
> "Ojos, cuya beldad entre mortales,
> hace inmortal la hermosura mía,
> ¿cuáles bienes el mundo perdería
> que a los males que dais fuesen iguales?
> Tenía, antes de os ver, por atrevidos,
> por locos temerarios los pastores
> que se osaban llamar vuestros vencidos;
> mas hora viendo en vos tantos primores,
> por más locos los tengo y más perdidos
> los que os vieron si no mueren de amores."

[To see if her eyes were those / whose fame extended out among the shepherds, / she gazed on them in a fountain one day, / did Dórida, and she says this, seeing them thus: / "Eyes, whose beauty among mortals, / makes my own beauty immortal, / what pleasures might the world lose / that would be equal to the wounds you deal? / I took them, before seeing you, as adventurers, / as madmen, those shepherds / who dared to call themselves your vanquished; / but now, seeing such charms in you, / I take as madder still, and more lost / those who looked upon you and do not die of love."]

Here, Dórida does not only *assume* the conventionally masculine position of the gaze; she *appropriates* it, identifying with that position, since, gazing on herself, she finds that the hyperbolic praise that would-be Petrarchans have lavished on their ladies for centuries, in songs that have provoked memorable retorts from a host of well-spoken ladies (one thinks of Cervantes's Marcela) is merited: men should find themselves lost once they have gazed on her. In fact, it is those who are immune to the beauty of her eyes who are truly mad.

Other poems in the series portray the relation between Vandalio and Dórida in terms of ecstatic erasure of self. Sonnet 28, for example, builds tension through an extended simile: "Como el pastor que, en la ardiente hora estiva, / la verde sombra, el fresco aire agrada, / y como a la sedienta su manada / alegra alguna fuente de agua viva (1–4) ("Just as the shepherd who, in the burning hour of the summer's day, / is pleased by the green shade, the cool air, / just as his thirsty flock is made / happy by a lively spring of water"). The release of tension that comes with the completion of the rhetorical structure intensifies the image of release figured by the melting snow and Dórida's melting rigor as it encounters Vandalio's ardor: "Ni menos se deshace el hielo mío, / Vandalio, ante tu ardor, cual suele nieve / a la esfera del sol ser derretida" (9–11) ("No less is my ice undone, / Vandalio, before your ardor, than is the snow / melted before the sphere of the sun").[22]

The apogee of the erotic scenes with Dórida is Sonnet 9 (LB). The poem opens with Vandalio fixed on the sensation of Dórida's foot as it presses on his heart:

Sonnet 9

Debajo de un pie blanco y pequeñuelo
tenía el corazón enamorado,
Vandalio tan úfano en tal cuidado,
que tiene en poco el mayor bien del suelo
Cuando movido Amor de un nuevo celo,
envidioso de ver tan dulce estado,
mirando el pie hermoso y delicado,
el fuego del pastor muestra de hielo.
En tanto, el corazón que contemplaba
el pie debajo el cual ledo se vía,
con lágrimas de gozo lo bañaba.
Y el alma, que mirando se sentía,
con fogosos suspiros enjugaba
las mancillas que el llanto en él ponía.

---

22. Cetina's ingenuity is evident in the final twist with the water imagery. Dórida is again speaking to the reflection of her image, this time in a river, not in a fountain: "Así decía Dórida en el río, / mirando su beldad, y el viento leve / llevó la voz que apenas fué entendida" (12–14) ("Thus spoke Dórida, / gazing at her beauty in the river, and the light breeze / stole away her voice, which could barely be heard"). Because Dórida speaks here as she looks upon her aqueous self, the water metaphors she employs create an image of her own thought and her own capacities to create figurative language out of experience. This polished manipulation of rhetoric is only one example of Cetina's talents as a poet.

[Beneath a tiny white foot / the heart of enamored Vandalio lay, / so content was it in its suffering, / that the greatest boons of this world were as nothing to him; / when Love, moved by a new whim, / and envious of his sweet state, / gazing upon the beautiful and delicate foot, / revealed the shepherd's fire as ice. / With that, the heart that contemplated / the foot, and its weight, / bathed it with tears of pleasure. / And the soul, which looked on, / dried with fiery sighs / the tears that sorrow had shed.]

This is another poem dedicated to the figuration of sensual tension and release, opening in a moment of extreme sensual delight that is followed by its rupture into an explosion of tears and sighs. The scene represents the climax of the Dórida poems: the close focus on the precise point of physical contact between the tiny white foot and Vandalio's heart presents an intense vision of masochistic delight. The poem also marks the pinnacle of Vandalio and Dórida's love, which begins to falter when the god of love disrupts the scene in the second quatrain. Once the god descends, the timeless stasis established in the first quatrain is broken. In lines 1 through 4, the shift from the narrative imperfect tense in the second line *(tenía)* to the present tense in the fourth *(tiene)* has permitted the poem to move seamlessly from past to present without affecting the lovers' experience. The foot stays on the heart, and Vandalio remains in ecstasy. When Amor enters the idyll, time resumes ("En tanto," line 9). The subsequent reinstatement of the imperfect tense sets the scene in motion again. However, with the resumption of time, Vandalio falls out of love ("el fuego del pastor muestra de hielo"; 8 ["reveals the shepherd's fire as ice"]).

Because the blissful scene is interrupted by the classical love god, we can say that one reason for the demise of Vandalio's passion is tied to the dawning of his awareness that his relationship with Dórida is not unique and self-invented, as the pinpoint specificity of the first quatrain suggests. Rather, it exists as one episode in a long tradition of poetry. This means that his ecstasies with Dórida are not private. They have been organized in terms by the conventions of amorous discourse and now-stale tropes such as fire and ice. As Vandalio moves into his second love affair, the relationship with Amarílida, he will maintain a self-conscious stance toward his desire, and we can take this as a legacy of the awakening to literary tradition that happens in Sonnet 9 (LB). But if Sonnet 9 represents a literary awakening, the poem resembles Sonnet 27 in representing the initiation of a socially and historically conditioned desire. The question regarding what motivates the crisis in

Vandalio's desire can be answered to some extent by considering the various conventions of Renaissance poetry—for example, by reading the sonnet as a sexual allegory, and/or by observing how it engages the Renaissance topos of mutability (that fate intervenes suddenly and inexorably and that the only constant is change). To read the poem as entirely literary in its scope, however, is to ignore the larger narrative of Vandalio's journey from idyll to world. The world, specifically, enters Sonnet 9 to take its own back after Vandalio, absorbed in Dórida, has vainly dismissed its attractions ("tiene en poco el mayor bien del suelo"). With a rapidity that imitates the punishments dealt out by the gods in the Metamorphoses, Amor intervenes to draw Vandalio from the bower and toward the worldly benefits that become available to shepherds willing to make their way out of their home provinces to the imperial center. In subsequent poems Vandalio departs from the Betis and makes his way towards Castile, and the Pisuerga river, where he will engage with peers at court and travel out into the empire to graze his flocks by the Rhine, the Ticino, and the Po. Poems such as Epistle 2, "Alma del alma mía, ya es llegada" ("Soul of my soul, it has come") and Song 4, "Betis, río famoso" ("Betis, famous river") attribute Vandalio's departure from the Betis to his newly discovered desire for, precisely, "el mayor bien del suelo," the success that awaits him in Valladolid. These poems indicate that Amor's interruption in Sonnet 9 (LB) is more than a titillating play of words conventional to Renaissance love lyric. It also is an allegory of imperial summons, when the nobleman, contented at home, is called to attend to imperial business at court or abroad. Again, politics and eros are shown as intertwined in Cetina's poetic imagination.

When we set Sonnet 9 (LB) into context within the range of poems that describe Vandalio's life and loves, it becomes an important key to the nature of the text Cetina was experimenting with. The poem represents, in sonnet form, the limitations of the kind of desire that is conventionally framed within courtly Petrarchan lyrics. It also posits the need for a new type of poetic discourse that can accommodate both erotic passion and worldly success. Both registers of interpretation, the literary and the historical, are important to an understanding of Cetina's ambitions for the pastoral text. On the one hand, Vandalio finds that he and Dórida have been playing at love in a borrowed language that is limited in its abilities to secure their idyllic space. This insight exposes the shortcomings of Petrarchism as a lyric discourse that is suited to represent all that there is of the modern imperial courtier's experience. On the other hand, Vandalio's desire for a successful military career leads him to accept the constraints imposed on his freedom and his desire by the empire. The compromise is represented by his departure from the shores of the Betis and his entry into a courtly world in which Petrarchan conventions are both called into question and expanded through recourse to supplementary poetic sources.[23]

The Poems of Exile from Dórida (Sonnet 45, Sonnet 191, Epistle 2, Epistle 4, Epistle 5, Song 8)

The poems of exile from Dórida express Vandalio's growing consciousness of the untenable nature of the union by the Betis. His relation with Dórida deteriorates through exposure to the social and political world that lies beyond Seville on the imperial map. Most of the poems are epistolary and thus inscribe references to an experience of physical separation breached only unsatisfactorily by means of a letter. Vandalio thus becomes aware of the gulf between self and other that exists even between lovers.

Differences between Dórida and himself first appear in the ways that they address their separation. While Vandalio, thinking as a poet, views absence as the motive to write and sing of his love in the tradition of the modern Petrarchan, Dórida invokes her reputation and imposes a vow of silence:

> Mandásteme, poco antes que partiese,
> que cuando más la ausencia me apretase
> no dijese mi mal ni lo escribiese.

---

23. Cetina's attitude toward the *Canzoniere* is best reflected in Epistle 6, written to the Princess of Molfeta, in which he describes himself as having been contented with his "antiguo fuego," or old flame, "Cuando por ocupar la fantasía / en ejercicio honesto y virtuoso / y para divertir el alma mía, / propuse, de atrevido y de curioso, / un lauro cultivar que había plantado, / casi a la par cruel cuanto hermoso (25–30) ("When, in order to occupy my imagination / in an honest and virtuous exercise / and to amuse my soul, / I proposed, in daring and curiosity, / to cultivate a laurel I had planted, / one nearly as cruel as it was beautiful"). The laurel here is just one more kind of tree; it has no priority over the elm it is about to supplant, nor is it associated with the senses of belatedness and anxiety about cultural inferiority that commonly follow on references to the laurel in most Renaissance poetry. Moreover, Cetina attributes falling in love with the (here) nameless lady represented by the laurel tree to his own hubris and his intellectual curiosity, and not to the machinations of Amor or the influence of his unlucky or lucky stars: "No me forzó el destino, el cielo, el hado: / antes fué arbitrio libre y voluntario, / . . . / quise probar así si con un vario / cuidado, otro del alma aflojaría" (31–35) ("Destiny did not force me, nor did the heavens or fate: / it was free will, and voluntary, / . . . / I wished to test if with a different care, I could weaken / another within my soul"). This view of the laurel as one tree among many in the forest shows Cetina's view of Petrarchism to have been informed by various miscellanies and the *Diverse* volumes, and not by the full *Canzoniere*, with its rich intratextual networks and densely interwoven subjective, religious, and worldly registers of significance.

> Decías que era mal que se mostrase
> manifiesto mi ardor entre las gentes,
> y que por él tu fama se manchase.
> . . . .
> Cuando más mi tormento me apretaba,
> mordiéndome los labios, padecía
> doblado mi dolor mientras callaba.
>
> (Epistle 4, 13–18; 31–33)

[You ordered me, just before I departed, / that when absence pressed me most / I speak not of my love, nor should I write of it. / You said that it was wrong / to show my ardor openly among the people, / thus staining your reputation / . . . / When my torment pressed me most, / biting my lips, I suffered / my pain doubled while I remained silent.]

The reference to *fama* signals the radical transformation of the terms of the relationship. Dórida no longer acts as the free and sensual shepherdess of the idyll. Rather, she plays the role of the circumspect lady of court who is watchful of her reputation. Having identified with the behavioral codes of gender and rank, she is no longer able to assume Vandalio's point of view, as she could in Sonnet 162, for example. For his part, Vandalio adopts the posture of the courtly lover and pleads,

> Consiénteme quejar la pena mía:
> de Dórida me quejo; a ella escribo;
> nadie sabe quién es, ni lo sabría.
> Dórida . . . el dolor rabioso, esquivo,
> que en mis entrañas tu beldad enciende
> de úfano me hace ir soberbio, altivo . . .
>
> (Epistle 4; 55–60)

[Permit me to complain of my suffering: / of Dórida I complain; to her I write; / no one knows who she is, nor will they know. / Dórida . . . the raging, wretched pain, / that your loveliness sets afire in my entrails / makes me walk proud, noble in my satisfaction . . .]

The exile poems depart from the conventions of courtly love. The separation and the unrequited desire that fuel amorous lyric erode the lovers' mutual faith. As the affair winds to a close, Vandalio's plaints become increasingly divided between pledges of his eternal love, "Y crea de mí que durará este fuego, / cuanto en tal fuego durará mi vida" (Epistle 2; 105–6) ("And believe me that this fire will last, / so long as my life, in such a fire, may last"), and detailed descriptions of how erotic musings, soured by exile and Dórida's strictures of secrecy, devolve into suspicion and jealousy:

> Júntanse al nuevo mal viejos cuidados;
> va la imaginación buscando cosas
> con que los hace al fin sentir doblados.
> Ponénseme delante mil celosas
> sombras, que me amenazan y maltratan;
> mil miedos, mil locuras sospechosas.
>
> (Epistle 4, 91–96)

[My old fears join with this new woe; / my imagination wanders looking for things / with which to make them seem, finally, doubled. / A thousand jealous shadows appear before me, / they threaten me and treat me ill; / a thousand fears, a thousand suspicious follies.]

When Vandalio voices his increasing despair in Sonnet 191 (addressed to the Duke of Sessa), the realistic note that sets him apart from other lovers is sounded once again. The inscription of "Sesenio" brings Vandalio's political and social circumstances, his world of diplomats and soldiers, to bear on an otherwise conventional lyric dilemma:

> Sesenio, pues que vas do vengo ahora,
> antes do siempre estoy, do ir quisiera,
> cuando a ver llegarás la gran ribera
> del Betis, que por tí tanto se honora
> . . . .
> A Dórida dirás que desespera
> la mía ya de verse alegre un hora.
>
> (1–4; 7–8)

[Sesenio, since you now go to where I arrive from, / where I always am, where I always wish to go, / when you arrive and see the great banks / of the Betis, which because of you is so honored /

... / To Dórida say that my [soul] now despairs / of even seeing itself joyful for one single hour]

The poem continues with an assertion that Vandalio's passion will outlast a trip across the river Lethe itself ("Pero si aquel antiguo nuestro río / fuera el otro do suelen los mortales / el peso descargar de sus cuidados, / no por eso dejara el ardor mío"; 9–12 ["But if that ancient river of ours / were that other one, where mortals / tend to unburden themselves of their woes, / not for that would I leave behind my ardor"). But the encroachment of the real world on the lovers that began at Sonnet 9 (LB) challenges the discourse of all-powerful bliss upon which such superhuman statements are founded. The oaths of constancy to Dórida prove hollow as the poems of transition begin.

The Transition Between Loves (Sonnet 10 [LB], Sonnet 21, Song 4)

The poems of exile from Dórida elaborate on the theme that the Betis idyll is untenable within the political and social world. The transition poems thematize and consolidate the breakdown of the "golden" relation while they simultaneously place increasing emphasis on Vandalio's engagement with his imperial career. His new identity is represented through his turn to Amarílida. But because the introduction of a second beloved is radically disruptive to a Petrarchan sequence, which turns around a lover's constancy to a single lady, the change of beloveds marks the dissolution of Vandalio's identity as a Petrarchan lover. Sonnets 10 (LB) and 21 represent successive crises of voice, reason, and self. Following on these poems, Vergil's First Eclogue is drawn into the text to serve, not only as a narrative device, but as the means by which poetic discourse can remain viable for the courtiers of a pan-European and transatlantic Spain.[24]

This complex set of poetic transactions is developed systematically. In Sonnet 10 (LB), Vandalio interrogates a silent and perhaps absent Dórida, and then himself, regarding his change of desire:

Dórida, hermosísima pastora,
cortés, sabia, gentil, blanda y piadosa,

---

24. Again, the incomplete nature of the pastoral makes it difficult to tell how direct a correspondence Cetina intended between Amarílida and Amaryllis. Cetina was also an admirer of Ariosto. As Nathalie Hester graciously pointed out to me, aspects of Amarílida make her resemble the temptress Armida; this is particularly during the transition, as Vandalio forsakes Dórida for the second lady.

¿cuál suerte desigual, fiera, rabiosa,
pone a mi libertad nueva señora?
El corazón que te ama y que te adora,
¿quién lo puede forzar que ame otra cosa?
¿Amarílida es más sabia o más hermosa que tu?
No sé. Contempla esta alma ahora
¿Fue jamás de Amarílida tratado
tan bien como de ti, tan sin fiereza?
¿No me acordabas tú si yo te amaba?
Pues sin mudarme yo, ¿quién me ha mudado?
Respondió el eco: "Yo, que en tanta alteza
mucho tiempo tan dulce ser duraba."

[Dórida, most beautiful shepherdess, / courtly, wise, gentle, tender and pious, / what chance unjust, wild, raging,/ sets a new mistress to my freedom? / That heart that loves you and adores you, / who can force it to love another? / Is Amarílida wiser or more beautiful than you? / I do not know. Let my soul contemplate that now. / Was I ever treated so well / by Amarílida as I am by you, so completely without fierceness? / Did you not remember me when I loved you? / Thus, as I did not change myself, who is it who has changed me? / The echo responded, "I, for this sweet state of being lasted for a long time."]

Formerly agile and inventive in their justification of love's logic, the lovers have nothing to say here. Dórida's silence in the face of Vandalio's questions, and Vandalio's inability to find his own answers indicate that the Betis idyll is spent. The poem thus concludes in the register of an agentless mandate of change, an echo with no discernible source.[25] Lines 13–14 correspond to a certain extent to the intervention of Amor in Sonnet 9 (LB). Vaguely Neo-Platonic, they invoke the same type of invisible but absolute authority that exists somewhere outside the poem and intervenes at whim. Sonnet 10 might also call to mind the "mudanza" sonnets of Juan Boscán, examined in the previous chapter.[26] However, whereas Boscán used the language of change to mask the social and political nature of the transformation

---

25. It seems possible that these lines are an imitation of an Italian text, poorly assimilated within Cetina's piece.

26. In Boscán's lyric sequence, discussed in Chapter 2, the mutability produced by the forces of the natural world and the cosmos was one of the principal motivating factors for the poetic

undergone by his Petrarchan lover—"mudanza" naturalized his shift from the unconstrained, maddening passions of his first affair to the moderate and contained love he shared with his eventual wife, aligning it with the movements of the seasons and the stars—Cetina uses the language of mudanza in a very different way. Just as inexorable as the laws of nature, mudanza for Cetina alludes to the experience of power. The word is not associated with a natural flow, but rather with violent and seemingly capricious disruptions to the natural state. Thus Sonnets 9 and 10 (LB) reveal Cetina's interest in describing how desire is transformed when it is inserted into a world structured by modern regimes of power and knowledge. In other poems Vandalio's change of heart is increasingly attributed to his having chosen the court over the idyll, the bureaucratic center of the empire over the home region of one's birth. Song 4 and Sonnet 21 link the problem of changed beloveds firmly to a tension between Vandalio's love of Seville and his desire for a career in Valladolid. Song 4, addressed to "Father Betis," retells the crisis allegorized in terms of fickle Amor in Sonnet 9 (LB), but this time with emphasis on Vandalio's decision to set forth from his home shores:

> Contento de mi suerte tal cual era
> por no andar peregrino
> buscando mejor pasto a mi ganado,
> pasaba yo mi vida en tu ribera,
> cuando nuevo camino
> para nuevo pesar me mostró el hado.
>
> (72–77)

[Contented with my luck such as it was / in order not to wander like a pilgrim / seeking better grass for my flock, / I passed my life on your banks, / when chance showed me a new path / for a new burden.]

As in Sonnet 9 (LB), Vandalio is moved here from a condition of stasis and contentment (line 72) to an opening toward a change; this time, the

---

speaker's embrace of discourses of Stoicism and courtly self-restraint. In the poetic narrative of Vandalio, Cetina breaks from conventional treatments of the phenomenon of change and insists on the worldly causes for transformations of desire. This worldly, political view is in keeping with the view of desire we saw framed in Sonnet 27, namely, that it is conditioned by contexts in the social and political worlds.

motivating force is fate and not love. However, it is significant that in Song 4 Vandalio's change of heart is inscribed on the Spanish map. The new road leads to Valladolid and thence to a new life on the banks of the Pisuerga, with the new love, Amarílida. The shift in rivers and the shift in beloveds are also intertwined formally in Sonnet 21 The poem repeats the dilemma presented in Sonnet 10 (LB), namely, the inexplicable nature of Vandalio's change in desire; in Sonnet 21, however, there is elaboration of its subjective effects. This is evident from the first line, in which Vandalio addresses himself as a nameless *mísero pastor*. The decision to leave the shores of the Betis calls into question his identity as an Andalucían (Vandalio). As a symptom of this breakdown, Vandalio's mode of speaking shifts from the conventional sonnet patterns of narration or logical argumentation, and devolves into a series of anguished cries:

Sonnet 21

¡Ay, misero pastor! ¿dó voy, huyendo?
¿Curar pienso un ardor con otro fuego?
¡Cuitado! ¿Adónde voy? ¿Estoy ya ciego
que ni veo mi bien ni el mal entiendo?
¿Dó me llevas, Amor? Si aquí me enciendo,
¿tendré do voy más paz o más sosiego?
Si huyo de un peligro, ¿á dó voy luego?
¿Es menor el que voy hora siguiendo?
¿Fue más ventura el Betis, por ventura,
que era ahora Pisuerga? ¿Aquél no ha sido
tan triste para mí como ese ahora?
Si falta en Amarílida mesura,
¿Cómo la tendrá Dórida, sabido
que llevo ya en el alma otra señora?

[Ay, miserable shepherd! Where do I run to as I flee? / Do I think to cure one passion with another fire? / Unhappy man! Where do I wander? Am I now blind / that I cannot see the good, nor understand what error is? / Where do you lead me, Love? If I burn here, / will I find more peace or more rest where I go next? / If I flee from one danger, where do I go? / Is the lady I now follow the lesser? / Was Betis more fortunate for me, perchance, / than Pisuerga was just now? Was that one not / as sad for me as this one is now? / If Amarílida lacks restraint, / how will Dórida show it when she learns / that I now carry a new woman in my heart?]

Vandalio's lack of a name here, added to his inability to answer the questions he poses both to love and to himself, show that the identity that was formed in terms of idyll and constancy has given way to a new mode of being on the banks of the Pisuerga. Over the course of the transition poems, the twin facts of Vandalio's ambition within the empire and his subjection to the mandates of an absolute authority variously troped as Amor and imperial command bar him permanently from participation in the idyllic space of the Betis, with all its overtones of naiveté, blissful self-absorption, and a historical golden age. However, they suit him perfectly to the pastoral space represented in Vergil's First Eclogue, where a shepherd's fields and his love are fashioned in correspondence to the imperial center.

Cetina and Vergil

To understand Vergil's usefulness to Cetina's text, it is helpful to recall the way in which themes of love and empire are worked in Vergil's Eclogue 1. The first point of contact between Vandalio's Amarílida and the shepherd Tityrus's Amaryllis is that both are second loves. In the Eclogue, Amaryllis steals Tityrus from Galatea: "After Amaryllis had us, and Galatea left" ("Postquam nos Amaryllis habet, Galatea reliquit"; Eclogue 1, 30).[27] Both women appear as solutions to the problems presented by the self-indulgent pleasures of both shepherds' youths—in the Dórida relation, the trope is sexual incontinence; in Vergil, it is Galatea's disastrous financial "spending" ("while Galatea held me / there was no hope of liberty or thought of thrift" ["dum me Galatea tenebat, / nec spes libertatis erat nec cura peculi"]; 31–32). As the Eclogue opens, Tityrus is depicted at rest, in a pastoral space, which we learn has recently been reorganized and redistributed by imperial mandate. Meliboeus, who has been forced to flee into exile by the new political order, salutes his friend: "Tityrus, lying back beneath wide beechen cover, / You meditate the woodland Muse on slender oat; / We leave the boundaries and sweet ploughlands of home. / We flee our

---

27. Vergil, *The Eclogues,* edited and translated by Guy Lee. Subsequent citations of Vergil are taken from this edition and will be referred to in the main text by line number. I have modernized the spelling.

homeland; you, Tityrus, cool in the shade, / Are teaching the woods to echo, *Lovely Amaryllis*" ("Tityre, tu patulae recubans sub tegmine fagi / silvestrem tenui Musam meditaris avena; /nos patriae finis et dulcia linquimus arva. / nos patriam fugimus; tu, Tityre, lentus in umbra / formosam resonare doces Amaryllida silvas"; 1–5). Tityrus responds, speaking of Augustus, "Oh, Meliboeus, a god has made this leisure ours. / Yes, he will always be a god for me" ("O, Meliboee, deus nobis haec otia fecit. / Namque erit ille semper deus"; 6–7).

Tityrus is an early and influential example of the subject whose ostensible autonomy is enabled and secured by a primary submission to power, here, Augustus. Tityrus reports that it is by the emperor's orders that he now carries on his pastoral way of life: "It was he who ordered me to graze cattle as before . . . and yoke bulls" ("pascite ut ante boves, pueri; summittite tauros" 45). Tityrus's embrace of the identity of imperial subject makes him a useful model for Cetina. Unlike the single-minded lovers of Petrarchan tradition and the bower, the songs of Tityrus embrace two objects of desire without conflict: the woods are still echoing with his song to Amaryllis as he begins to sing the emperor's praises to Meliboeus, indicating that his passion for Amaryllis does not conflict with his embrace of the emperor and his position within the imperial state. For this reason, his love is able to exist within the historical and political world. But in exchange, it becomes subject to imperial mandate. Tityrus thus serves as the model for Cetina's Vandalio, who embraces ambitions for both love and the success that can be secured when a shepherd agrees to trade the autonomous bower for the productive and (it was hoped) fruitful existence of a life lived under imperial shade. Cetina indicates that Vergil's text reflects on his own plot both by fixing Amaryllis as Vandalio's second beloved and by making continuous associations between Amarílida and Valladolid: Vandalio's embrace of Amarílida signifies in the Spanish text, as it does in the Latin, an embrace of subjection, or of a mode of being that is founded first and foremost on submission to the structuring authority of the imperial state. But since the primary tropes for identity are locations (the Betis, the Pisuerga, Andalucía, Valladolid), the narrative also begins to inscribe a subtext about the political and administrative remapping of Spain under the institutions of early modern, imperial government. Vandalio's love for his home river is rewritten and revised into experiences of shifting identification with various sites of activity within the territories of the empire: the Po, the Tiber, the Rhine. As a consequence, the loves with Amarílida are pastoral in the generic sense, if not bucolic and self-enclosed in the idealized way that love was experienced by the Betis.

While they retain the references to flocks, pastures, rivers, and riverbanks, the bucolic fantasy is constantly mediated by Vandalio's subjection to the whims of his emperor and his captains, whose summons from place to place have a greater impact on the way he lives his life than do the moods and demands of his lady.

As an additional point, the Eclogue provides a poetics, as well as a narrative, through which to express the subjectivity of the new political order. In Vergil's poem, conflicting points of view regarding the rise of Augustus remain unresolved with the onset of evening:[28] Tityrus embraces the new order, while Meliboeus, forced into exile, laments it. But as night falls, Tityrus calls a halt to Meliboeus's lament by inviting him to set his cares aside and enjoy a rustic hospitality.[29] We have seen Cetina deploy a version of this strategy above, in Sonnet 27, where the looming threat of death is deflected into an aesthetic register in which suffering is no longer associated with the fear of actual pain and actual death. In the Vandalio poems, the association of evening with the suspension of conflict suggests that Cetina was thinking of Vergil as he arrived at his solution for how to represent the complex subject of Spanish Empire. Furthermore, since Dórida represents the life by the Betis and Amarílida life in Valladolid, Vandalio displays a change of attitude here that goes far beyond the conventional contradictions of amorous discourse ("I freeze/I burn"). When Cetina turns to emulate Vergil's text, the dialogic structure of the eclogue form, in which multiple singers voice discrete songs within the framework of a single poem, replaces the single-mindedness of the Petrarchan sequence. The fulfillment of the Amarílida series takes place when Vandalio expresses his heart as capable of holding both ladies and both constellations of desire, one centered on home, one centered on the empire, without conflict.

---

28. Alpers comments on the pastoral convention of suspending conflict, *What Is Pastoral?* 67–69.

29. [Meliboeus:] "'Look where strife has led / Rome's wretched citizens: we have sown fields for these! / Graft pear trees, Meliboeus, now, set vines in rows. / Go, little she-goats, go, once happy flock of mine. / Not I hereafter, stretched full length in some green cave, / Shall watch you far off hanging on a thorny crag; / I'll sing no songs; not in my keeping, little goats, / You'll crop the flowering Lucerne and bitter willow.' Tityrus: 'However, for tonight you could rest here with me / Upon green leafage: I can offer you ripe fruit / And mealy chestnuts'" ("en cuo discordia ciuis / produxit miseros: his nos conseuimus agros! / insere nunc, Meliboee, piros, pone ordine uitis. / ite meae, felix quondam pecus, ite capellae. / non ego uos posthac uiridi proiectus in antro / dumosa pendere procul de rupte uidebo; / carmina nulla canam; non me pascente, capellae, / florentem cytisum et salices carpetis amaras.' / Tityus: 'Hic tamen hance mecum poteras requiescere noctem / fronde super uiridi: sunt nobis mitia poma, / castaneae molles,'" 71–81).

The Amarílida Relation (Sonnets 35, 46, 72, 87, 88, 98, 109, 212, 4, 27, 120, Song 5, Epistle 10)

Both through its intertextual links to the First Eclogue and as the worldly second love that replaces the unbridled and unconstrained loves of Vandalio's youth, the relationship with Amarílida figures the young courtier's subjection to the Hapsburg regime. The experience is ambivalent. Vandalio's new life as an imperial subject extends him opportunities for travel and for interchange with other courtly shepherds, but his renunciation of autonomy also gives rise to the troubling symptom of impotence. Vandalio proceeds through various scenarios of frustration and self-induced restraint in this series. His reduced sexual powers are ascribed in some poems to jealousy and uncertainty about his new lady's love for him. In others, they are associated with the jaded views that both he and Amarílida hold of the lasting powers of love. In Sonnet 87, for example, Vandalio is about to possess his lady, "El dulce fruto en la cobarde mano / casi puesto en la hambrienta boca" (1–2) ("The sweet fruit in the cowardly hand, / almost set in his hungering mouth"), but he finds himself unable to complete the act: "de turbado lo suelta, y no lo toca, / vencido de un temor bajo, villano" (3–4) ("flustered, he lets it fall, and does not touch it, / defeated by a base and vile fear"). In Sonnet 35, details of the scene are changed, but the frustration is the same. Vandalio is nearly dead with amorous longing and laments to a grieving and compliant Amarílida, "Poca seguridad, menos firmeza, / no me dejan gozar vuestros favores; / que un recelo mortal me los desvía" (12–14) ("Uncertainty and, even more, a lack of will, / keep me from enjoying your favors; / for a mortal dread deflects me from them"). The word *recelo* (dread) also appears in Sonnet 98 ("Entre osar y temer, entre esperanza" ["Between daring and fear, between hope"]) and Sonnet 120 ("La nueva luz en nacer el día" ["The new light at the dawn of day"]). In each case, the emotion fulfills a self-sanctioning function, disciplining Vandalio from consummating his desire for an Amarílida who is nearly always represented as willing. The emphasis in these poems on the frustration of erotic passion stands in clear contrast with the Dórida series and underscores the association of Amarílida with subjection and with a life lived in conditions that depend on the caprices of the monarch and the state. Perhaps the strongest illustration of the trope appears in Sonnet 46, which describes a scene of lovers' communion that contrasts sharply with poems in the Dórida group, such as Sonnet 9 (LB). Where the Dórida poem represents the lovers engaged in an experience of erotic pleasure that overcomes the boundaries of difference that distinguish body, time, and the world, the lovers in Sonnet 46 are pitiably bound by their separate mortal experiences. Vandalio lies in Amarílida's arms, but there is none of the mingling of selves that takes place in the Dórida poems:

Sonnet 46

> Con aquel poco espíritu cansado
> que queda al que el vivir le va dejando,
> en brazos de Amarílida llorando
> Vandalio, de salud desconfiado
> "No me duele el morir desesperado
> —Dijo—pues con mi mal se va acabando;
> mas duéleme que parto y no sé cuando,
> Señora, ¿habrás dolor de mi cuidado?"
> La ninfa que con lágrimas el pecho
> del mísero pastor todo bañaba:
> "Sin premio no será tu amor," decía.
> Mas él, puesto en el paso más estrecho,
> mucho más que el morir, pena le daba
> no poder ya gozar del bien que oía

[With that small and weary quantity of spirit / that remains to a man from whom life is departing, / weeping in the arms of Amarílida, / Vandalio, doubting his health, spoke; / "It is not the despair of death," / he said, "since my suffering ends with me; / what hurts me is that I will depart, and I do not know when, / My lady, will you feel pain for my suffering?" / From the nymph who with tears / bathed the breast of the wretched shepherd: / "Your love will not go without reward," she said. / But he was now entering the narrowest passage; / much more than by death he was pained / by not being able to take pleasure from the good news he heard.]

Vandalio's cry in the second quatrain reflects his awareness that his will and his powers are not his own to enjoy; rather, they are subject to summons by an empire that requires soldiers and a governmental structure that needs viceroys, governors, and diplomats. Certain that he will have to abandon this embrace as he has been forced to leave others before it, he is unable to take pleasure in Amarílida's proffered favors. However, Vandalio's frustrations do not lead him to challenge the conditions of his new position. He is Tityrus, not Meliboeus.[30] One of the elements that suggests that the Vandalio poems were conceived of as two parts of a longer text is the psychological and emotional logic that informs his loves. By the Betis, Vandalio was able to enjoy Dórida's favors, but he was insensible to the social, political, and imperial world around him. With Amarílida, what he has lost in prowess is compensated by the satisfactions of life lived in the circles of court.

In this regard, Song 5 serves an analogous function in the Amarílida series that Sonnet 9 (LB) serves within the Dórida one. The poem is a close imitation of Ariosto's "Quando'l sol parte, e l'ombra il mondo cuopre" ("When the sun departs, and the world is covered in shadow"). The Spanish poem takes on a significance that is not found in the Italian one, namely, the chastened pleasures of a second love when one has learned one's lessons in the first. The poem opens with Vandalio and Amarílida singing of their love for one other. Vandalio sings, "Amarílida mía, ¡oh tú, que sola / doquiera que yo sea / en el alma me estás!" (34–36) ("My Amarílida, oh you alone who, / no matter where I am / are in my soul!"). Subsequently, the two draw together in amorous bliss:

> Amor, después que calla mi pastora,
> desciende a confirmar tan dulce efeto.
> Allí se asienta en los hermosos pechos;
> ora en los ojos arde y se enamora,
> ora entre los cabellos va secreto,
> de tanto bien tan loco,
> que el mundo tiene en poco;
> mas, ¿quién lo tendrá en más, quien sea discreto?
>
> (57–64)

[Love, after my shepherdess has fallen silent, / descends, confirming the sweet effect. / There he seats himself, between her beautiful breasts; / now he burns and lights her eyes with love, / now among her locks he wanders in secret, / mad with joy, / he holds the world in little regard; / but what man of judgment would hold it dearer?]

Whereas in Sonnet 9 (LB) Amor's entry precipitated a crisis, his arrival in lines 56–57 of the song *confirms* the love between Vandalio and his lady.

---

30. And not Garsilaso. See my discussion of Garcilaso's Sonnet 33 and Elegy 2 in Chapter 2.

The difference between the two scenes is the difference between the closed relationship that has taken place in the autonomous Petrarchan bower and the triangulated desire experienced by fully socialized subjects who identify with their positions within the networks of power that surround them. Such subjects understand that authority both constrains and enables. The anxieties Amor triggered in the Betis idyll do not interfere with these older, wiser lovers' bliss. They speak openly of possible rivals for each other's affections in a clear allusion to the rivalries and affairs that proliferate within the narrow society of court, and they accept Amor's subtle interventions as they consummate their love.

Ultimately, Song 5 is the most tender and erotic of the Amarílida poems, but it is also represented as a *scene,* that is, as an experience of love that is on the one hand deeply felt and on the other understood as a performance and a display for readers of poetry and for fellow courtiers. Thus the version of the moment of folly from Sonnet 9 (LB), Vandalio's disdain for "el mejor bien del suelo" appears in line 63 of Song 5, "el mundo tiene en poco" ("he holds the world as little"); but the significance of the statement is undermined as it is immediately opened outward when the speaker asks, "who wouldn't?" ("¿quién lo tendrá en más . . . ?" 64). The question limits the extent of the two lovers' self-absorption by reminding us that even in the moments of deepest intimacy the Amarílida relation takes place in the social world.[31]

It also takes place within the hearts of complex subjects. As I indicated earlier, the final resolution of conflict in the Vandalio poems takes place in this song, with its atmosphere of evening and register of pastoral suspension, as Vandalio finds room in his heart for both women, Dórida and Amarílida. Dórida appears on the scene unexpectedly, as one of the Hispanizations of Ariosto's three rival ladies in the Italian version of the poem:

> Dórida renueva
> los antiguos ardores;
> Alba me ruega que me duela della;

---

31. Furthermore, this is overtly the world of court. The mention of *discreción,* the art of judgement, in line 64, suggests Vandalio's "quién" is addressed to an audience of courtiers. The list of rival shepherds Amarílida enumerates reinforces the sense of court, though it is peopled with the figures of pastoral: "Tirso y Fausto, pastores extremados, / mozos sueltos, ligeros, / y ambos a dos hermosos sin enmienda . . . / entre ambos en amor suelta la rienda / sin temor de fatiga . . . . / Mas, ¿quién será él que de otro amor me encienda / Vandalio . . ." (67–78) ("Tirso and Fausto, shepherds of great skill, / free and casual youths / and both of them beautiful without flaw . . . / between the two, love lets loose his reins / without fear of the whip . . . / But who will be the one, Vandalio, who will inflame me with another love").

> ambas mozas, hermosas como flores,
> una y otra de amor hacen gran prueba;
> Alba es sanguina, colorada y bella
> como las frescas rosas;
> de azucenas hermosas
> es color de Dórida; mas ella
> ni otra habrá jamás que a amor me estringa
>
> (79–88)

[Dórida renews / the old ardor; / Alba begs me to pine for her; / both comely, beautiful like flowers, / one and the other give great shows of love; / Alba is sanguine, colorful, and lovely / like fresh roses; / Dórida is the color of beautiful lilies; / but neither she / nor another will ever have that which drives me to love]

In contrast to his wretchedness in Sonnets 10 (LB) and 21, Vandalio here speaks sweetly of his old and new loves, referring not only to Dórida and Amarílida, but also to "Alba." His tone reflects the sprezzatura of the seasoned courtier, and Song 5 opens the way for the poems of exile from Amarílida as he is sent off on missions to pastures across Europe. This set of exile poems underscores the transformation of Vandalio's identity, as he longs for the Pisuerga and not for the Betis. His notion of home has shifted from the local region to the seat of imperial power.

The Exile from Amarílida (Sonnets 3, 5, 97, 140, 193, Song 11)

The poems of exile from Amarílida show the emotional distance that Vandalio has traveled in his struggles to accommodate his life within the empire. In Song 5, he fears that he will be summoned to leave the banks of the Pisuerga. In Sonnet 97 he is at war; and Sonnets 3, 5, and 140 and Song 11 show him grazing his flocks by the Ticino, the Po, and the Rhine, respectively; these are foreign rivers that designate sites of imperial battles. Notably, these poems do not portray the inner conflict that was a theme in the poems written in exile from Dórida. Instead, Vandalio expresses uncomplicated longing for home, and "home" is by the Pisuerga: "Paced, mis ovejuelas, pues los hados, / la invidia ajena y la aspereza altiva / de la ribera de Piserga os priva" (Sonnet 5, 9–11) ("Graze, my lambs, for the fates, / foreign envy and bitter pride / keep you from the banks of the

Pisuerga"). Sonnet 140 expresses envy at another shepherd's dispatch back to Spain:

> Dichoso tú; tú sólo eres dichoso,
> que vuelves do verás tan presto el Tago,
> y el bien que te hace ir tan presuroso.
> "Yo, misero, llorando me deshago,
> de sólo ver Pisuerga deseoso:
> ¡Mira cuál es de Amor, Tirreno, el pago!"
>
> (9–14)

> [Fortunate you; you alone are fortunate, / for you return soon to the Tagus, / and that pleasure that makes you travel with speed. / "I, wretched, am undone by weeping, / desiring only to see the Pisuerga: / Look what is the reward, Tirreno, of Love!"]

In Sonnet 193, directed to Montemayor, Vandalio sighs: "Si como vas, Lusítano, yo fuese / do el alma dejé, que no debiera; / si como verás, presto la ribera / del hermoso Pisuerga así la viese" (1–4) ("If I traveled, Lusítano, as you do / to where I left my soul, which I should not have done; / if, just as you will see, close to the banks / of the beautiful Pisuerga, I saw her like that").

Both in terms of tone and in the rich pastoral imagery they contain, these poems correspond to the lyrics directed to the Betis; but they mourn the loss of the Pisuerga. In this way they reflect Vandalio's successful accommodation to the subjectivity of the courtier of the centralized Spanish Empire. Vandalio's notion of home has been transformed from the local region of his birth to the bureaucratic center. The poems therefore testify to the success of Cetina's experiment in fashioning a new poetic discourse for the modern courtier.

There are no subsequent developments that continue the adventures of Vandalio, Amarílida, and Dórida beyond Vandalio's departure from Spain into the wider world of the empire.

As has been mentioned, Cetina's contemporaries did not make reference to his having worked on an extended text. However, thematic and formal unities in the Vandalio poems distinguish the group of poems that treat the loves of Vandalio from other pastoral sonnets and mini-sequences composed by peers such as Hernando de Acuña and Jerónimo de Urrea as they traded masked accounts of courtly dalliances and rivalries.[32] Cetina's work can be seen as forming a bridge between the courtierizing aims of Boscán, in his new lyric, and the impulse to recuperate Spanish greatness within poetry, an impulse that gains momentum over the course of the century. Cetina's views on poetry draw close to those of Boscán in that he rejects traditions of epic and ballad. But while the question posed through much of Cetina's writing is the same one explored by Boscán—how does one shape a discourse proper to the modern Spanish subject?—the motivation for his poetic experiments was different. It was not the imperative to contain Spanish greatness that informed the crafting of his more extended text. Rather, it was his encounter with the limits of Petrarchism and bucolic escapism as he sought to represent the subjectivity of the contemporary imperial Spanish courtier.

---

32. The Damon-Silvia and Silviano-Silvia poems, which appear as brief groups within the collected poetry of Hernando de Acuña, are particularly appealing and reveal an unexpected tender and erotic tone for a poet who generally takes the stance of a man's man.

4

HEROIC LYRIC

Proxima heroica maiestate lyrica nobilitas . . .

—Scaliger, *Poetices* VII.1.47

FERNANDO DE HERRERA (1534–1597) WAS THE poet of light. A skilled composer of odes and an innovator in early modern genres from literary criticism and history to saintly biography, Herrera chose light and the sun as the favored metaphors for his ambitions in the field of letters. He composed the critical *Las obras de Garcilaso de la Vega con anotaciones* (The Poetry of Garcilaso de la Vega with Annotations, 1580) to shed light on proper compositional strategies and to lead Spanish writing out of obscurity;[1] and the erudite Petrarchan poetry with which he is most commonly associated—sonnets (primarily) directed to the celebration of the lady "Luz," or "Light" (also referred to as Heliodora, Aurora, and Estrella, among other luminous names)—have inspired critics to refer to his "radiant" poetics. López Bueno observes that "en la poesía herreriana, el mundo se subsume en el objeto amoroso, que irradia desde su heliocentrismo" ("in the poetry of Herrera, the world is subsumed into the object of desire, which radiates forth in a heliocentric order") (*La poética cultista,* 51).

---

1. On Herrera and discourses of obscurity and illumination, see Paul Julian Smith, *Writing in the Margin,* 32–37. See also 43–49, and Herrera himself: "Ni . . . pretendo descubrir más luz que la que conviene a los ojos flacos y cortos de vista. . . . Pero deseo que sea esta mi intención bien acogida de los que saben, y que se persuadan a creer que la honra de la nación . . . me oblig[ó] . . . a publicar estas rudezas de mi ingenio" ("nor . . . do I intend to reveal more light than that which is suitable for weak and myopic eyes. . . . But I wish that my intentions are welcomed by those who have knowledge, and that I may persuade them that the honor of the nation . . . obliged me to publish these crude results of my wit"); *Annotations,* 264. Page references to the *Annotations* refer to the 2001 Cátedra edition of the text.

The formulation is particularly useful. Whereas the lasting poetic fame marked by the laurel structures the Petrarchan universe, light, as a source of illumination and also as a source of energy, is the trope that motivated and organized Herrera's verbal enterprises both in poetry and in prose.[2] "Donde no hay luz ni entendimiento" he wrote in the *Annotations,* "no se puede conocer ni entender cosa alguna" ("where there is neither light nor understanding . . . one cannot know or understand anything at all").[3] We can compare this line with Boscán's formulation, discussed in Chapter 1: the new art "consiste en ingenio y en juicio, no teniendo estas dos cosas más vida de cuanto tienen gusto" ("depends entirely on wit and on judgment, neither of which have life apart from pleasure"). Written half a century or so before Herrera composed the *Annotations,* these words link Boscán to a fundamentally different epoch from that of his Sevillian successor. To Boscán, composing poetry was an activity of courtly *otium;* furthermore, it was informed by pressures to mediate and diffuse the energies and passions of the nobleman, and thereby assist in his accommodation to the new social and political regimes to which he was subject. Herrera forged his precepts and his practice for a *new* "new poetry" in the late 1500s, as Spanish captains were celebrated as glorious agents of a heroic modern age in which a modern Catholic king—not Ferdinand, but Philip II—would secure the hegemony of the true religion across the globe in a "second Reconquest." At the same time, Spanish noblemen were subordinate as never before to the powers of God and of the king. Counter-Reformation ideologies cast the Spanish fighter's heroic *diestro braço* as an instrument of divine will: God guided the aim and provided the force for each successful blow. Within this context, the discourse of courtly lyric was invested with a new mandate. While it still participated in promoting and naturalizing the nobleman's subjection, it was also required to *disguise* the fundamental disruption of Spanish masculine identity that had been brought about by the discourses of messianic imperialism, and to proclaim the virtue and the virility of the modern age.

2. Herrera's known canon of writing was diverse as well as prolific. On the historical writing and the *Tomás Moro,* see Randel, *The Historical Prose,* as well as Lara Garrido, *Del Siglo de Oro* (133–48). On the *Annotations,* see the introduction by Pepe and Reyes, in Herrera, *Annotations,* 17–83. Morros Mestres ("La idea de la lírica") is also a very useful scholar and commentator on the text, since he tracks the sources of Herrera's opinions in the work; Montero situates the *Annotations* within the context of the controversy that followed on its publication.

3. This line is also quoted by Lara Garrido, 138. His brief but incisive comments on Herrera's poetics underscore some of the principal points in López Bueno. See *Del Siglo de Oro,* 133–48.

Viewed from this perspective, the observation made by Mary Gaylord Randel some time ago, that Herrera's works are joined by a "common heroic *vision*," takes on a particular significance (Randel, *The Historical Prose*, 4, my emphasis). In keeping with mannerist aesthetics, Herrera can be understood as working to recuperate a measure of the heroic Spanish agency that was excluded by modern conditions through his manipulation of poetic discourse to achieve powerful visual effects. Smith has pointed out that Herrera maintained an affinity for the trope of *enargeia*, in particular, and he glosses the term: "The form of the thing is to be so expressed in the word that it is seen rather than heard, and the orator's linguistic gesture will provoke emotions appropriate to this graphic persuasiveness." Sixteenth-century rhetoricians deployed these figures in the interest of securing the *eficacia* of language to compensate for absent things, "to represent the object in an excellent way."[4] Herrera made no secret of his opinion that male agency, or *virtud*, was the definitive "lost object" for contemporary Spanish poetry.[5] But his sense of this loss was complex, given that it was brought about by God's decision to favor the Spanish nation with the completion of His will. The *Annotations*, Herrera's nationalist odes, and his Petrarchan poetry to the lady Luz cohere as an organic whole when we understand them as informed by an acute sense of the obsolescence of traditional ideals of Spanish masculinity and of poetry itself in a modern age that was making new and perhaps exaggerated claims for those ideals. Across the spectrum of Herrera's writings, we find him working to bring virile Spanish glory into life and presence on the page while maintaining a rhetorically licensed

---

4. Quotations from Smith, *Writing in the Margin*, 45 and 44. On the rhetoric of visual effect in the late sixteenth century, see the important study by Bergmann (*Art Inscribed*). On metaphors of vision in the Petrarchan poetry, see also Navarrete (*Orphans of Petrarch*, 151–69).

5. Two examples from the *Annotations* characterize Herrera's view. The first is his opening defense of his project: "Los españoles, ocupados en las armas con perpetua solicitud hasta acabar de restituir su reino a la religión cristiana, no pudiendo entre aquel tumulto y rigor acudir a la quietud y sosiego de estos estudios, quedaron por la mayor parte agenos de su noticia y apenas pueden dificilmente ilustrar las tinieblas de la oscuridad en que se hallaron por tan largo espacio de años" (278) ("The Spanish, occupied with the perpetual cares of completing the restitution of their kingdom to the Christian religion, and unable, amid the tumult and the demands of that time to welcome the quiet and the leisure of such studies, remained for the most part alien to news of it, and it is only with difficulty that one can illustrate the darkness and the obscurity in which they found themselves during a long period of years"). The second appears in Herrera's comments on Cetina, whose sonnets we found praised by Herrera in Chapter 3. As he continues his remarks, however, he attributes Cetina with a certain lassitude: "fáltale el espíritu y vigor, que tan importante es a la poesía; y así dice muchas cosas dulcemente, pero sin fuerzas" (280) ("he lacks spirit and vigor, and these are quite important to poetry; and thus he says many things sweetly, but without force").

ambiguity regarding the substance that lay behind those words, and a politic attitude regarding the place of human agency in the physical world.

From Action to Essence

Herrera was born in the environs of Seville in 1534 and remained a resident of the area until his death in 1597. His adult years corresponded to the reign of Philip II (1527–1598).[6] Herrera, who was described by his biographer, Francisco de Pacheco, as the descendant of an honorable but modest family, gained his livelihood through a position in the parish of St. Andrés. However, despite his marginality with respect to the court, and despite a propensity for secluding himself in his study, he was a member of an ambitious and productive intellectual circle.[7] Judging from allusions to Herrera that appear in Pacheco and in the writings of other near-contemporaries, such as Rodrigo Caro, in *Los claros varones de Sevilla*, and also judging from the list of dedicatees to whom Herrera directed his writing or with whom he exchanged sonnets and songs, it is clear that he consorted with fellow humanists and intellectuals of various ranks, including members of the power elite.[8]

This association with members of the old and new Spanish nobility very likely enhanced his sensitivity to political and ideological factors that were transforming ideals of Spanish masculinity and prowess. In the final third of the sixteenth century, the conditions were ripe for an efflorescence of heroic Spanish poetry.[9] Imperial forces were occupied in nearly continuous warfare against the Turks to the east, against Protestants to the north, against rebellious Moriscos internally, and in the Americas, in continuing wars of

---

6. Philip's rule formally commenced in 1555 and 1556 and lasted until his death in 1598. In effect, however, he had governed from about 1543, when the emperor began granting him increasing responsibility for matters on the Peninsula (Kamen, *Philip of Spain*, 1997).

7. The principal source of biographical information regarding Herrera has always been his contemporary Pacheco, in the *Libro de verdaderos retratos de los hombres ilustres de Sevilla* (1599). Macrí amplified the context of Pacheco's brief remarks. See *Fernando de Herrera*, 23–48.

8. The best known are the Count and Countess of Gelves, since generations of scholars have argued for a love affair or at least an unrequited passion on Herrera's part for the Countess. Equal numbers of critics are skeptical about the possibility of a historical beloved. I argue below that Herrera's Petrarchan sequence was "about" love only in the most rhetorical sense: Herrera praised Petrarch most of all for using poetic and rhetorical strategies in a manner so dexterous that he elevated the trivial theme of love to an exalted status.

9. On the sixteenth century as a climate for epic, see Davis, *Myth and Identity*, as well as Simerka, *Discourses of Empire*.

conquest. Official propaganda promoted celebrated captains such as don García de Toledo, Juan of Austria, Sebastian of Portugal, and the king himself as divine agents crusading for the final global victory of the True Church. But as we have already encountered a number of times in this book, the composition of the military ranks and the technologies and fighting strategies employed in war were no longer what they had been under the medieval system. Furthermore, Philip II had been imbued with a messianic triumphalist notion of Spanish destiny by his father, Holy Roman Emperor Charles V; and his royal astrologers, jurists, biographers, and chroniclers surpassed their precursors in elaborating on the idea that Spain was the chosen instrument of divine will.[10] In the wake of the Spanish victory at Lepanto (1571), in particular, Spanish triumphalism no longer associated military valor and honor with the aristocracy. With new social organizations taking over within imperial fighting ranks and within the context of an ideology that presented victory as a gift from God, any Spanish man, regardless of his rank, could claim a share of a Spanish national myth as "the daring Spaniard" (*el osado español*) and the *diestro braço* lost a degree of purchase on the social imagination.[11]

We have seen how a number of Spanish writers responded to these conditions. Notably, we might recall the nostalgic lament of Sánchez de Lima for a lost generation of aristocratic warrior poets, discussed in Chapter 1. In contrast to Sánchez de Lima, Herrera's writings reflect a distinctly un-nostalgic view of a modern era in which Spain's valiant men had the good fortune to be chosen by God to participate in the revelation of His will.[12] However, a sense of a fundamental hermeneutic, as well as a historical, gulf

---

10. John Headley has analyzed many of the memoranda and letters of council by which the young Charles of Burgundy was guided to represent himself as, simultaneously, a "new Caesar," and, in a more Christian vein, the fulfillment of God's promise to unite the world under one sovereign. Headley focuses on the shaping role of Mercurio de Gattinara in the young emperor's formation and in his ultimate acceptance by the Spanish grandees. See Headley, "The Hapsburg World," 93–127. See also the discussion of the discourse of universal monarchy in Geoffrey Parker, *Success Is Never Final*, 19–38. One point Parker reminds us of is that most of the European states claimed that providence was on the side of their military and imperialistic policies.

11. The discourse of "el osado español" and its variants has received some discussion. See, for example, Michael Gerli on "el gallardo español" as it appears in Ercilla and is taken up by Cervantes (Gerli, "Aristotle in Africa") and Anthony Cascardi, *Ideologies of History*. It seems clear that Cervantes and Herrera, at the very least, understood the social implications of employing terms for generalized male Spanish force.

12. Two distinguishing features of Herrera as a writer are his mannerism and nationalism; but a third striking aspect of his worldview is his presentism, as Randel, among others, has pointed out. In her discussion of Herrera's defense of Lepanto as the most heroic battle ever fought (*The Historical Prose*, 84–86), she notes that his claim is based on the "technical superiority of modern weaponry,

that separated the Spanish past from the revealed modern age informed Herrera's scholarship into classical and emergent forms and genres, from the ode, the elegy, and the eclogue through the sonnet and prose forms such as the historical account (*relación*), the saintly life, and the expanded critical commentary. In this new epoch it was the patriotic and spiritual duty of the man of letters to fashion the Castilian language into forms adequate to the representation of Spain's glory. As Lara Garrido has described, referring to Herrera's cultural moment, "El destino de los pueblos está regido por una instancia superior: la voluntad divina, cuya presencia en la Historia debe ser subrayada frente a la común ceguedad. Es así como cobra un nuevo sentido . . . la figura del hombre de letras y del poeta, en las conexiones entre relato histórico y canción heroica—desvelamiento de la grandeza mesiánica de los españoles que 'no puede tener morada en la estrechura de la tierra' porque defienden con las armas 'la honra de Jesucristo'" (*Del Siglo de Oro,* 140) ("The destiny of peoples is ruled by a superior cause: divine will, whose presence in History must be underscored in the face of their common blindness. It is thus that . . . the figure of the man of letters and the poet gain a new meaning, in the connections between the historical account and the heroic song—the revealing of the messianic greatness of the Spanish, 'who cannot find a dwelling place in all the wide earth' because they defend with arms 'the honor of Jesus Christ'"). Such "revealing" is the stated purpose of Herrera's *Annotations,* which opens with the well-known claim: "Deseo que sea esta mi intención bien acogida de los que saben, y que se persuaden a creer que la honra de la nación y la nobleza y excelencia del escritor presente me obligaron a publicar estas rudezas de mi ingenio" (264) ("I desire that my intentions be welcomed by those who have knowledge and that they are persuaded to believe that the honor of the nation and the nobility and the excellence of the present writer [Garcilaso] obliged me to publish these crude fruits of my wit"). A number of astute studies of this ambitious critical work, a true sixteenth-century masterpiece and one of the first European works of literary criticism, have emphasized the ways in which Herrera championed Spanish writers to compensate peninsular cultural belatedness with respect to Italy. The significance of Herrera's meditations on genre in the work has received less consideration, but the *Annotations*

---

which makes an enemy more fearful than ever, and individual survival still more tenuous" (86). Herrera's view thus differs substantially from what is expressed by other writers discussed in this book, such as Aldana, who mourns the end of sword fighting (see Introduction), and Cetina, who expresses terror before modern guns (see Chapter 3).

fits more completely into the cultural context of Counter-Reformation Spain and into Herrera's ambitions as a man of letters, first, when we take him at his word that his critical work was motivated by a concern for the condition of language in the Spanish nation,[13] and, second, when we recall that both contemporary political and religious discourses promoted the difference between the heroic Spanish past and the present age. Herrera voices his dismay at the current state of a discourse that is no longer capable of memorializing Spanish glory because the fundamental bases for representation have been transformed. The most significant example for our purposes appears in the course of comments on Garcilaso's Eclogue 2:

> ¿En qué región se hallaron reyes tan fuertes, tan guerreros, tan religiosos como los que sucedieron a Pelayo? ¿Quien mereció la gloria, el nombre y opinión, traída de la famosa antiguedad, como Bernardo del Carpio? ¿Quién puede exceder la fortaleza y piedad del Conde Fernán González, esclarecido capitán de Cristo? ¿Quién fue tan belígero y bien afortunado como el Cid Ruy Díaz? . . . Pues ya la felicidad, prudencia y valor del rey católico son tan grandes, y sobran con tanto exceso los hechos de los otros reyes, que no sufren que se les compare otro alguno . . . Mas, ¿para qué me alargo con tanta demasía en estos ejemplos, pues sabemos que no faltaron a España en algún tiempo varones heroicos? ¡Faltaron escritores cuerdos y sabios que los dedicasen con immortal estilo a la eternidad de la memoria! Y tuvieron mayor culpa de esto los príncipes y los reyes de España, que no atendieron a la gloria de esta generosa nación y no buscaron hombres graves y suficientes para la dificultad y grandeza de la historia; antes escogieron los que les presentaba el favor y no sus letras y prudencia. Y hasta ahora sentimos esta falta con profunda ignorancia de las hazañas de los nuestros, porque no hay entre los príncipes quien favoresca a los hombres que saben y pueden tratar verdadera y eloquentemente, con juizio y prudencia, las cosas bien hechas en paz y en guerra. (902–4)

> [In what region were there found kings so strong, such warriors, men so devout as those who followed after Pelayo? Who deserved

---

13. Unlike Boscán, who sought to reform poetry for "nuestra España," Herrera used the word *nación* as is seen in the quotation above.

the glory, the name, and the opinion, brought forth from famous ancient times, as much as Bernardo del Carpio? Who can exceed the force and the piety of Count Fernán González, distinguished captain of Christ? Who was so warlike and so fortunate as the Cid Ruy Díaz? . . . But now that the happiness, the prudence and the valor of the Catholic King are so great, and surpass by so great an extent the deeds of other kings that he does not suffer comparison to another. . . . But, why do I go on for such great length with these examples, for we know that Spain did not lack heroic men at any time. What were lacking were sane and wise writers who commended them to eternal memory with immortal style! And they had the greatest fault in this the princes and the kings of Spain, who did not attend to the glory of this generous nation and did not seek out men of sufficient gravity for the difficulty and the grandeur of history; rather, they chose those who presented them with favor and not with their letters and their prudence. And until now we have felt this lack through the deep ignorance of the deeds of our own men, because there is not one among the princes who favors those men of knowledge who can treat truthfully and eloquently, with judgment and prudence, those things well done in peace and in war.]

This outburst is most immediately motivated by perceived calumnies of Italian writers who criticized the actions of the imperial armies (Bembo, specifically, had called their behavior during the Sack of Rome "barbaric," and the term sent Herrera into a frenzy).[14] However, this passage has a larger point that Herrera reiterated in various ways throughout the *Annotations*: Spanish and imperial wars were misunderstood because they were not represented in the proper way. Answering to vain and shortsighted kings and

14. "No sé que ánimos se puedan hallar tan pacientes que toleren los oprobios y denuestos con que vituperan a los españoles los escritores de Italia. . . . No se disculpa Bembo con la imitación antigua, que ya no tiene ahora lugar esta respuesta, si no es porque le parece más elegante modo de hablar, y por eso nombra al turco Rey de Tracia, que es la menor parte de su imperio . . . no son los españoles tan inhumanos y apartados de la policía . . . que merescan ese apellido" ("I do not know what souls can find the patience within themselves to tolerate the opprobrium and the denouncements with which the writers of Italy vituperate the Spanish. . . . Bembo is not excused for the reason of his having imitated the ancients, for there is no longer any place for that response, no, he said it because it appears to him to be a more elegant mode of speaking, and for that reason he calls the Turk the King of Thrace, when that is the smallest part of his empire . . . the Spanish are not so inhuman nor so isolated from politesse . . . that they deserve such a name"); *Annotations*, 899–900.

patrons, Spanish writers had emphasized individual human achievements without fitting them into the greater pattern of universal Christian history. Fixed within the mere worldly context, the actions of Spain's medieval heroes and the imperial forces were at best flat and devoid of meaning; at worst, they could appear brutal and destructive. But Herrera and his generation had been blessed with the insight that achievements from the victories of Pelayo (the Asturian king credited with launching the "Reconquest" in the eighth century) through the triumphs of Charles V, Philip II, and Juan of Austria were not simply *events* in Spain's national history. They were *portents* of something far greater: the fulfillment of Christian history. And the deeds of Spain's individual captains, kings, and heroes were smaller signs that fit into this larger pattern. As a consequence, the modern age did not require poets so much as it did men of "prudence," that is, those who could read and interpret divine signs and demonstrate the true significance of the triumphs, the defeats, and the heroic actions they commemorated.[15]

Herrera's views were clearly shaped by the ideological climate of late sixteenth-century Spain (Hernando de Acuña's "Ya se acerca, Señor, o ya es llegado," discussed in Chapter 1, was composed at roughly the same time). But they received support from contemporary social conditions, for instance, the successful deployment of formations such as the Spanish *tercios* and the Swiss pikemen, blocs of soldiers drawn from the general ranks of the populace. As the success of various imperial wars was credited to the increased use of these kinds of troops (a decision informed, always, in the background, by God's will), a discourse of generalized male Spanish prowess displaced references to the *diestro braço* in Spanish poetry and prose. References to the *osado español* (the daring Spaniard), to the *gallardo español* (the brave Spaniard), and to the *esforzado español* (the powerful Spaniard) are rife throughout sixteenth-century heroic poetry and prose, from Eclogue 2 of Garcilaso de la Vega through compositions by Ercilla, Herrera, and Cervantes, among others. Therefore, in Spain, as acutely as anywhere else in Europe, the question loomed: was epic still the noble discourse through

---

15. Unlike his father, Philip II did not take to the battlefield. Rather, he styled himself as the "prudent" king and occupied himself with the management of the realm, with securing the dynasty through attempts to father an heir, and with meditation and prayer that he might correctly interpret the signs of God's will. His half-brother, don Juan of Austria, was selected to suppress the Morisco rebellions in the Alpujarras region in 1569. Don Juan was successful and went on to lead the Holy League to victory against the Ottoman navy at Lepanto, in 1571. Propagandists joined the two victories together to represent Christian Spain as bringing about a "Second Reconquest" of Islam. On tensions between the prudent king and his "impulsive" half-brother, see Kamen, *Philip of Spain*, 134–40.

which the greatest events in history were best represented? Had the long tradition of Homer's art come to an end? Certain writers—notably Tasso, in Italy, and Juan Rufo and Alonso de Ercilla, among others, in Spain—addressed themselves to the task of reforming epic to accommodate the ideologies of the messianic present.[16] Other men of letters argued that traditional forms were not suited to commemorating Spanish victories in the contemporary age and confronted a paradox. Providence had revealed that the true heroes of history were God, Christ, and the True Church. However, both patrons and an eager public demanded stirring and colorful nationalist poetry.[17] Furthermore, men and women of prudence, as we have already seen, understood themselves as bearing a moral responsibility to represent the great events of the triumphal era in ways that were accessible to the less enlightened.[18]

16. Herrera may have composed an epic in his youth—his friend Francisco de Rioja claimed that he did, in introductory comments to the 1619 *Versos*. But given the relative absence of mention of an epic within contemporary accounts of Herrera's career, his assertion seems unreliable. Serious poets tended to be credited with having composed an epic, whether or not they did so.

17. Macrí notes that Herrera and Rufo maintained a hostile relationship. Rufo referred to Herrera as arrogant and outspoken, a view which most likely derived from what Herrera had to say of the court favorite's great work. "Rufo debió encontrarse con Herrera en el salon del marqués de Tarifa. Acostumbrado al fácil éxito mundano, le pinta como un 'hombre leído y estudioso ... bronco, arrogante y despejado, y poeta áspero y terrible'" ("Rufo must have met Herrera in the salon of the Marquis of Tarifa. Accustomed to easy worldly success, he paints him as a 'well read and studious man . . . brusque, arrogant, and outspoken, and a harsh and terrible poet'"); Macrí, *Fernando de Herrera*, 24. The anecdote supports the contention that Herrera not only did not write epic himself, but attacked those who did on literary and doctrinal grounds. Having said that, it should be noted that Herrera praised the Portuguese Camoes in the *Annotations* for his majestic style. He seems to have ignored Ercilla, perhaps because he seems to have had little interest in the New World.

18. A brief look at the openings of parts one and two of *La Araucana* demonstrates the impact of Counter-Reformation culture on heroic, or Homeric, epic. The different ways in which Ercilla framed the two parts of his poem for his cultured and courtly readership indicates the challenges faced by a poet attempting to accommodate epic to the ideologies and the social organization of early modern Spain. Part one, published in 1569, opens with two rhetorical commonplaces, each properly "Renaissance" in perspective and rhetoric. The first statement is contained in the prologue and is an apology and justification for publishing: "Si pensara que el trabajo que he puesto en esta obra me había de quitar tan poco el miedo de publicarla sé cierto de mí que no tuviera ánimo para llevarla al cabo. Pero considerando ser la historia verdadera y de cosas de guerra, a las cuales hay tantos aficionados, me he resuelto en imprimirla, ayudando a ello las importunaciones de muchos testigos que en lo más dello se hallaron, y el agravio que algunos españoles recibirán quedando sus hazañas en perpetuo silencio, faltando quien les escriba, no por ser ellas pequeñas, pero porque la tierra es tan remota y apartada y la postrera que los españoles han pisado por la parte del Pirú;" Ercilla, *La Araucana*. vol. 1, Prólogo, 121. ("If I thought that the labor I have taken with this work would lessen by so little the fear of publishing it, I know for certain that for my part I would not have had the spirit to bring it to completion. But considering that this is a story that is true and relates things of war, of which there are so many followers, I have resolved to publish it, this resolution being aided by the requests of many who were found to have witnessed it, and by the injury

For Herrera, the best path toward solving this conundrum lay in combining aspects of Counter-Reformation logic with the advanced science of contemporary rhetoric. The task of the prudent writer would be to portray Spain's heroes in exalted, powerful language (*eficacia*). This language would represent their achievements effectively. More important, however, it would call attention to the significance of representation itself by means of

---

received by those Spanish men whose deeds were relegated to perpetual silence, lacking someone to write of them, not because they were small ones, but because the land is so remote and distant, and the most recent in the regions of Peru to have been trod upon by the Spanish"). The second is the supplication to Philip II: "No las damas, amor, no gentilezas / de caballeros canto enamorados, / ni las muestras, regalos y ternezas / de amorosos afectos y cuidados; / mas el valor, los hechos, las proezas, / de aquellos españoles esforzados / . . . / Suplícoos, gran Felipe, que mirada / esta labor, de vos sea recibida" (1–6; 17–18) ("Not the ladies, or love, not the pleasant witticisms / of knights in love do I sing, / nor the signs, prizes, and tender exchanges / of sentiments of love and care; / but the valor, the deeds, the spoils, / of those strong Spaniards / . . . / Great Philip, I beseech that, having been gazed on / this work is accepted by you"). Part two of the *Araucana* was published in 1578, and its opening inscribes the text within the mature social, poetic, and religious ideologies of the Counter-Reformation, and illustrate the penetration of the institutions of State and Church into late sixteenth-century poetic discourse: "Quisiera mil veces mezclar algunas cosas diferentes; pero acordé de no mudar estilo porque lo que digo se me tomase en descuento de las faltas que el libro lleva, autorizándole con escribir en él el alto principio que el Rey nuestro señor dio a sus obras con el asalto y entrado de San Quintín, por habernos dado otro aquel mismo día los araucanos en el fuerte de la Concepción" (Prólogo) ("I would have wished a thousand times to mix in other, different things; but I decided not to change my style so that what I say could avoid being discounted for the faults that the book presents. I am authorized to write here of the great beginning that the King our sovereign gave to his labors with the assault and the entry into San Quentin by the fact that the Araucans had given us another assault that same day in the fort of La Concepción"). "Salga mi trabajada voz, y rompa / el son confuso y mísero lamento / con eficacia y fuerza que interrompa / el celeste y terrestre movimiento. / La fama con sonora y clara trompa, / dando más furia a mi cansado aliento / derrame en todo el orbe de la tierra / las armas, el furor y nueva guerra. / Dadme, ¡oh sacro Señor!, favor, que creo / que es lo que más aquí pueda ayudarme, / pues en tan gran peligro ya no veo / sino vuestra fortuna en que salvarme; / mirad dónde me ha puesto el buen deseo, / favoreced mi voz con escucharme, / que luego el bravo mar, viéndoos atento, / aplacará su furia y movimiento. / Y a vuestra nave el rostro revolviendo, / la socorred en este grande aprieto, / que, si decirse es lícito, yo entiendo / que a vuestra voluntad todo es sujeto (1–20) ("Let my weary voice sing out, and break / the confused sound and the miserable lament / with efficaciousness and force that will interrupt / the movement of heaven and earth. / Let fame, trumpeting resonant and clear, / giving more fury to my tired breath / spread through all the orb of the earth / the arms, the fury, and this new war. / Give me, oh Holy Lord! favor, for I believe / that that is what can most here aid me, / for in such great danger I can no longer see / how to find my salvation if not from your favor: / look where my good desires have placed me, / favor my voice by listening to me, / for the great sea, observing you attentive, / will placate its furious movement. / And turning your face to your ship, / grant it succor in these straits, / for, if it is permitted that I speak thus, I understand / that all is subject to your will.")

In part one, Ercilla portrays himself as invested with the responsibility of commemorating heroes and the actions they undertake in remote reaches of the globe. In part two, his task is different: now he must inscribe, using all the persuasive power of modern rhetoric, the subjection of the world and its inhabitants to God and the Sovereign. The openings of the first two parts of the

striking visual and acoustic effects. The artificial, self-consciously aesthetic aspects of his style would illuminate the deeper truth that informed these works, namely, that the men celebrated were themselves signs of God's plan; their force, their strength, their courage, and their mental agility were in fact dross in comparison with what they signaled: the noble essence of the soul of the Spanish people who had been chosen by God as his instruments.[19] Herrera's frequent comments on manly virtue (*virtud*) in the *Annotations* all turn on this fundamental translation of physical characteristics into metaphysical ones, from action to essence. For example his note on the word *valiente* (valiant) locates the strength of the nobleman, not in his fighting arm, but rather in his soul. He opens his comment by redefining *fortaleza*, which means strength or fortitude:

> La fortaleza es una levantada virtud del ànimo, no vencida de algún temor, y constante en las cosas adversas, y en emprender y sufrir generosamente todos los peligros y incitada a las cosas altas y difíciles, y menospreciadora de las humildes y bajas. Pero no todos los que son prontos a poner las manos en cualquier peligro y sin temor alguno acometen todos los hechos peligrosos se pueden llamar fuertes, a opinión de Aristóteles, porque los que por deseo de alcanzar una pequeña gloria y por esperanza de aquistar riquezas y robar se arrojan a los peligros y combaten sin miedo con los contrarios, no merecen ni gozan esta alabanza. (897)

> [Fortitude is an exalted virtue of the spirit, one never vanquished by fear, and constant in adverse events, and generous in undertaking and in suffering danger, and incited to great and difficult tasks, and disdainful of humble and low ones. But not all those who are quick to set their hand to whatever danger, and who commit those dangerous deeds without fear can be called strong, in the opinion

---

Araucana therefore can be said to reflect the subjection of epic discourse to the hegemony of the political state. As a result, efficacious speaking ("eficacia," line 3) begins to be valued over efficacious action, even in the action-packed genre of the epic. In part two of the poem, great noble captains will be named in long lists, and their daring and virtue praised (see lines 19.69–76), but the epic character of the poem no longer turns on the heroism of the noble individual; rather, it is sustained by a messianic doctrine of a globe subsumed under God's will.

19. This is the ideological undergirding of mannerist aesthetic excess. On the ideological aspects of mannerism, see Baena, "Spanish Mannerist Detours," as well as Smith, *Writing in the Margin*.

of Aristotle, because those who, desiring to gain a little bit of glory and acquire some riches by looting, throw themselves into dangers and fight without fear with the adversary, do not deserve or enjoy such praise.]

Nearly every writer we have studied up to this point has employed a conceit of "private" internal space whose ideological function can be exposed. In sixteenth-century poetry, in particular, the hidden regions of the heart and of the soul are the sites in which lyric speakers internalize their complex experiences of power and embrace ideology as their own private desire. The entry on *valiente* represents another iteration of this same process. The man of *fortaleza* demonstrates a greater quality of spirit than does the vainglorious and avaricious strongman who rushes into battle. By associating physical bravery with base motives and appetites, Herrera makes a virtue of self-restraint, the discipline that is most crucial to great men who sought to eke their living within the Hapsburg political regime. We have encountered examples of this discourse of inner strength before. In Chapter 1, we noted that Herrera praises the sonnet form in the *Annotations* by drawing on the late fifteenth-century writings of Lorenzo de'Medici. Lorenzo's discourse of pragmatic virtù presents subjection and constraint as enabling conditions for a particular variety of nobility. Roughly a century later, Herrera demonstrated the impact of Counter-Reformation doctrine on the courtier's strategies of accommodation. In Herrera's writings, self-restraint is no longer a willed, pragmatic act. It is a noble quality conferred upon the soul by God. A similar view also informs Song 2 (1582), a poem that was perhaps composed for his friend and patron Fernando de Enríquez de Ribera, the Marquis of Tarifa.[20]

Song 2

No celebro los hechos
del duro Marte, y sin temor osados
los valerosos pechos,
la siempre insigne gloria
de aquellos españoles no domados
. . . .

---

20. Cuevas credits Coster with identifying the poem as a wedding song composed for the marquis and marquise, in 1580 (Cuevas, *Poesía*, 391).

No basta, no, el imperio
ni traer las cervizes humilladas
presas en cautiverio
con vencedora mano,
ni que, de las banderas ensalzadas,
el cita y africano,
con medroso semblante,
y el indo y Persia sin valor se espante

que quien al miedo obliga
y rinde el corazón, y desfallece
de la virtud amiga,
y va por el camino
do la profana multitud perece
sujeto al yugo indino,
pierde la gloria y nombre,
pues siendo más se hace menos hombre.

Los heroes famosos
los niervos derribaron,
que ni en los engañosos
gustos, ni en lisonjeras
voces de las sirenas peligraron,
ante las ondas fieras
atravesando fueron
por do ningunos escapar pudieron.

Seguid, Señor, la llama
de la virtud, que en vos sus fuerzas prueba

(9–13; 41–66)

[I do not celebrate the deeds / of harsh Mars, and the fearlessness, the daring, / the valiant breasts of / the always distinguished and glorious / Spaniards, never conquered / ... / No, empire is not enough, / nor is it enough to lead those humbled necks / imprisoned in captivity / by your conquering hand, / nor, by unfurling your banners, /

and with a fearsome face, / to strike fear in the Turk and the African, / and in India and cowardly Persia / for he who pleases / to give his heart over to fear, and forsakes / his friend virtue / and pursues the path / down which the profane multitude disappears, / subjected to the undignified yoke, / he loses his glory and his name, / or being greater in the eyes of the world he makes himself less of a man. / The sinews of the famous heroes were destroyed / —for while neither through deceiving / appetites, nor by the flattering / voices of the sirens did they wander into danger—they crossed over the fierce waves / from whence none could escape. / Follow, Sir, that flame / of virtue, for it tests its force in you]

Using the ancients as examples, Herrera admonishes his young friend that apparently heroic acts such as the conquest of empires and the subjection of the infidel are not, in fact, sufficient to preserve the honor of one's name. Indeed, the greater the power a man wields, the less he is a man ("siendo más se hace menos hombre"; 56). The desire to spread fear is a base appetite that must be conquered if a man is to reveal his true virtue, which lies in his capacities for self-restraint.

Songs for the *Varón máximo*

While Song 2 is another example of Herrera substituting a mystical discourse of essence for the nobleman's previously celebrated characteristics, his physical strength and his agency, the poem is also notable inasmuch as it is a lyric. Along with doctrine and rhetoric, the *form*s in which contemporary heroic achievements were to be commemorated was a central preoccupation for Herrera. While he was ambitious on behalf of poetry, he was aware of important developments in alternative genres and not at all convinced that poetic discourse still had a significant role to play in the modern age.[21] At the same time, he was not prepared to dispense with the art altogether. It is notable that his entry on the failure of poets to adequately represent the role of Spanish and imperial wars in history appears as a comment on Garcilaso's Eclogue 2, in a section in which Garcilaso had inserted a brief narrative of the battle of Gelves. Herrera was intrigued by this experiment in setting

---

21. On Herrera's ambivalent views on historical writing as an emergent genre, see Randel, *The Historical Prose*. Lara Garrido, *Del Siglo de Oro*, emphasizes Herrera's saintly lives (see 139).

historical material into the eclogue form.[22] Thus, drawing on a selection of old and new textual authorities—on Lorenzo, on Quintilian, on contemporary rhetoricians such as Scaliger, Ruscelli, and Minturno—Herrera set out to forge the poetry suitable for Spain's great men.[23] This poetry would suit Aristotelian doctrines of decorum in that it would occupy an appropriately subordinate place in the hierarchy of the genres: it would be lyric, not epic. At the same time, this contemporary "new lyric" would be noble in its own way. Herrera's ambitions for his lyric are expressed most clearly as he defines the genre of the ode:

> Después de la magestad heróica, dieron los antiguos el segundo lugar a la nobleza lírica, poema nacido para alabanzas y narraciones de cosas hechas, y deleites y alegrías y convites. Requiere este verso ingenio vivo y espiritoso, voluntad cuidadosa y trabajadora, juicio despierto y agudo, las voces y oración pulida, castigada eficaz y numerosa y particularmente, la jocundidad, como los élegos la lacivia y los epigramas los juegos. Y así como la poesía eróica tomó nombre del canto . . . así la lírica se apellidó . . . porque no se pronunciaban sin el canto de la lira. (477–78)

> [After the majesty of the heroic meter, the ancients gave second place to the nobility of the lyric, a poem born for encomia and the narration of feats achieved, of delights and pleasures and festivals. This verse requires a lively and spirited wit, a will to careful work, an attentive and sharp judgment, and voices and sentences that are polished, carefully considered, efficacious, and measured; particularly it requires jocularity, just as elegies require license, and epigrams contests. And just as heroic poetry took its name from the great song . . . so the lyric was named . . . because it was not pronounced without the song of the lyre.]

22. Overall the *Annotations* make the case that Garcilaso was an excellent poet and man of letters who achieved the best results possible given the limited verbal resources available to him at the time. The *Annotations* work to supplement Garcilaso's work with modern rhetorical theory and useful examples from ancient and modern writers whose relevance has been revealed to the present age.

23. On Herrera's sources, see the detailed analysis by Morros Mestres (*Las polémicas literarias*), as well as the introduction by Pepe and Reyes to the Cátedra edition of the *Anotaciones*. The discussions by Randel (*The Historical Prose*), Lara Garrido (*Del Siglo de Oro*), López Bueno (*La poética cultista*), and Navarrete (*Orphans of Petrarch*) also set Herrera's ideas in the contexts of Italian mannerist rhetoric.

Following Scaliger, Herrera presents the lyric as essentially subordinate. The ode, for example, is "second in majesty" to heroic great song.[24] But within these constraints, the lyric offered some important resources. For one thing, while it was not epic, it was still privileged discourse, retaining a measure of grandeur, even if it was "second." In addition, contemporary lyric forms such as the sonnet and many types of song were not subject to ancient prescriptions by the worthies. They did not have to follow the rules and codes set down, for example, in Aristotle. The new lyric thus lent itself to enhancement through modern rhetorical devices and vocabularies.[25] Herrera suggests this in his remarks on the sonnet:

> Es el soneto . . . tan extendida y capaz de todo argumento que recoge en sí sola todo lo que pueden abrazar estas partes de poesía, sin hacer violencia alguna a los preceptos y religión del arte, porque resplandecen en ella con maravillosa claridad y lumbre de figuras y exornaciones poéticas la cultura y propriedad, la festividad y agudeza, la magnificencia y espíritu, la dulcura y jocundidad, la aspereza y vehemencia, la comiseración y affectos, y la eficacia y representación de todas. (266–67)

> [The sonnet . . . is so extensive and capable of any argument that it gathers into itself all that these other kinds of poetry can embrace, without doing a single violence to the precepts and the doctrine of the art, because in it shine forth with marvelous clarity and light of figures and poetic adornments, culture and propriety, festivity and wit, magnificence and spirit, sweetness and humor, bitterness and vehemence, commiseration and the affects, and the efficaciousness and representation of them all.]

These two features of the new lyric, its inherited privilege as poetic discourse and its potential for modernization, appealed to Herrera as he sought to forge a heroic art for the contemporary age. Before the lyric could come into its own as a discourse for the contemporary age, however, Herrera needed to recuperate it from the damages wrought by Boscán.

---

24. See Morros Mestres on this passage (*Las polémicas literarias*, 216).

25. For a slightly different view of Herrera's ideas of epic, lyric, and the present, see Navarrete, *Orphans of Petrarch*, 151–57, 165–67, in which he touches on Herrera's comments on the epic and the phrase "el osado español," and 177–79.

Early in the *Annotations,* Herrera contrasts Tuscan with Spanish. The former is "muy florida, abundosa, blanda y compuesta, pero libre, laciva, desmayada, y demasiadamente enternecida y muelle y llena de afectación" (277) ("very florid, abundant, smooth, and composed, but free, lax, weak, and too tender and soft and full of affectation"). Spanish, in contrast, is

> grave, religiosa, honesta, alta, magnífica, suave, tierna, afectuosísima y llena de los sentimientos, y tan copiosa y abundante que ninguna otra puede gloriarse de esta riqueza y fertilidad . . . es más recatada y observante, que ninguno tiene autoridad para osar innovar alguna cosa con libertad; porque ni corta ni añade sílabas a las dicciones, ni trueca ni altera forma, antes toda entera y perpetua muestra su castidad y cultura y admirable grandeza y espíritu . . . Finalmente la española se debe tratar con más honra y reverencia y la toscana con más regalo y llaneza. (277–78)

> [Our (tongue is) grave, religious, honest, elevated, magnificent, smooth, tender, very full of affect and sentiments, and so copious and abundant that no other can glory in such richness and fertility . . . it is more circumspect and observant, for no one has the authority to dare innovate anything with liberty; because one neither cuts nor adds syllables to its diction, nor does one exchange or alter a form, but rather, sufficient unto itself, it perpetually displays its restraint and its refinement and its admirable greatness and spirit . . . Finally, Spanish should be treated with more honor and reverence, and Tuscan with more ornament and simplicity.]

These two descriptions have a context in a contemporary humanist discourse. As Patricia Parker has demonstrated, vernacular derivatives of the Latin words *mollis, nervus,* and *viriliem* appear throughout the writing of sixteenth-century rhetoricians and testify to an anxiety regarding the possible effeminacy of the pursuit of letters. This anxiety was enhanced when the field of letters turned to the elaboration of style, the "'futile and crippling study of words,' to the detriment of the 'things' that are the 'sinews' (*nervi*) of discourse."[26] A preoccupation with "virile style"

---

26. Parker, "Virile Style," 203; embedded quotations are of Quintilian, in the *Institutes,* 8.18–22, in the 1936 Loeb edition, as cited by Parker. Parker's discussion establishes the principal source for sixteenth-century preoccupations with "virile style" as Quintilian, although she observes that

(Parker) clearly informed Herrera's comments on Spanish and Italian. His attribution of the quality of *muelle* to Tuscan represents the opening salvo in his attempt to recuperate masculine force for Spanish lyric, and it can serve to focus our attention on the vocabulary of virility, heroism, glory, spirit, and magnificence that is omnipresent through the seven-hundred-plus pages of the *Annotations*. Herrera's poetics of the lyric is really a poetics of masculinity, motivated by the persistent cultural ambivalence about masculine agency and the ideal of the Spanish hero. When Herrera makes a claim for the enjambed line as "virtuous" ("cortar el verso . . . no es vicio sino virtud, y uno de los caminos principales para alcanzar la alteza y la hermosura del estilo, como en el heróico latino, que romper el verso es grandeza del modo del decir"; 270 ["to break the line . . . is not a vice but a virtue, and one of the principal paths by which to achieve the elevation and the beauty of the style, as in the Latin heroic line, where to break the line is greatness in the mode of speech"]), or when he calls for Spanish poetry to be instilled "not only with flesh and blood, but with sinews" ("no sólo . . . carne y sangre, pero niervos"; 560), he reveals his greater purpose: an invigoration that was also a re-masculinization of the Spanish language.

In the *Annotations* in particular, this re-masculinization is represented as a recovery from sprezzatura. The target in the early pages of the text is clearly Boscán, in his aspect as the author of a movement to modernize and nationalize Castilian poetry by tailoring it to the discourses and practices of docile courtiers on the order of Castiglione. As we saw in Chapter 1, Boscán's remarks on poetics linked style to politics, directing writers and readers away from close rhyme and meter and toward Italian hendecasyllables in a language that only loosely disguised the additional distinction he was drawing between *caballero*-style warriors and the peaceable, urbane courtiers who were his ideal modern Spanish subjects: happily married neighbors, improving friends. Herrera was similarly inclined against rhyme and meter, and he agreed with Boscán that regular verse privileged music over reason, thereby producing an inferior poetry. However, he was repelled by the common and vulgar nature of poetry composed in the mode of sprezzatura.

---

nervus is also an important word for Horace. The arguments she cites in the essay—from Erasmus, Montaigne, Eloyt, among others—will strike a familiar note with readers of Herrera, whose *Annotations* bear numerous traces of the discourse of "virile style" (ibid., 203–4).

In the following passage, Herrera directly engages Boscán's discussion of consonance and issues a firm reproof:

> que no decienda a tanta facilidad que pierda los numeros y la dignidad conveniente. Y en este pecado caen muchos, que piensan acabar una grande hazaña cuando escriben de la manera que hablan, como si no fuese diferente el descuido y llaneza, que demanda el sermón común, de la observación que pide el artificio y cuidado de quien escribe. No reprehendo la facilidad, sino la afectación de ella, porque singular virtud es decir libre y claramente sin cansar el ánimo del que oye . . . y no se puede dejar de conceder que regala mucho al sentido ver que ningunos vínculos y ligaduras de consonancias impiden el pensamiento para no descubrirse con delgadeza y facilidad. Más, ¿quién no condenará el poco espíritu y vigor, la humildad y bajeza que se adquiere con el conseguimiento della? ¿y quién no estima por molestia o disgusto oír palabras desnudas de grandeza y autoridad cuando importa representarla? (267–68)

> [(a poem) should not descend into such simplicity that it loses its measure and the appropriate dignity. And many fall into this fault, thinking that they have achieved a great deed when they write in the manner in which they speak, as if the ease and simplicity demanded by the common sermon were no different from the circumspection and care demanded of those who write with artifice. I do not reprove simplicity, but rather the affectation of it, because it is a singular virtue to speak freely and clearly, without tiring the spirit of he who hears . . . and one cannot fail to concede that it is pleasing to the sense to find that no chains and bindings of consonance impede thought from revealing itself with subtlety and ease. But who will not condemn the lack of spirit and vigor, the humility and lowness that is acquired in achieving this? And who does not esteem it an annoyance or displeasure to hear words denuded of their grandeur and their authority when it is important to represent that quality?]

Boscán's Italianate reform, according to Herrera, reflected a fundamental misunderstanding of Spanish masculinity. In an epoch in which Hapsburg power had not only been consolidated, but determined to be divinely willed, the tender and graceful mode of dissembling promoted by Castiglione and Boscán represented an effeminate affectation (*afectación*) that was now revealed to be entirely foreign to the Spanish soul.[27] In Herrera's view, true Spanish spirit should be recognized for its vigor, its grandeur, and its authority, which would inform the contemporary courtier's necessary circumspection. Herrera's ideals thus resembled the *varon máximo* celebrated some years later by Gracián, the prudent and circumspect figure formed "prudente, Séneca; sagaz, Esopo; belicoso, Homero; Aristótiles, filósofo; Tácito, político; y cortesano, el Conde" ("in prudence, by Seneca; wisdom, Aesop; as a warrior, Homer; Aristotle, philosopher; Tacitus, a politician; and as a courtier, Castiglione").[28] To represent this authentic and modern nobleman, a new "new art" was required, one that represented Spanish men in their essential Spanish virility. The balance of this chapter will be devoted to considering the two principal subgenres Herrera worked with in his experiments with heroic lyric: the ode and Petrarchism.

The Ode: Variety and Grandeur

A relatively early ode, the "Canción en alabanza de la divina majestad, por la victoria del Señor don Juan," which Herrera appended to his historical account of the Battle of Cyprus (*Relación de la guerra de Cipre*, 1572), is representative of his attempts to frame grave subject matter in a worthy style that was also accommodated to Counter-Reformation doctrine.[29]

---

27. Later in the text Herrera provides an ambiguous defense of Boscán: "Boscán, aunque imitó la llaneza de estilo y las mismas sentencias de Ausias y se atrevió traer las joyas de Petrarca en su no bien compuesto vestido, merece mucha más onra que la que le da la censura y el rigor de jueces severos; porque si puede tener desculpa ser estranjero de la lengua en que publicó sus intentos y no exercitado en aquellas disciplinas que le podían abrir el camino para la dificultad y aspereza" (279) ("Boscán, although he imitated the plain style and the very sentences of Ausias and dared to bring the jewels of Petrarch into his own ill-composed garments, deserves much more honor than that which the censure and the rigor of severe judges gives him, because he can indeed be excused for being a stranger to the language in which he published his efforts"). We can interpret Herrera's remark as waspishness or as a sign of his commitment to truthful rigor. In either case, a historical irony came to bear on the remark when the *Annotations* came under attack by Juan Fernández de Velasco ("el Prete Jacopín"), who, speaking for the *catedráticos* of Salamanca, challenged the Sevillian Herrera's arrogance in commenting on and criticizing the poetry of the Toledan Garcilaso (Seville was technically part of Castile, but north-south tensions ran high in the sixteenth century). On the "controversy" generated by the *Annotations*, see Montero, *La controversia*. On Herrera and Boscán, see Navarrete, *Orphans of Petrarch*, especially 162–65.

28. Bernat Vistarini and Madroñal, eds., *El Héroe* (Madrid: Clásicos Castália, 2003).

29. On the *Relación*, see Randel, *The Historical Prose*.

The poem opens with an extended and solemn call to praise God in his aspect of "Dios de las batallas." The first ten lines demonstrate Herrera's principal strategies for composing heroic ode:

> Cantemos al Señor, que en la llanura
> venció del mar al enemigo fiero.
> Tú, Dios de las batallas, tu eres diestra,
> salud y gloria nuestra.
> Tú rompiste las fuerzas, y la dura
> frente de Faraón, feroz guerrero.
> Sus escogidos príncipes cubrieron
> los abissos del mar, y decendieron
> cual piedra en el profundo, y tu ira luego
> los tragó, como arista seca el fuego.
>
> (1–10)

[Let us sing to the Lord, who across the wide reaches of the sea / defeated the fierce enemy. / You, God of battle, you are the skill, / the safety, and the glory of us all. / You broke the strength, and the harsh / brow of Faraón, the fierce warrior. / His select princes covered / the deep seas, and they descended / like stones into the deep, and then your ire / swallowed them, as fire does dry tinder.]

This poem may at first seem to be a variation on epic or ballad; however, the style is more stately than that of a ballad, while Herrera replaces the muse-inspired song of arms and a man with a virtuous community who gather to praise a virile and warlike God. The opening lines thereby imbue the ode with the plenitude and the grandeur that Herrera argued for in the *Annotations,* but they also establish the poem as unfolding in a subordinate register, and this circumspection with respect to divine and earthly rank licenses Herrera's subsequent use of epic conventions. For example, lines 7 through 10 contain an epic simile. The Turkish princes are scattered over the water and sink like stones into a deep that swallows them in the same manner that fire consumes straw. The comparison is saved from catachresis by Herrera's brevity, which turns a contradiction into an agindeza. Complex, allusive and nested as it is, the image disappears as quickly as the straw and the Turks. Herrera's descriptions of the heroic actions of Juan of Austria bring the poem similarly close to epic:

> Por la gloria debida de tu nombre,
> por la venganza de tu muerta gente,
> y de los presos por aquel gemido,
> vuelve el braço tendido
> contra aquél que aborrece ya ser hombre;
> y las honras que a ti se dan consiente;
> y tres y cuatro veces su castigo
> dobla, con fortaleza, al enemigo,
> y la injuria a tu nombre cometida
> sea el duro cuchillo de su vida.
>
> (70–79)

[For the glory that is due to Your name, / for the vengeance of Your slain men, / and for the imprisoned, for their groans, / he turns his strong arm / against that one who is abhorrent to the state of man; / and bestows the honors that are due to you; / and three and four times redoubles / the force of his punishment, of the enemy, / and the injury committed to your name / will serve as the harsh blade to his life.]

The anaphora that builds the momentum of the coming blows in lines 70–71 and 72, and in lines 75, 76, and 78 of this passage, and the impact of the enjambments between lines 73 and 74—and especially between lines 76 and 77, as the prince extends his valiant arm and deals out his just punishment to his foes—contribute to building the vivid scene. However, Herrera continues to work a careful balance between the representation of heroism and the subordination of human greatness. The prince's actions are represented in lines addressed to God, as the prince fights in God's service. Furthermore, the lines demonstrate Herrera's prudence as a reader of divine signs. As Juan of Austria's sword becomes forged out of the Turkish slights to God in lines 78 and 79, the heroic *braço tendido* is revealed as having been animated by divine force; and the voice that sings the song thereby remains *recatada,* or observant of its place, "second in majesty."[30]

---

30. This subordination is enhanced by the variable rhyme and the length of the verses. It can also be argued that their irregularity endows them with subjectivity: the poem varies according to the voice, which speaks in an irregular pattern of eleven- and seven-syllable lines. The effect is that the ode appears to emerge from inside a human body and not from the totalizing registers of history and epic.

As another representative example of Herrera's experiments with the ode, the first song of the 1582 lyric sequence is a lament for the heroic death of the Portuguese King Sebastian. The vocabulary of the poem is, again, characteristic of Herrera's heroic style, and his use of enjambment and variation in the rhythm of the lines works to underscore the solemnity and power of the grieving voice:

Song 1 [1582]

Voz de dolor y canto de gemido,
y espíritu de miedo envuelto en ira
hagan principio acerbo a la memoria
de aquél día fatal, aborrecido,
que Lusitania mísera suspira,
desnuda de valor, falta de gloria;
y la llorosa historia
asombre con horror funesto y triste,
dend'el áfrico Atlante y seno ardiente
hasta do el mar d'otro color se viste
y do el límite rojo de Oriente,
y todas sus vencidas gentes fieras,
ven tremolar de Cristo las banderas.

(1–13)

[A pained voice and a groaning song, / and a shuddering spirit wrapped in ire / give the bitter opening to the memory / of that fatal day, hateful, / for which miserable Lusitania sighs, / denuded of valor, devoid of glory; / and let the grievous story / shock with its horror, funereal and sad, / that between the Atlantic and the burning breast of Africa, / to where the sea clothes itself in a different color / and where the red limits of the east, / and all her fierce and conquered peoples, / see the banners of Christ shudder.]

The rhythm and rhyme of the abbreviated line 7 ("y la llorosa historia") cause it to echo the final dactyl and iamb of line 6 ("falta de gloria"). This formal variation inscribes a stately pause in the lament and illustrates Herrera's assertion that the *eficacia* of the ode will arise from lines that are considered, polished, and measured ("pulida . . . eficaz y numerosa").

Finally, one last poem merits mention as an example of Herrera's heroic song. Sonnet 54, collected among Herrera's sueltos, is unusual among the sonnets we have examined in this book.[31] The poem makes relatively little use of elements such as the volta and is actually a mini-ode, fitting an elevated vocabulary into fourteen rhythmic lines:

Sonnet 54

Alégrate Danubio impetuoso
de quien huyó el tirano de Oriente;
tú, Alfeo sacro y Ebro caudaloso,
sujetos a ese bárbaro y vil gente;
que la preza con lazo riguroso
que enfrena el curso a vuestra gran corriente,
Betis quebrantará victorioso
y vuestro imperio juntará a Ocidente.
Veréis al fiero y áspero tirano
dejar del largo Eufrates esta parte,
por fuerza y sangre y hierro y fuego y muerte.
Y cerradas las puertas del dios Iano,
sossegará, domesticado, Marte,
con vuestra diestra y gloriosa suerte.

[Rejoice, impetuous Danube / for the tyrant of the Orient has fled; / And you, sacred Alfeo and abundant Ebro, / subject to that barbarous and vile people; / for the enslavement that with its rigorous ties / binds the course of your great current, / has been broken by victorious Betis / and your empire has been joined to the Occident. / You will see the fierce and harsh tyrant / leave behind the great Euphrates, / perforce, and with blood, and iron, and fire and death. / And once the portals of the god Janus are closed, / Mars, domesticated, will be soothed, / by your fitting and glorious fortune.]

This poem represents a variety of sonnet that has not to this point made an appearance in this book; it is a sonnet in the sense of the "little song" that fits

---

31. Cuevas collects this sonnet, which he dates to 1578, among Herrera's loose Italianate lyric. The poem did not form part of the 1582 edition.

Herrera's description in the *Annotations:* "el soneto . . . tanto es más difícil, por estar encerrado en un perpetuo y pequeño espacio . . . puede fácilmente juzgar con la experiencia quien ha compuesto sonetos, y recogido en una sujeta y sutil materia con gran dificultad, ha esquivado la oscuridad y dureza del estilo" (268) ("the sonnet . . . is more difficult, for being enclosed in a perpetual and small space . . . this can be easily judged from experience by the person who has written sonnets, and, having gathered a tamed and subtle material with great difficulty, has vexed it with obscurity and roughness of style"). In fact, unlike many writers studied in this book, Herrera was not engaged by the conceit of sonnetization.[32] His sonnets tend to fit into the category of abbreviated odes or Petrarchan fragments. However, while Herrera made little use of the disciplining function of the volta, for example, or of puns and ambivalent representations of the lyric "I," many of his sonnets show evidence of a similarly modern and perhaps more radical poetic experiment, one that again reveals the form's adaptability to early modern views. In his Petrarchan sonnets, in particular, Herrera deployed formulas

---

32. There are some exceptions. Sonnet 64 (1582) is a celebration of just Christian empire that was probably composed around the time that Philip II inherited the crown of Portugal: "Ya que el sujeto reino lusitano / inclina al yugo la cerviz paciente, / y todo el grande esfuerzo de Ocidente / tenéis, sacro señor, en vuestra mano, volved contra el suelo órrido africano / el firme pecho y vuestra osada gente; / que su poder, su corazón valiente, / que tanto fue, será ante el vuestro en vano. / Cristo os da la pujanza de este imperio / para que la fe nuestra se adelante / por donde su santa nombre es ofendido. /¿Quién contra vos, quién contra el reino esperio / bastará alzar la frente, que al instante / no se derribe a vuestros pies rendido?" ("Now that the subject Lusitanian realm / inclines its patient neck to the yoke, / and all the great strength of the West, / Sacred Sir, is held in your hand, / once again turn your stalwart breast and your brave people against the horrid African soil; / for its power, its valiant heart, / which was once so great, will strive in vain before your own. / Christ propels you into this empire / so that this our faith may proceed forward / to those places where His sainted name is offended. / Who against you, who against the western realm / will be sufficient to raise his brow, who in that instant / will not fall vanquished at your feet?") Spanish propagandists treated the Spanish inheritance of the Portuguese throne as providential. According to contemporary writers, God had prevented King Sebastian from fathering children and had sent him to his glorious death (Sebastian died in a daring, if imprudent, crusade) so that Portugal could be "restored" to Spain (as Dian Fox discusses, he suffered from numerous ailments and expressed a strong dislike of women; she mounts a convincing argument for the king's homosexuality; see Fox, "'Frente a Frente'"). Sonnet 64 presents Portugal's patient acquiescence to providence as the final sign that the time has come to take up the perennial Spanish struggle to conquer North Africa (lines 1–8). Although the Africans have resisted in the past (lines 7–8), they will not do so in the coming battle because Christ animates the Spanish forward charge (lines 9–14). The poem corresponds formally to sonnetization, since Herrera deploys the rules of the sonnet form to underscore a Counter-Reformation discourse of Christian might. Christ enters the poem at the crucial point of the volta, the space in which the poetic utterance "turns" on itself, after the completion of the quatrains and before the opening of the new rhyme scheme in the tercets. From this position, God's son can be said to bend the poem to His will. The speaker's prediction of success in Africa, voiced in the second quatrain, becomes transformed retroactively from courtly flattery to divine

abstracted from the *Canzoniere* in the manner of a verbal technology that would represent Spanish virility in its radiant essence. My use of the word *technology* here is deliberate. Herrera's views on Petrarchism anticipated the Heideggerian formulation of modern poetic revealing as techne that was opposed to poiesis, "not . . . a bringing-forth in the sense of *poiesis* . . . a challenging . . . which puts to nature the unreasonable demand that it supply energy that can be extracted and stored" (15).[33] The final section of this chapter is devoted to a discussion of Herrera's Petrarchan technology of heroic lyric.[34]

Irradiation

Like other scholarly minded poetic reformers, Herrera admonished lax contemporaries for their fundamental misunderstanding of the *Canzoniere*. Unlike many of his peers, however, Herrera directed equal attention to imitatio and to the mechanisms of Neo-Platonic sublimation that undergirded the work. Most discussions of Herrera overlook the latter; however, the

---

prophecy, since after line 9 Spanish victory is no longer a matter of speculation but rather a divine truth awaiting revelation. In addition to doctrine, the poem inscribes late sixteenth-century political hierarchies as well. The Portuguese kingdom is peaceably subjected to the yoke of Spanish monarchy (lines 1 and 2), and the poem's African kingdoms will also bow their heads to Spanish power (lines 13 and 14). Ultimately, however, Sonnet 64 represents a Counter-Reformation political vision. The fates of Philip and of Spain are subject to the power of Christ, the prime mover of Spanish *imperium* who wields force over the poem itself.

33. I have discussed Herrera's proto-Heideggerian ideas before. See Middlebrook, "Fernando de Herrera Invented the Internet."

34. One final, paradigmatic example of Herrera's ideals for his heroic lyric song is Elegy 3, "No bañes en el mar sagrado y cano" ("Do not bathe in that sacred, gray sea"), which has been discussed by López Bueno, among other critics (*La poética cultista*, 49–50). The poem appears in the 1582 Petrarchan sequence and is unusual in that it represents a rare moment in which the poetic speaker enjoys erotic fulfillment: "Aquí donde el grande Betis ve presente / l'armada vencedora qu'el Egeo / manchó con sangre de la Turca gente, / quiero decir la gloria en que me veo / . . . / Lo demás qu'entre nos passó, no es dino, / noche, d'oír el austro pressuroso / . . . / Mete en el ancho piélago espumoso / tus negras trenzas, y húmido semblante, / que'en tanto que tú yaces en reposo, / podrá Amor darme gloria semejante." (7–10; 67–73) ("It is here, where the great Betis beholds / the conquering armada that stained / the Aegean with the blood of the Turkish people, / that I wish to speak of the glory in which I find myself / . . . / What happened between us is not worthy, / oh night, to be overheard by the rushing south wind / . . . / Hide away your dark locks and your watery face, / in the broad and foamy depths, / for while you take your repose / love grants me a similar glory"). The commemoration of the historical event of the launch of the Spanish ships toward their victory at Lepanto licenses Herrera's speaker's reflection on his own conquest of his beloved. This theme of amorous license establishes the poem as an elegy, according to Herrera's classicist criteria.

poetics of Petrarchan sublimation are the key to understanding Herrera's aesthetics.[35] In the *Annotations,* Herrera argues that Petrarch invented a specific verbal operation that set the *Canzoniere* apart from other kinds of texts and established it as an important model for the ennobling and the reinvigoration of Spanish poetry:

> Petrarca . . . dejó atrás con grande intervalo en nobleza de pensamientos a todos los poetas que trataron de cosas de amor, sin recibir comparación en esto de los mejores antiguos . . . Dessean algunos más cosas en los escritos de Petrarca, no considerando que el poeta élego no tiene necesidad de mucha más erudición; y le imponen culpa de vestir y aderezar con palabras las sentencias comunes, no consistiendo su excelencia en esquivar los conceptos vulgares. ¿Y cuál puede ser mayor alabanza de Petrarca que hacer con el género de decir suyo aventajadas y maravillosas las cosas comunes? (271–72)

> [Petrarch . . . in the nobility of his thoughts outstripped by a great distance all poets who treated the theme of love, in this, not even the best of the ancients compared with him. . . . Some desire more things from the writings of Petrarch, not considering that the elect poet has no need for more erudition; and they fault him for clothing and appointing common sayings by means of his words, for his excellence does not consist in disguising vulgar ideas. But what can be greater praise of Petrarch than to make common things privileged and marvelous by means of his mode of speech?]

Herrera perceived Petrarch as having expanded the power of secular vernacular letters, endowing language with a transformational force. Petrarch's fourteenth-century skills in *elucutio* and *dispositio* enabled him to defeat the categories that bound the material plane and to elevate base things to the order of the privileged and the marvelous. In the poetic register, these base elements were love lyrics; in the human one, they were the appetites:

---

35. In pages I have already cited in this chapter, critics such as Cuevas, Lara Garrido, Navarrete, and López Bueno all make reference in passing to Herrera's interest in sublimation. As is evident from my discussion, López Bueno's discussions of irradiation are particularly relevant to the argument I am forwarding here. Lacking up to this point has been an explanation of how Herrera's Petrarchism fits into his larger project of transforming action into essence, thereby recuperating heroic poetry for modern Spain. This is the gap I am proposing to fill.

Escribió para mostrar la fuerza del deseo sensual, que combatía con la razón, y así dijó:
> la voglia et la ragion combattuto ánno
> sette et sette anni, et vincerá il migliore.

Y en otra parte rompe con este afecto:
> Pigmalión quanto lodarti dei
> de l'imagine tua, se mille volte
> n'havesti quel, ch'io solo una vorrei.

Pero pinta esto tan poéticamente y tan apartado y lleno de honestidad en las voces y el modo que es maravilloso su artificio. Y todo él se emplea y ocupa en el gozo de los ojos más que de otro sentido, y en el de los oídos y entendimiento, y en consideración de la belleza de su Laura y de la virtud de su ánimo. (272)

[He wrote to show the power of sensual desire, which he combated by means of reason, and thus he said, "Desire and reason have battled for seven and seven years, and the better one will win out." And in another place he breaks with this affect: "Pygmalion, how glad you should be of your statue, because you received a thousand times what I yearn to have just once." But he paints this so poetically, and with such detachment, and with a voice and a manner so full of honesty that his artifice is marvelous. And he is occupied most of all with the pleasure of the eyes more than any other sense, and with that of the ears and of the understanding, and with the consideration of the beauty of his Laura, and of the virtue of her soul.][36]

Informed by the same preoccupations that motivate passages we have examined earlier in this chapter—in the entry on *valiente,* for example, and the song in praise of true virtue (Song 2 [1582])—these passages provide the key to fitting Herrera's Petrarchism into the wider context of his ambitions for modern letters. Each turns on the challenge of redefining masculine nobility for an era in which men are subject to political and metaphysical regimes that appropriate their agency. But whereas the *valiente* passage and the song are proscriptive and didactic, and rely on accompanying exempla and visual figures to *persuade* readers that the modern condition is an exalted one, Herrera's discussion of Petrarch frames

---

36. The translations of Petrarch's Poem 101 and Poem 78 embedded in this quotation are from Durling (*Petrarch's Lyric Poems*, 1976).

the *Canzoniere* as a sophisticated verbal device by which to *transform* men's appetites for action into glorious essence. Furthermore, the mechanisms by which the sequence transformed the base into the elevated and appetite into understanding could be abstracted from the original text and adapted to modern conditions, for "no todos los pensamientos y consideraciones de amor y de las demás cosas que toca la poesía cayeron en la mente del Petrarca y del Bembo y de los antiguos" ("not all the thoughts and the considerations of love and of the other things that poetry touches upon came to mind for Petrarch and Bembo and the ancients"); and "no supieron inventar nuestros precessores todos los modos y observaciones de la habla" (274) ("our predecessors did not know all the modes and the aspects of language"). Moreover, to employ Petrarchan sublimation significantly enhanced a writer's efficaciousness in revealing (by which Herrera also meant representing) "many things": "por esta vía se abre lugar para descubrir muchas cosas" (273) ("by this path the way is opened to reveal many things"). Therefore, while Petrarchan poetics furnished the fourteenth-century writer with a means to transform erotic desire into marvelous artifice, Herrera, writing in his own day, his language fortified by modern discoveries in the rhetorical arts, selected a beloved who would serve as a source of *force* as well as transformation. "Luz," or "light," provided Petrarchism with the fuel to achieve effects of heroic lyric. The function of light and its energy for the sequence is established in the opening sonnet of the 1582 *Algunas obras de Fernando de Herrera*:

Sonnet 1

Osé y temí, más pudo la osadía
tanto que desprecié el temor cobarde;
subí a do el fuego más me enciende y arde
cuanto más la esperanza se desvía.
Gasté en error la edad flórida mía;
ahora veo el daño, pero tarde:
que ya mal puede ser que el seso guarde
a quien se entrega ciego a su porfía.
Tal vez pruevo (mas, ¿qué me vale?) alzarme
del grave peso que mi cuello oprime,
aunque falta a la poca fuerza el hecho.
Sigo al fin mi furor, porque mudarme

no es honra ya, ni justo que se estime
tan mal de quien tan bien rindió su pecho.

[I dared and I feared, but my daring so strong / that I disdained cowardly fear; / the more I climb to where the flame lights and burns, / the more my hope is led astray. / I wasted the flower of my youth in error; / now I see the danger, but too late: / for the mind can offer little protection / to a man who delivers himself blindly over to his daring. / Perhaps I will break loose (but what good does it do me?) / of that grave weight that oppresses my neck, / although I lack even that little force to achieve the deed. / I follow my madness along, in the end, because to change / would no longer bring honor, nor would it be just that / one who rendered his breast to one so exalted be held in such low esteem.]

The challenges posed to interpreting the 1582 volume have puzzled Herrera's readers over time. Sonnet 1 provides a promising opening to a late sixteenth-century Petrarchan sequence: the poem imitates the principal conventions of an introductory poem (then and now, wasted youth, error), and it is composed in a rhythm and a vocabulary that demonstrate Herrera's facility with the precepts of humanist poetic reform. Taken as a whole, however, the collection of poems diverges from the model. Herrera's lyric speaker does not achieve salvation or transcendence by the final poem; indeed, there is no real conclusion to the narrative. The text simply leaves off with a cry of frustration.[37] Finally, the collection lacks balance between the individual fragments, many of which are strikingly beautiful, intensely visual works, and the whole, which fails to cohere. Herrera himself is reported to have rejected the 1582 volume as juvenilia further along in his career.

While I do not propose to provide a comprehensive account of the relationship of the 1582 sequence to the *Canzoniere,* certain aspects of the collection make more sense when we follow cues that are presented in Sonnet 1, first about the poem's relationship to Herrera's wider preoccupations with the virility of the Spanish subject, and, second, about the relationship

---

37. López Bueno provides an overview of the criticism of the sequence, as well as a very useful account of the struggle between passion and reason in the work (*La poética cultista,* 35–60). See also Navarrete, *Orphans of Petrarch,* 168–99, on the sequence, and Cuevas on the editions of Herrera's work (Herrera, *Poesía,* 87–99).

of action and appearance, and the value that Herrera attached to each. The speaker represents himself as having suffered through a heroic struggle between daring and fear. "Osé y temí" reproduces the terms for noble self-mastery that appear in the entry on *valiente,* in the *Annotations.* Moreover, Sonnet 1 represents the same ambivalent outcome of the internal struggle that is found both in the *valiente* entry and the wedding song. Daring is the stronger force in the sonnet (line 1), and the speaker thus corresponds to Herrera's modern masculine ideal of the noble soul that struggles against itself but emerges triumphant. While the struggle is heroic, however, it is also self-defeating. At the end of the poem, the speaker claims that he does not have "even that little force" (*la poca fuerza,* line 11) that will enable him to free himself from his oppression. Moreover, were he to do so, the struggle would not bring him honor (line 13).

Sonnet 1 therefore presents us once again with an image of noble subjection. The speaker's daring is all display: "osé y temí" makes for a vigorous opening in comparison to other versions of the line we have seen before, such as "Entre osar y temer," by Cetina.[38] His power is limited to the domain of representation; however, having noted that, we see that Sonnet 1 also goes on to take the innovative turn as Herrera leads the poem and the sequence into his own terrain in line 3, "subí a do el fuego más me enciende y arde." The line introduces the element that inspires the speaker's daring, a radiant light that implies the sun, and that will take shape across the sequence as the beloved Luz. The line suggests the myth of Phaeton, a common topos in baroque and mannerist poetry. The vainglorious son of Helios serves as an example or *escarmiento* against overreaching. But while Sonnet 1 clearly alludes to Phaeton, the passages from Herrera's writings that we have been examining in these pages suggest an alternate interpretation, namely, that the crucible of Petrarchan desire transforms the mere brash daring available to any "osado español" into the true nobility that can be found within the elect few. Luz illuminates this nobility, fueling it into presence in Sonnet 1. In subsequent poems she will continue to transform action into display by serving as the source of illumination for the color-saturated and richly embellished fragments that work by means of *enargeia.* At the opening of this chapter, I referred to critical discussions of Herrera's use of visual figures and provided an initial definition of *enargeia* as the art of placing an object before the eyes. An additional definition supplied by Joseph Campana, "forceful visuality," helps explain Herrera's investment in

---

38. See Chapter 3.

the beautiful Petrarchan fragment as sublimated heroic force.[39] The poems that celebrate light and the visual register, in particular, are often entirely detached from any kind of moral or autobiographical narrative and function in and of themselves as pure *enargeia,* forceful presence that compensates for the "lost object" that is masculine Spanish agency in the modern age. They thus fulfill the demand for heroic lyric. Subsequent poems in the 1582 sequence and in the loose lyrics not included in the volume will elaborate on the ennobling sublimation of forceful action into aesthetic effects. For example, read apart from Herrera's theories of lyric, the quatrains of Sonnet 45 (1582) appear to be meaningless, if lovely, ornament:

> Clara, suave luz, alegre y bella,
> que los safiros y color del cielo
> teñis de la esmeralda con el velo
> que respandece en una y otra estrella;
> divino resplandor, pura centella,
> por quien, libre mi alma, en alto vuelo
> a las alas rojas bate y huye el suelo,
> ardiendo vuestro dulce fuego en ella

(1–8)

[Clear, soft light, happy and beautiful, / you who tinge the sapphires and the color of the sky / with emerald by the veil / that shines out from one and another star; / divine refulgence, purest spark / toward whom my soul, freed, in soaring flight / beats its red wings and flees the ground, / your sweet fire burning within it]

Considered within the context of Herrera's aims to forge a persuasive heroic lyric, however—poetry that was simultaneously "second in majesty" and resplendent and forceful in revealing the virile nobility of the Spanish soul—Sonnet 45 (1582), or Sonnet 33 (1582), which begins with "Ardientes hebras, do se ilustra el oro / de celestial ambrosia rociado" (1–2) ("Shining strands, where gold, / bedewed with celestial ambrosia shines forth") and goes on to evoke "Purpúreas rosas, perlas de Oriente, / marfil terso, y angélica armonía" (9–10) ("Purpled roses, pearls of the orient, / smooth marble,

---

39. Campana ("On Not Defending Poetry") draws a distinction between *enargeia* as "forceful visuality" and *energeia,* a figure that stirs the affective experience of presence.

angelic harmonies"), or Sonnet 10, "Rojo sol, que con hacha luminosa / coloras el purpúreo y alto cielo" (1–2) ("Red sun, who with your shining brush / colors the exalted purple sky"),[40] assume significance as statements of glorious presence are informed by the possible emptiness that subtends their fabric. Ultimately, Herrera's Petrarchan strategies may best be set off in the somewhat overlooked Sonnet 59 (1619).[41]

Sonnet 59

Rayo de guerra, grande honor de Marte,
fatal ruina al bárbaro africano,
que, en la temida España, de el Romano
Imperio levantaste el estandarte:
Si la voz de la Fama, en esa parte
do estás, puede llegar al reino vano,
teme, con el vencido italiano,
d'el osado español la fuerza y arte.
Otro mayor que tú, en el yugo indino
lo puso, y un gran Leiva la vitoria
d'Italia conquirió en sangrienta guerra.
Y al fin, un nuevo César, qu'al latino
en clemencia y valor ganó la gloria,
y añadió mar al mar, tierra a la tierra.

[Lighting bolt of war, great honor of Mars, / fatal ruin of the barbarous African, / you who, within fearsome Spain, raised the standard / of the Roman Empire: / If the voice of Fame can reach to that place where you are, / that vain kingdom, / be fearful, along with the defeated Italian, / of the force and the art of the daring Spaniard. / Another greater than you placed him under the ignoble yoke / and the great Leiva conquered Italy in victory, /

---

40. The use of aesthetic language in this poem has been commented on by Smith (*Writing in the Margin*, 58–59).

41. Poems that appear in the 1619 *Versos de Fernando de Herrera* have tended to be treated with caution by critics. The volume's editor, Herrera's friend Francisco de Pacheco, referred to having repaired and completed poems that had been damaged in a shipwreck, and scholars have therefore hesitated to treat poems that appear only in that volume as authentically Herrera's own (see Cuevas, 87-99). The question of attribution is not critical to my argument here. If Pacheco or another member of Herrera's circle amended Sonnet 59, they were certainly working from a deep understanding of their deceased friend's poetics and his ambitions for *enargeia*.

in bloody war. / And in the end, a new Caesar gained / the glory of the Latin one in clemency and in valor, / and joined sea to sea, shore to shore.]

Opening with an invocation of the great Roman general Scipio, a worthy whose conquest of Spain pales in comparison with the victories secured by the Spanish captains Fernando González de Córdoba (the "Great Captain") and Antonio de Leiva (the Marquis of Vasto), and whose domains cannot equal the global empire secured by Charles V, the modern Caesar, Sonnet 59 (1619) is informed by the Spanish triumphalist and messianic view of history. But in the aesthetic register, the poem also represents the transformation of virile masculine identity in the context of that history. This is most evident in the first line of the poem, where the brilliant general's battlefield force is represented *as* brilliance, with the striking visual figure of the lightning bolt, or "rayo de guerra." The line is a textbook example of *enargeia*. The figure transforms action into essence, as the physical power of the general's fighting arm is transformed into a flash of light. Moreover, the visual effect is supported by an acoustic one: the charge is reinforced by stress on the first syllable of the word. Since *rayo* is also the first word of the poem, the sonnet is propelled into presence and motion.

But the deftly worked aesthetics in this poem speak directly to the paradoxical nature of Spanish nobility and glory in the late sixteenth century, since *enargeia* is used here to *displace* the famed general. Furthermore, this displacement is enacted by a modern constellation of Spanish ideological and historical circumstances. Scipio's individual powers are outstripped by the Spanish Caesar, whose ascendance to the throne, as we have seen throughout this chapter, marked a new epoch for Spain. Charles V was the monarch and the emperor who had been blessed to carry out God's final will on earth, and his reign inaugurated a new historical and cosmological epoch. However, while the new Caesar was supported by providence, in this poem he is also supported by the "osado español." When in line 8 this figure precedes the named captains, he reflects a transformation in the way in which Spain now appeared to itself, both as a society and as a force on the globe. No longer identified with the heroic individual valor of the medieval era, Spain was privileged collectively, as a nation.

Sonnet 59 employs Petrarchan technologies of illumination and poetics to both display and mask the conflicting social and ideological forces that trouble the poetic representation of greatness and military glory in Herrera's epoch. In this way, the poem fulfills the potential that he observed in the

Canzoniere as a text with specific utility in the modern age. And yet, in the end, were the circumstances of Spanish modernity suitable for representation in poetry? Is the *rayo de guerra* an exaltation or a statement of defeat, an evacuation? In recent years, critics have begun to look past the apparently empty excesses of mannerist aesthetic elaboration to argue that in certain ideological climates, hollow ornament has a point. In fact, it *is* the point in periods of radical cultural change in which old forms are evacuated of meaning and new forms are rising up to take their place. Setting the image of the *rayo de guerra* against that constant Spanish backdrop, the Castilian hero, the wielder of the sovereign *diestro braço*, the figure against which Juan Boscán wrote so conscientiously in his 1541 "Letter" and sequence, Sonnet 59 comes into focus as no mere exercise in ornamentation and hyperbole. Rather, it becomes an ambivalent image that emblematizes what has been variously referred to as the "crisis of disorientation of the Counter-Reformation" and the "culture of the baroque."[42]

Herrera's efforts in the field of letters consistently reflect his attempts to secure Spanish identity in the face of the early modern culture shock. Were his experiments with heroic lyric a success? In his view, they were not. Herrera appears to have been content with some of his odes; however, he rejected his Petrarchan poetry as juvenilia and requested that it be destroyed. He turned to the longer and weightier projects enumerated by Pacheco—a general history of Spain, a saintly "Life" of Thomas More (1590), a long poem on Proserpine.[43]

Members of Herrera's circle, however, and patrons such as the Count and Countess of Gelves held the lyric in higher esteem.[44] If Herrera's noble patrons liked the work but Herrera himself did not, the discrepancy suggests that Petrarchan poetry did not, in the end, manage to transcend its limitations as a base subgenre. The displacement of the noble Spanish hero into

---

42. "La crisis y la desorientación de la edad contrarreformista, entre la abstracción neoplatónica del ejemplarismo heroico y la preocupación historicista de las criaturas del arte" ("crisis of disorientation of the Counter-Reformation, between the neoplatonic abstraction of the heroic exemplar and the historicizing preoccupation of those creatures dedicated to art"); Macrí, *Fernando de Herrera*, 29. For "culture of the baroque," see Maravall, *Culture of the Baroque*.

43. The *Tomás Moro* was published. The other two works, if completed, have not been located.

44. The simple fact of the 1619 edition suggests that at least one friend, Francisco de Pacheco, and perhaps others, recognized Herrera's aims with Petrarchan poetry and with the new lyric, more widely. Pacheco, who edited and introduced the volume, reported that he had saved it from a shipwreck and had restored many of the pages that had been damaged in the event (*Poesía original*, 87–99). This admission has led scholars to avoid working with the poems contained in the edition,

efficacious and brilliant discourse yielded spectacular results, but they testified to power—to the empire and the elite patrons and rulers who occupied the higher ranks of its political regime—not to the cultural memory. In the struggle between poiesis and politics in which Herrera sought to play a part, politics appeared to have won.

---

since they cannot be attributed with certainty to Herrera himself; but arguably, authorship is less important here than content. Many of the 1619 poems are decidedly mannerist in style. Moreover, several of them are strong statements of imperialist triumphalism. Whether Herrera composed them or not, or whether he composed parts of them or not, the works provide support for the idea that his use of aesthetics was bound up with the question of the changing nature of Spanish virility in his profoundly nationalist and messianic age. The question of whether his view was shared by fellow writers in his intellectual circle or whether it was a view he held on his own is a relatively minor one.

CODA: THE TOMB OF POETRY

WHEN THE LICENSE, THE PRESTIGE, and the energies of poetry are appropriated by the hegemonic institutions of the church and the state, and when they are directed to the political end of glorifying state-sponsored subjects, are they still poetic energies?

The Introduction and chapters of this book have traced a long circle. We opened in the melancholic tenor of the baroque and with Francisco de Aldana's bitter Sonnet 45, in which the heroic Castilian fighting arm is portrayed as having been crushed beneath the discursive and representational armatures of the contemporary age. I then traced the path by which the new lyric movement of which the sonnet formed an important part became aligned with Hapsburg modernity. As Juan Boscán reoriented Spanish poetry from its traditional function of celebrating Castilian heroes in song, he appropriated the authority of poetic discourse to stabilize the identity of a new Spanish nobleman. The Italian-styled mode of courtliness he promoted through his lyrics and his writings on poetics answered to the demands that were being placed on men by the nascent Spanish Hapsburg regime and thus participated in transformations in notions of the self that are commonly associated with the onset of social modernity. But in a manner that is perhaps less immediately visible, the adoption of the new lyric also marked an important threshold for poetic modernity, as the role assigned to poetry within culture changed. To adopt the forms and the stylistic conventions of the new lyric entailed breaking with the idea of singer-poets existing in a continuum across the generations as human channels for the transmission of native tradition. The new lyric reflected and helped to normalize a new social mandate for a poetry whose scope was significantly reduced. The private, urbane poet is not celebrated for his or her capacities to conserve the fundamentals of culture and history; he or she is praised for skill in mastering and channeling poetic language such that it can be accommodated to modern dimensions: the rational and circumspect individual who is bound, circumscribed, and traversed by human-authored regimes of power and knowledge in a desacralized—if not necessarily a secular—world. What makes the sixteenth century of special interest to those of us who think about poetics is the fact that this was the first time that this more modest poetry, the lyric, became associated with privilege and authority.

But did this shift represent, in fact, the end of poetry, in its premodern sense? Discussing the rise of the lyric—the substitution of a poetics of Horace for the poetics of Homer—Susan Stewart has observed that the lyric poet works "under a threat of overdetermination (that the Orphic creator might turn back tragically against himself, inadvertently losing the work through adherence to habit or convention), and under a threat of underdetermination (that the freedom of creation could be rooted only in the particular history of the creator)" (12).[1] More recently, Virginia Jackson has complicated the epic/lyric distinction by taking a more concrete and historicizing perspective on poems in culture. The "lyricization" of poetry, a process that she understands to have culminated in the nineteenth century, produced the strange situation in which we find ourselves at the end of the first decade of the twenty-first, as poetry is simultaneously overvalued as essential to our cultural survival and mourned as irretrievably marginal to the information-centered and resolutely prosaic contemporary world. This dilemma may be more acute in academic circles in the United States than it is among poets and scholars in Europe, and, specifically, in Spain. As Jesús Munárriz pointed out in his anthology *Un siglo de sonetos en español,* the lyric tradition, and most especially the tradition of the sonnet, has thrived continuously in Spain and in the Spanish Americas (10). But Jackson's point is that the hegemony of lyric poetry in the post-Romantic era has confounded our ability as critics to discuss the nature and function of poetic discourse. "Poetry," at present, serves as a sort of shorthand term for a vast spectrum of poems, "songs, riddles, epigrams, sonnets, epitaphs, blazons, leider, elegies, marches, dialogues, conceits, ballads, epistles, hymns, odes,

---

1. In these comments, Stewart (*Poetry and the Fate of the Senses*) is engaging in dialogue with remarks by Grossman in *The Sighted Singer*. In particular, she builds on Grossman's point, mentioned in the Introduction (note 7) of this book, that poetics break on the distinction between Homer and Horace, and that the Horatian model threatens to devolve into "mere" self-legitimation. As I mentioned, Horace himself called attention to the potential trap, and the Homer-Horace distinction becomes a touchstone through critical writings on poetry.

eclogues and monodramas considered lyric in the Western tradition before the early nineteenth century," all of which have been conflated into a single genre:

> When the stipulative functions of particular genres are collapsed into one big idea of poems as lyrics, then the only function poems can perform in our culture is to become individual or communal ideals . . . the more ideally lyric poems and poetry culture have become, the fewer actual poetic genres address readers in specific ways. That ratio is responsible for our twenty-first century sense that poetry is all-important and at the same time already in its afterlife. (183)

This insight holds true for European critics and poets as well as those reading and writing in the United States. Moreover, as we have seen perhaps most clearly in the writings of Garcilaso and Herrera, some sixteenth-century writers were acutely aware of their position on the frontiers of a discursive movement aimed at severing the relationship between poetry and "real life." Jackson fixes her argument to the context of "the single abstraction of the post-Romantic lyric" (183), but in Chapter 4 of this study we observed Herrera struggling to create a heroic lyric that would compensate for the obsolescence of epic and ballad forms rendered obsolete by the religious and courtly ideologies by which Counter-Reformation Spanish culture was organized under Philip II.

The lyrics by Herrera and his close contemporary Aldana studied here ultimately responded to the new order of things in the melancholic key that Fernando Rodríguez de la Flor has diagnosed as the principal note of the Spanish baroque: "energías amargas, discursos de la desesperanza del mundo y también articulaciones de la *atra bilis,* del 'humor negro,' que fueron entonces la marca del intellectual entregado a lo que pronto se le relevaría como *vanas cogitaciones,* y al que amenaza siempre una inminente remisiónde la voz" (*Barroco,* 21) ("Bitter energies, discourses of despair for the world and also articulations of the *atra bilis,* the 'black bile,' which were then the mark of the intellectual absorbed in what would soon be revealed as *vanas cogitaciones,* and which were threatened, always, by an immanent postponement of the voice"). In a more jocular and prosaic vein, Miguel de Cervantes (1547–1616) presented his own view of the complete evacuation of traditional ideals of both heroism and poetry in the era of the Hapsburgs. His satirical *soneto con estrambote,* or "sonnet with a tail," "Al Túmulo del Rey Felipe II En Sevilla," puts paid to the quest for heroic lyric:

Al Túmulo del Rey Felipe II En Sevilla

Voto a Dios que me espanta esta grandeza
y que diera un doblón por describilla!,
porque, a quién no suspende y maravilla
esta máquina insigne, esta braveza?
Por Jesucristo vivo, cada pieza
vale más de un millión, y que es mancilla
que esto no dure un siglo, o gran Sevilla,
Roma triunfante en ánimo y riqueza!
Apostaré que el ánima del muerto,
por gozar este sitio, hoy ha dejado
el cielo, de que goza eternamente.
Esto oyó un valentón y dijo: "Es cierto
lo que dice voacé, seor soldado,
y quien dijere los contrario miente."
Y luego, incontinente,
caló el chapeo, requirió la espada,
miró al soslayo, fuése, y no hubo nada.

[To the Coffin of King Philip II, in Seville: "I swear to God I'm amazed by this grandeur, and I'd give a gold piece to be able to describe it! for who is not overwhelmed and astounded by this spectacular structure, this fierceness? By Jesus, every item is worth a fortune, and it's a shame that it can't last a century, oh great Seville, a Rome triumphant in spirit and in wealth! I'll bet that the soul of the departed, to enjoy this place, today has come down from heaven, where he enjoys eternal glory." A braggart heard this and replied, "It's true what you say, mister soldier, and anybody that says otherwise lies." And then, straightaway, he set his cap, clutched at his sword, looked askance, walked off, and there was nothing.][2]

2. This poem is collected by Rivers in *Muses and Masks* (42–43). I have used his translation, with a minor adjustment to the ending, which Rivers translates as, "and nothing happened."

Obliquely based on a conventional scene of feudal loyalty, in which the mourning vassal visits the tomb of his master, this poem invokes heroic and virile preoccupations: great oaths (lines 1 and 5), the humble man's wonder at the great monuments erected by his king (lines 1 through 6), Rome and her legacies of imperial splendor (line 8), the passage of time (lines 6 and 7). But while the language is present, the culture that once infused it with meaning is not. Cervantes undermines grandiose contemporary conventions with his characteristic virtuosity: the solemn oath becomes a mild curse of wonder issuing from the mouth of a common infantryman; his awe at the great monument derives from his estimation of its cost, a fortune perceived as all the more striking because he assumes that the masterpiece is ephemeral.

In the coarse, burlesque language of the poem and the wry interchange of its two interlocutors, Cervantes is as usual injecting a dose of pragmatic realism into the representation of the Spanish monarch and his relationship with his subjects. But he is also saying something important about contemporary poetry and, specifically, about the new lyric and the sonnet form that was its clearest emblem. Far from commemorating the sayings and the actions of the great, the sonnet had become, by the time Philip II died,[3] the tomb of poetry, a verbal artifact whose significance in the late sixteenth century resided most powerfully in its rectangular, blocklike shape that resembles both a stamp of authority and a funerary monument. The words that constitute this kind of poem, according to Cervantes, have no capacity to mean. The soldier-speaker would give a gold piece to complete a successful act of description, but he cannot, and when the work indulges in contemporary decadent permissiveness to allow itself three extra lines, the result is precisely, nothing: *nada* (line 17). Bloated and distorted by the addition of the three extra lines, the poem performs the exact opposite of a commemorative function, fixing no image in place, erroneously foretelling the fall of the monument and claiming ignorance of the king's name.

In content and attitude, Cervantes's sonnet resembles certain of the *novelas ejemplares,* and reminds us of his position on the fulcrum between the Spain of poetry and the Spain of prose. The era in which the lyric was overtaking epic as the principal poetic mode was also the era in which poetry was losing ground to this rival discourse, which was crossing over from the field of legislation to assume increasing popularity and prestige as

---

3. Philip II died in 1598.

the language by which to represent human existence and experience. And it is notable that the first volume of the *Quijote,* published in 1605, opens with an extended lampoon of what had by then become a reflexive gesture in the early modern publishing world, namely, the inclusion in the prefatory pages of a book of as many sonnets as an author and a publisher could muster. Cervantes takes evident pleasure in including among his sonneteers a figure no less authoritative than Babieca, the famed steed of the Cid, who sets forth his praise for Rocinante in a suitable Renaissance encomium. By 1615, as Cervantes was publishing the second part of the work, it no longer seemed necessary to acknowledge the tattered remains of poetic prestige. In part due to the changes he himself had wrought on the Spanish culture of letters, Cervantes felt licensed to open the novel in the key of the novel, with his attack on the false *Quijote,* before embarking down the convoluted and ever more powerful modern course of metafiction.

On the other hand, if we examine Cervantes's writings and the culture of peninsular poetry more carefully, it emerges that it was not all poetry that was consigned to the tomb. While flatly suspicious of any use of the forms and conventions of the new lyric that fell outside the range of the amatory, Cervantes viewed the Castilian ballad, or *romance,* as a still-viable form. Furthermore, in the Americas, both the romance and the emergent *silva,* a type of poem that maintained strong links to Dantean canzone and the prophetic biblical songs that would ground it in the idea of poetry as poiesis, flourished as members of the Creole and European-identified lettered elites sought to stabilize the identity of the Spanish-American subject.[4] While peninsular writers experienced poetic modernity as a substitution of Horace for Homer, mid- to late-sixteenth century lettered elites working in the Americas attempted to *displace* the restrictions of Horace and set Dante and Ovid in place as the poetic foundations for a transatlantic identity as citizens of a global city of letters.[5] In the vice-realms of the Americas, the rise of the lyric held forth the tantalizing promise of expansion, both in the spectrum of viable modern identities and in the genre of poetry itself. In the Old World, however, the intersection of poetry and Hapsburg politics had transformed the genre of the *diestro braco* into a reliquary.

---

[4]. On the career of the new lyric in the New World, see the excellent overview provided by Gónzalez Echevarría in "Colonial Lyric."

[5]. The phrase is taken from the classic study by Rama, *La ciudad letrada.*

BIBLIOGRAPHY

Acuña, Hernando de. *Varias poesías.* Edited by Luis F. Díaz Laríos. Madrid: Cátedra, 1982.
Agamben, Giorgio. *The End of the Poem: Studies in Poetics.* Translated by Daniel Heller-Roazen. Stanford: Stanford University Press, 1999.
Albi de la Cuesta, Julio. *De Pavía a Rocroi: Los tercios de infantería española en los siglos XVI y XVII.* Madrid: Balkan, 1999.
Alcazar, Bartolomé de. "Al soneto, vecinos, al malvado." In *La poesía de la edad de oro,* vol. 1, edited by José Manuel Blecua, 220. Madrid: Clásicos Castália, 1984.
Aldana, Francisco de. *Poesías castellanas completas.* Edited by José Lara Garrido. Madrid: Cátedra, 1985.
Alpers, Paul. *What Is Pastoral?* Chicago: University of Chicago Press, 1996.
Althusser, Louis. *Lenin and Philosophy and Other Essays.* Translated by Ben Brewster. New York: Monthly Review Press, 1971.
Anderson, Perry. *Lineages of the Absolutist State.* London: N.L.B., 1974.
Aram, Bethany. *Juana the Mad: Sovereignty and Dynasty in Renaissance Europe.* Baltimore: Johns Hopkins University Press, 2005.
Argote de Molina, Gonzalo. "Discurso sobre la poesía castellana." In *La retórica en españa,* edited and translated by Elena Casas et al. Madrid: Editorial Nacional, 1980.
Armisén, Antonio. *Estudios sobre la lengua poética de Boscán: La edición de 1543.* Zarazoga: Departamento de Literatura Española, Universidad de Zarazoga, 1982.
Baehr, Rudolf. *Manual de versificación española.* Madrid: Editorial Gredos, 1973.
Baena, Julio. "Spanish Mannerist Detours in the Mapping of Reason: Around Cervantes' *Novelas Ejemplares.*" In *Reason and Its Others: Italy, Spain, and the New World,* edited by David Castillo and Massimo Lollini, 204–20. Nashville: Vanderbilt University Press, 2006.
Barja, Juan, "El destino de Si: El soneto como forma material." In *Welterfahrung-Selbsterfahrung: Konstitution und Verhandlung von Subjektivität in der spanischen Literatur der früen Neuzeit,* edited by Wolfgang Matzat and Bernhard Teuber. Tübingen: Niemeyer, 2000.
Barnard, Mary E. *The Myth of Apollo and Daphne from Ovid to Quevedo: Love, Agon, and the Grotesque.* Durham, N.C.: Duke University Press, 1987.
Bembo, Pietro. *Prose Della Volgar Lingua di Pietro Bembo.* Milano: Cisalpino, 2000.
Berger, Harry, Jr. *The Absence of Grace: Sprezzatura and Suspicion in Two Renaissance Courtesy Books.* Stanford: Stanford University Press, 2000.
Bergmann, Emilie L. *Art Inscribed: Essays on "Ekphrasis" in Spanish Golden Age Poetry.* Cambridge: Harvard University Press, 1979.

Beverley, John. *Against Literature*. Minneapolis: University of Minnesota Press, 1993.

———. *Aspects of Góngora's "Soledades."* Amsterdam: J. Benjamins, 1980.

———. "Gracián, o la sobrevaloración de la literatura (barroco y postmodernidad)." In *Relecturas del barroco de Indias,* edited by Mabel Moraña, 17–30. Hanover, N.H.: Ediciones del Norte, 1994.

Blecua, José Manuel. *La poesía de la edad de oro*. Vol. 1. Madrid: Clásicos Castália, 1984.

Boscán, Juan. *Obra completa*. Edited by Carlos Clavería. Madrid: Cátedra, 1999.

Brown, Gary, J. "Fernando de Herrera and Lorenzo De' Medici: The Sonnet as Epigram." *Romanische Forschungen* 87 (1975): 226–38.

Butler, Judith. *The Psychic Life of Power: Theories in Subjection*. Stanford: Stanford University Press, 1997.

Calderón de la Barca, Pedro. *El alcalde de Zalamea. La vida es sueño*. 22d ed. Pitágoras, Mexico: Espasa-Calpe Mexicana, 1985.

Campana, Joseph. "On Not Defending Poetry: Spenser, Suffering, and the Energy of Affect." *PMLA* 120, no. 1 (2005): 33–48.

Caro, Rodrigo. *Varones insignes en letras naturales de la ilustrísima ciudad de Sevilla*. Edited by Luis Gómez Canseco. Sevilla: Diputación Provincial de Sevilla, 1992.

Casas, Elena, et al., eds. *La retórica en España*. Madrid: Editorial Nacional, 1980.

Cascardi, Anthony J. *Ideologies of History in the Spanish Golden Age*. University Park: Pennsylvania State University Press, 1997.

Castiglione, Baldassarre. *The Book of the Courtier*. Translated by George Bull. Harmondsworth: Penguin Books, 1967.

Castillejo, Cristóbal de. *Obra completa*. Edited by Rogelio Reyes Cano. Madrid: Biblioteca Castro, 1998.

Castillo, David. *(A)wry Views: Anamorphosis, Cervantes, and the Early Picaresque*. West Lafayette, Ind.: Purdue University Press, 2001.

Cave, Terence. *The Cornucopian Text: Problems of Writing in the French Renaissance*. New York: Oxford University Press, 1979.

Cetina, Gutierre de. *Obras de Gutierre de Cetina, con introducción y notas del doctor D. Joaquín Hazañas y la Rua*. Sevilla: Francisco de P. Díaz, 1895.

———. *Sonetos y madrigales completos*. Edited by Begoña López Bueno. Madrid: Cátedra, 1990.

Cheney, Patrick Gerard, and Frederick Alfred de Armas, eds. *European Literary Careers: The Author from Antiquity to the Renaissance*. Toronto: University of Toronto Press, 2002.

Colombí-Monguió, Alicia de. "Boscán frente a Navagero: El nacimiento de la conciencia humanista en la poesía española." *Nueva Revista de Filología Hispánica* 40, no. 1 (1992): 143–68.

———. "Petrarca sin petrarquismo: De Santillana a Boscán." In *Homenaje a don Luis Monguió*, edited by Jordi Aladro Font, 119–43. Newark, Del.: Cuesta, 1997.

———. *Petrarquismo Peruano: Diego Dávalos y Figueroa y la poesía de la miscelánea austral*. London: Tamesis, 1985.

Cornejo Polar, Antonio. *"Discurso en loor de la poesía": Estudio y edición*. Edited by José Antonio Mazzotti. Lima: Centro de Estudios Literarios "Antonio Cornejo Polar," Latinoamericana Editores, 2000.

Cruz, Anne J. "Arms vs. Letters: The Poetics of War and the Career of the Poet in Early Modern Spain." In *European Literary Careers: The Author from Antiquity to the Renaissance,* edited by Patrick Gerard Cheney and Frederick Alfred de Armas. Toronto: University of Toronto Press, 2002.

———. *Imitación y transformación: El petrarquismo en la poesía de Boscán y Garcilaso de la Vega.* Amsterdam: J. Benjamins, 1988.

———. "Self-Fashioning in Spain: Garcilaso de la Vega." *Romanic Review* 83, no. 4 (1992): 517–38.

Dante Alighieri. *De vulgari eloquentia.* Edited and translated by Steven Botterill. Cambridge: Cambridge University Press, 1996.

Darst, David H. *Juan Boscán.* Boston: Twayne Publishers, 1978.

Davis, Elizabeth B. *Myth and Identity in the Epic of Imperial Spain.* Columbia: University of Missouri Press, 2000.

Elias, Norbert. *Power and Civility: The Civilizing Process.* Translated by Edmund Jephcott. Vol. 2. New York: Pantheon, 1982.

Elliott, John Huxtable. *Imperial Spain: 1469–1716.* New York: New American Library, 1977.

Ercilla, Alonso de. *La Araucana.* Edited by Marcos A. Morínigo and Isaías Lerner. 2 vols. Madrid: Editorial Castalia, 1979.

Flor, Fernando R. de la. *Barroco: Representación e ideología en el mundo hispánico, 1580–1680.* Madrid: Cátedra, 2002.

Foucault, Michel. *The Order of Things: An Archaeology of the Human Sciences.* New York: Vintage Books, 1994.

Fox, Dian. "'Frente a Frente': Francisco de Aldana and the Sublimations of Desire." *Calíope: Journal of the Society for Renaissance and Baroque Hispanic Poetry* 11, no. 1 (2005): 65–85.

Freccero, John. "The Fig Tree and the Laurel: Petrarch's Poetics." In *Literary Theory/ Renaissance Texts,* edited by Patricia Parker and David Quint, 20–32. Baltimore: Johns Hopkins University Press, 1986.

Friedman, Edward. "Creative Space: Ideologies of Discourse in Góngora's *Polifemo.*" In *Cultural Authority in Golden Age Spain,* edited by Marina S. Brownlee and Hans Ulrich Gumbrecht, 51–78. Baltimore: Johns Hopkins University Press, 1995.

Fuchs, Barbara. *Mimesis and Empire: The New World, Islam, and European Identities.* Cambridge: Cambridge University Press, 2001.

Gaylord, Mary M. "Góngora and the Footprints of the Voice." *MLN* 108, no. 2 (1993): 230–53.

Gerli, E. Michael. "Aristotle in Africa: History, Fiction, and Truth in *El Gallardo español.*" *Cervantes: Bulletin of the Cervantes Society of America* 15, no. 2 (1995): 43–57.

González Echevarría, Roberto. *Celestina's Brood: Continuities of the Baroque in Spanish and Latin American Literatures.* Durham, N.C.: Duke University Press, 1993.

———. "Colonial Lyric." In *The Cambridge History of Latin American Literature,* edited by Roberto González Echevarría and Enrique Pupo-Walker, 191–230. New York: Cambridge University Press, 1996.

Gracián, Baltasar. *El héroe: Oraculo manual y el arte de prudencia.* Edited by Antonio Bernat Vistarini and Abraham Madroñal. Madrid: Castalia, 2003.

Graf, E. C. "From Scipio to Nero to the Self: The Exemplary Politics of Stoicism in Garcilaso de la Vega's *Elegies.*" *PMLA* 116, no. 5 (2001): 1316–33.

Greene, Roland. *Post-Petrarchism: Origins and Innovations of the Western Lyric Sequence.* Princeton: Princeton University Press, 1991.

———. *Unrequited Conquests: Love and Empire in the Colonial Americas.* Chicago: University of Chicago Press, 1999.

Greene, Thomas M. *The Light in Troy: Imitation and Discovery in Renaissance Poetry.* New Haven: Yale University Press, 1982.

Grossman, Allen R., with Mark Halliday. *The Sighted Singer: Two Works on Poetry for Readers and Writers.* Baltimore: Johns Hopkins University Press, 1992.

Hauser, Arnold. *Mannerism: The Crisis of the Renaissance and the Origin of Modern Art.* Translated by Eric Mosbacher. New York: Knopf, 1965.

Headley, John M. *The Emperor and His Chancellor: A Study of the Imperial Chancellery Under Gattinara.* Cambridge: Cambridge University Press, 1983.

———. "The Hapsburg World Empire and the Revival of Ghibellinism." In *Medieval and Renaissance Studies: Proceedings of the Southeastern Institute of Medieval and Renaissance Studies, Summer 1975,* edited by Siegfried Wenzel, 93–127. Chapel Hill: University of North Carolina Press, 1975.

Heiple, Daniel L. *Garcilaso de la Vega and the Italian Renaissance.* University Park: Pennsylvania State University Press, 1994.

Helgerson, Richard. *A Sonnet from Carthage: Garcilaso de la Vega and the New Poetry of Sixteenth-Century Europe.* Philadelphia: University of Pennsylvania Press, 2007.

Hermida Ruiz, Aurora. "Historiografía literaria y nacionalismo espanõl: Garcilaso de la Vega o el linaje del hombre invisible." Ph.D. diss., University of Virginia, 1999.

Herrera, Fernando de. *Anotaciones a la poesía de Garcilaso.* Edited by Inoria Pepe and José María Reyes. Madrid: Cátedra, 2001.

———. *Poesía castellana original completa.* Edited by Cristóbal Cuevas García. 2d ed. Madrid: Cátedra, 1997.

Horace. *Satires, Epistles, and Ars Poetica.* Translated by H. Rushton Fairclough. Cambridge: Harvard University Press, 1978.

Hurtado de Mendoza, Diego. *Poesía.* Edited by Luis F. Díaz Larios and Olga Gete Carpio. Madrid: Cátedra, 1990.

Iventosch, H. "The Renaissance Pastoral and the Golden Age: A Translation of a Sonnet of Giraldi Cinthio by Gutierre de Cetina." *MLN* 85 (1970): 240–43.

Javitch, Daniel. *Poetry and Courtliness in Renaissance England.* Princeton: Princeton University Press. 1978.

Kamen, Henry. *Philip of Spain.* New Haven: Yale University Press, 1998.

———. *Spain, 1469–1714: A Society of Conflict.* 3rd ed. New York: Pearson/Longman, 2005.

Kennedy, William J. *Jacopo Sannazaro and the Uses of the Pastoral.* Hanover, N.H.: University Press of New England, 1983.

Kittay, Jeffrey, and Wlad Godzich. *The Emergence of Prose: An Essay in Prosaics.* Minneapolis: University of Minnesota Press, 1987.

Langer, Ullrich. *Perfect Friendship: Studies in Literature and Moral Philosophy from Boccaccio to Corneille.* Geneva: Librairie Droz, 1994.

Lapesa, Rafael. "La poesía de Gutierre de Cetina." In *Hommage à Ernest Martinenche: La segunda edad de oro en la literatura española,* edited by Homero Seris. Paris: Editions d' Artrey, 1939.

Lara Garrido, José. *Del Siglo de Oro: Métodos y relecciones.* Madrid: Universidad Europea-CEES Ediciones, 1997.

López Bueno, Begoña. *Gutierre de Cetina: Poeta del renacimiento español.* Sevilla: Excma. Diputación Provincial de Sevilla, 1978.

———. *La poética cultista de Herrera a Góngora: Estudios sobre la poésia barroca andaluza.* Sevilla: Alfar, 1987.

López Pinciano, Alonso. *Filosofía antigua poética.* Edited by Pedro Muñoz Peña. Valladolid: Impr. y Libreria Nacional y Extranjera de Hijos de Rodriguez, 1894.

Lorenzo, Javier. "Displacing Petrarch: Christomorphism and Exemplarity in Juan Boscán's *Libro Segundo.*" *Calíope: Journal of the Society for Renaissance and Baroque Hispanic Poetry* 7, no. 2 (2001): 23–36.

Lynch, John. *Spain Under the Hapsburgs.* 2 vols. New York: Oxford University Press, 1964–69.

Macrí, Oreste. *Fernando de Herrera.* Translated by María Dolores Galvarriato. Madrid: Gredos, 1959.

Maravall, José Antonio. *Las communidades de Castilla: Una primera revolución moderna.* Madrid: Revista de Occidente, 1963.

———. *Culture of the Baroque: Analysis of a Historical Structure.* Translated by Terry Cochran. Minneapolis: University of Minnesota Press, 1986.

Mazzotta, Giuseppe. *The Worlds of Petrarch.* Durham, N.C.: Duke University Press, 1993.

Mazzotti, José Antonio, ed. *Agencias criollas: La ambigüedad "colonial" en las letras hispanoamericanas.* Pittsburgh: Instituto Internacional de Literatura Iberoamericana, 2000.

McNerney, Kathleen. *The Influence of Ausiàs March on Early Golden Age Castilian Poetry.* Amsterdam: Rodopi, 1982.

Medici, Lorenzo de'. "A Commentary on My Sonnets." In *Lorenzo de' Medici: Selected Poems and Prose,* edited by Jon Thiem et al., 103–117. University Park: Pennsylvania State University Press, 1991.

———. *Opere.* Edited by Tiziano Zanato. Torino: Giulio Einaudi editore, 1992.

Menocal, Maria Rosa. *Shards of Love: Exile and the Origins of the Lyric.* Durham, N.C.: Duke University Press, 1994.

Middlebrook, Leah. "En Arcadia Betis: The Imperial Lyric of Gutierre de Cetina." *Bulletin of Hispanic Studies* 78, no. 3 (2001): 297–317.

———. "Fernando de Herrera Invented the Internet: Technologies of Self-Containment in the Early Modern Sonnet." In *Reason and Its Others: Italy, Spain, and the New World,* edited by David Castillo and Massimo Lollini, 61–78. Nashville, Tenn.: Vanderbilt University Press, 2006.

Mirollo, James V. *Mannerism and Renaissance Poetry: Concept, Mode, Inner Design.* New Haven: Yale University Press, 1984.

Montemayor, Jorge de. *Los siete libros de La Diana.* Edited by Asunción Rallo Gruss. Madrid: Cátedra, 1991.

Montero Delgado, Juan. *La controversia sobre las anotaciones herrerianas.* Seville: Servicio de Publicaciones de Excmo. Ayuntamiento de Sevilla, 1987.

Montolí Bernadas, Victor. *Introducción a la obra de Gutierre de Cetina.* Barcelona: PPU, 1993.

Moraña, Mabel, ed. *Angel Rama y los estudios latinoamericanos.* Pittsburgh: Instituto Internacional de Literatura Iberoamericana, 1997.

———. *Relecturas del barroco de Indias.* Hanover, N.H.: Ediciones del Norte, 1994.

Morreale, Margherita. *Castiglione y Boscán: El ideal cortesano en el renacimiento español*. Madrid: CSIC, 1959.
Morros Mestres, Bienvenido. "La idea de la lírica en *Las Anotaciones a Garcilaso* de Fernando de Herrera." In *La idea de la lírica en el renacimiento: Entre Italia y España*, edited by María José Vega Ramos and Cesc Esteve, 211–29. Vilagarcia de Arousa, Pontevedra, Spain: Mirabel, 2004.
———. *Las polémicas literarias en la España del siglo XVI: A propósito de Fernando de Herrera y Garcilaso de la Vega*. Barcelona: Quaderns Crema, 1998.
Munárriz Peralta, Jesús. *Un siglo de sonetos en español*. Madrid: Hiperion, 2000.
Murrin, Michael. *History and Warfare in Renaissance Epic*. Chicago: University of Chicago Press, 1994.
Navarrete, Ignacio Enrique. *Orphans of Petrarch: Poetry and Theory in the Spanish Renaissance*. Berkeley and Los Angeles: University of California Press, 1994.
Oppenheimer, Paul. *The Birth of the Modern Mind: Self, Consciousness, and the Invention of the Sonnet*. New York: Oxford University Press, 1989.
Padrón, Ricardo. *The Spacious Word: Cartography, Literature, and Empire in Early Modern Spain*. Chicago: University of Chicago Press, 2004.
Parker, Geoffrey. *Success Is Never Final: Empire, War, and Faith in Early Modern Europe*. New York: Basic Books, 2002.
Parker, Patricia. "Virile Style." In *Premodern Sexualities*, edited by Louise Fradenburg and Carla Freccero, 199–222. New York: Routledge, 1996.
Pastor Bodmer, Beatriz. *Discursos narrativos de la conquista: Mitificación y emergencia*. Hanover, N.H.: Ediciones del Norte, 1988.
Petrarca, Francesco. *Petrarch's Lyric Poems: The Rime Sparse and Other Lyrics*. Edited and translated by Robert M. Durling. Cambridge: Harvard University Press, 1976.
Pierce, Frank. *La poesía épica del Siglo de Oro*. 2nd ed. Translated by J. C. Cayol de Bethencourt. Madrid: Gredos, 1968.
Plett, Heinrich F. *Rhetoric and Renaissance Culture*. New York: De Gruyter, 2004.
Poema del Cid. Edited by Francisco López Estrada. Madrid: Castalia, 1974.
Prieto, Antonio. *La poesía española del siglo XVI*. Madrid: Cátedra, 1984.
Quint, David. *Epic and Empire: Politics and Generic Form from Virgil to Milton*. Princeton: Princeton University Press, 1993.
———. *Origin and Originality in Renaissance Literature: Versions of the Source*. New Haven: Yale University Press, 1983.
Rama, Angel. *La ciudad letrada*. Hanover, N.H.: Ediciones del Norte, 1984.
Ramón Resina, Joan. "The Role of Discontinuity in the Formation of National Culture." In *Cultural Authority in Golden Age Spain*, edited by Marina S. Brownlee and Hans Ulrich Gumbrecht, 284–303. Baltimore: Johns Hopkins University Press, 1995.
Randel, Mary Gaylord. *The Historical Prose of Fernando de Herrera*. London: Tamesis, 1971.
Reichenberger, Arnold G. "Boscán and the Classics." *Comparative Literature*, no. 2 (1951): 97–118.
———. "Boscán's 'Epístola a Mendoza.'" *Hispanic Review* 17, no. 1 (1949): 1–17.
Reyes Cano, Rogelio. *Estudios sobre Cristóbal de Castillejo: Tradición y modernidad en la encrucijada poética del siglo XVI*. Salamanca: Ediciones Universidad Salamanca, 2000.

Rivers, Elías L. *Francisco de Aldana: El divino capitán*. Badajoz: Institución de Servicios Culturales, 1955.
———. *Muses and Masks: Some Classical Genres of Spanish Poetry*. Newark, Del.: Cuesta, 1992.
Roche, Thomas P., Jr. *Petrarch and the English Sonnet Sequences*. New York: AMS Press, 1989.
Ruiz Silva, Carlos. *Estudios sobre Francisco de Aldana*. Valladolid: Universidad de Valladolid, 1981.
Sánchez de Lima, Miguel. *El arte poética en romance castellano*. Edited by Rafael de Balbín Lucas. Madrid: CSIC, 1944.
Sannazaro, Jacopo. *Arcadia*. Edited by Francesco Erspamer. Milan: Mursia, 1990.
Simerka, Barbara. *Discourses of Empire: Counter-epic Literature in Early Modern Spain*. University Park: Pennsylvania State University Press, 2003.
Smith, Paul. *Discerning the Subject*. Minneapolis: University of Minnesota Press, 1988.
Smith, Paul Julian. *Writing in the Margin*. New York: Oxford University Press, 1988.
Spiller, Michael R. G. *The Development of the Sonnet: An Introduction*. New York: Routledge, 1992.
Stewart, Susan. *Poetry and the Fate of the Senses*. Chicago: University of Chicago Press, 2001.
Tanner, Marie. *The Last Descendant of Aeneas: The Hapsburgs and the Mythic Image of the Emperor*. New Haven: Yale University Press, 1993.
Tylus, Jane. *Writing and Vulnerability in the Late Renaissance*. Stanford: Stanford University Press, 1993.
Valdés, Juan de. *Diálogo de la lengua*. Edited and with introductory notes by Juan M. Lope Blanch. Madrid: Castalia, 1969.
Vega, Garcilaso de la. *Obras completas: Con comentario*. Edited by Elias L. Rivers. Madrid: Editorial Castalia, 1981.
Vega, María José. "La poética de la lírica en el renacimiento." In *La idea de la lírica en el renacimiento: Entre Italia y España*, edited by María José Vega Ramos and Cesc Esteve, 15–43. Vilagarcia de Arousa, Pontevedra, Spain: Mirabel, 2004.
Vergil. *The Eclogues*. Edited and translated by Guy Lee. London: Penguin, 1984.
Vickers, Nancy J. "Diana Described: Scattered Woman and Scattered Rhyme." In *Writing and Sexual Difference*, edited by Elizabeth Abel, 95–108. Chicago: University of Chicago Press, 1982.
Walters, D. Gareth. *The Poetry of Francisco de Aldana*. London: Tamesis Books, 1988.
Weinberg, Bernard. *A History of Literary Criticism in the Italian Renaissance*. Chicago: University of Chicago Press, 1961.

INDEX

Acuña, Hernando de, 11, 14–17
  "A un buen caballero, y mal poeta, la lira de Garcilaso contrahecha" (To a good knight and bad poet, the lyre of Garcilaso, unstrung), 31–32, 53
  Boscán's work and, 48
  Cetina and, 136–37
  Damon-Silvia/Silviano-Silvia poems of, 137 n. 32
  El caballero determinado, 30, 31 n. 19
  form and politics in sonnets of, 28–32, 50, 146–47
  Memorial, 15 n. 2
  Poema del Cid, 21–25
  poetics of, 102, 110
  rational subjects in poetry of, 25–28
  Sonnet 30, 25–28, 32 n. 20, 33, 35, 59–60
  Sonnet 45, 15–25, 28, 30, 32–33, 35, 50, 51, 59–60, 82, 96; courtly subjects in, 18–25; form and politics in, 28, 30, 32, 50, 51; masculine ideal in, 59–60, 96; rational subjects in, 25; Renaissance wit in, 28, 35; song-sonnet relationship in, 32 n. 20; structure of, 33, 82
  Sonnet 94, 29–32
Acuña, Pedro de, 14–15
Against Literature (Beverley), 110
agency
  in Acuña's poetry, 18–25
  in Herrera's lyric poems, 138–52
  of rational subjects, 25–28
  discourse versus discourse of subject, 3 n. 5
Albi de la Cuesta, Julio, 8 n. 18
Alcázar, Bartolomé de, "Contra un mal soneto" (Against a bad sonnet), 52–53
Aldana, Francisco de, 4–10, 34 n. 22, 143 n. 12, 175, 177

"Epístola a Arias Montano" (Epistle to Arias Montano), 7 n. 15
  Sonnet 45, 4–11, 7 n. 15, 108, 113 n. 17, 175
Althusser, Louis, 24
"Al Túmulo del Rey Felipe II En Sevilla" (Cervantes), 178–79
Anabaptists, 53–54
anamorphosis, 9
Arcadia (Sannazaro), 11, 107, 113–14
Aretino, Pietro, 49
Argote de Molina, Gonzalo, 43 n. 31
Ariosto, Ludovico, 105, 124 n. 24
Aristotelian poetics, 2, 153–54
Armisén, Antonio, 61 n. 2, 62 n. 3, 66 n. 8, 73 n. 12, 84 n. 23
arms and letters, 17, 19–20, 22–23, 24, 97–98, 99 n. 30
arte mayor form of poetry, 33, 46–47
Augustine of Hippo (Saint Augustine), 64 n. 5
"A un buen caballero, y mal poeta, la lira de Garcilaso contrahecha" (To a good knight and bad poet, the lyre of Garcilaso, unstrung) (Acuña), 31–32, 53

Baehr, Rudolf, 34 n. 22
ballad
  Cervantes' view of, 180
  memorializing role of, 60
Bembo, Pietro
  Cetina and, 105
  poetics of, 2, 81, 145
beschouwer figure, 6–7
Beverley, John, 110
blazon, 9 n. 19–20
Book of the Courtier, The (Castiglione), 48–50
  Boscán's translation, 61, 68–69, 82
  Horatian influence on, 66 n. 8

Boscán, Juan, 10–11, 26 n. 15
  Cancionero General and, 45
  Castillejo and, 53–57
  Cetina and, 105, 125–26
  courtierization of song by, 59–102, 175
  "Epístola a Mendoza" (Epistle to Mendoza), 66 n. 8, 83 n. 22, 89 n. 25
  Herrera's discussion of, 155–58
  "Letter to the Duchess of Soma" (Carta a la duquesa de Soma), 41, 44–45, 46 n. 34, 53, 60–62, 68–69, 72–73, 90, 173
  new art of poetry of, 32 n. 20, 35–38, 38 n. 25, 40–52
  Obras completas, 42, 60–69, 72–82, 95
  Petrarch and, 43–44, 60–61, 72–77
  Poem 8, 64
  Poem 11, 63
  Poem 12, 64–65
  Poem 19, 65–66, 70, 92
  Poem 21, 63
  Poem 29, 74
  Poem 30, 75–76
  Poem 33, 76–77
  Poem 47, 69–72, 76, 95
  Poem 53, 77–78
  Poem 57, 78
  Poem 58, 78
  Poem 64, 82
  Poem 66, 77, 79–81
  Poem 67, 81–82
  Poem 68, 82
  Poem 71, 73, 86–87
  Poem 78, 73, 83–84, 87
  Poem 79, 73, 84–85, 87
  Poem 80, 73, 85–87
  Poem 95, 87
  Poem 101, 82 n. 22
  Poem 112, 87
  Poem 114, 72, 90–91
  Poem 115, 60, 72, 73, 93–95
  Poem 116, 88, 94–95
  Poem 119, 91, 110
  Poem 120, 90–91
  Poem 123, 92
  Poem 124, 92
  Poem 126, 90–92
  Poem 127, 88–89, 92
  Poem 128, 95
  Poem 129, 95–96
  Poem 130, 67, 92, 95
  Poem 159, 85
  poetics of, 102, 105, 139, 173

  second lady in poetry of, 83–87
  sonnet form and, 34 n. 22
"broken foot" *(pie quebrado)* form, 55 n. 41
Brown, Gary J., 36–37
Butler, Judith, 3 n. 5, 24, 100

caballero determinado, El (The steadfast knight) (Acuña), 30–31, 31 n. 19
Calderón de la Barca, Pedro, 6–7
Campana, Joseph, 169–70, 170 n. 39
"Canción en alabanza de la divina majestad, por la victoria del Señor don Juan" (Herrera), 158–60
canzone
  Dante's discussion of, 2, 37–38, 180
  little songs and, 32–33
  Petrarchism and, 14
  sonnets and, 45
Canzoniere (Petrarch), 11–12, 64, 68, 73–77, 87, 93, 103, 112, 121 n. 23, 164–74
Caro, Rodrigo, 141
Cartagena, Alfonso de, 55
Cascardi, Anthony J., 4 n. 9, 8 n. 17, 20 n. 9, 23 n. 12
Castiglione, Baldassare, 19, 26 n. 15, 38 n. 25, 41, 49–50, 65, 66 n. 8, 73 n. 12, 81, 156–58
Castilian culture
  Acuña's knowledge of, 29–30
  Boscán's relations with monarchy in, 46 n. 34
  caballeros, in Boscán's poetry, 45–52, 59–60
  Herrera's lyric poetry and, 40
  identity and poetry in, 42
  imperialist ideology and, 144
  language and, 43–44
  poetry and, 7–10
Castillejo, Cristóbal de, 11, 46, 53–58
Castillo, David, 9 n. 21
Catullus, 61 n. 2
Cervantes, Miguel de, 12, 142 n. 11, 146, 177–80
  "Al Túmulo del Rey Felipe II En Sevilla," 178–79
Cetina, Gutierre de, 11, 103, 142 n. 12, 169
  Amarílida relation in poetry of, 131–35
  Dórida relation in poetry of, 115–21
  Epistle 10, 131–35
  exile poems of, 122–24, 135–37
  imperialism in work of, 103–37
  Song 4, 124–28
  Song 5, 131–35

Song 11, 135–37
Sonnet 3, 135–37
Sonnet 4, 131–35
Sonnet 5, 135–37
Sonnet 9, 118–21, 124–26
Sonnet 10, 124–28, 135
Sonnet 21, 124–28, 135
Sonnet 27, 108–15, 119–20, 131–35
Sonnet 35, 131–35
Sonnet 46, 131–35
Sonnet 72, 131–35
Sonnet 87, 131–35
Sonnet 88, 131–35
Sonnet 97, 135–37
Sonnet 98, 131–35, 169
Sonnet 109, 131–35
Sonnet 120, 131–35
Sonnet 140, 135–37
Sonnet 162, 122
Sonnet 191, 123–24
Sonnet 193, 135–37
Sonnet 212, 131–35
Vandalio poems of, 106–8, 113–37
Vergil and, 128–30
Charles V (Holy Roman Emperor), 30–31, 41, 44 n. 32, 104, 141 n. 6, 142, 146, 172
Christian Reconquest, 2, 42–43, 59
Cid, poetic images of, 21–22, 59
Cinthio, Giambatista Giraldi, 115
Cisneros regency, 57 n. 43
civilizing process, sonnets and, 25–28
Colombí-Monguió, Alicia, 38 n. 25
Comento de' miei sonetti (Lorenzo de' Medici), 38–40, 106 n. 8
comuneros revolts, 41, 46, 57 n. 43
Confessions (Augustine), 64 n. 5
consonance, 45, 45 n. 33, 59–60, 65–66, 71, 103, 157
"Contra un mal soneto" (Against a bad sonnet) (Alcázar), 52–57
copla form, Boscán's use of, 45, 68–69
"Coplas por la muerta de su padre" (Verses on the death of his father) (Manrique), 54 n. 41
Cortegiano II (The book of the courtier) (Castiglione), 48–49
  Boscán's translation, 61, 68–69, 82
  Horatian influence on, 66 n. 8
Counter-Reformation, Herrera's poetry and, 144, 148–52, 158–59, 163 n. 32, 173

courtierization, in Spanish lyric poetry, 3–4, 8–12, 17–18
  Boscán's courtierization of song, 60–61, 70–73
  in Boscán's new poetry, 40–52
  Cetina's work and, 108–13
  discourse of reason and, 25–28
  form and politics and, 28–32
  Petrarchan influence on, 72–77
  in Sonnet 45 (Acuña), 18–25
Cruz, Anne J., 100 n. 32
Cuevas García, Cristóbal, 162 n. 31, 165 n. 35
culture
  form and politics and, 28–32
  ideology of sonnet form and, 57–58
  poetry genres and, 8–10
  politics and, 28–32

da Lentino, Giacomo, 32, 33 n. 21, 34 n. 22
Dante Alighieri, 2, 25, 32 n. 20, 37, 38 n. 25, 38–39, 81, 88
d'Arezzo, Guittone, 33 n. 21
Darst, David, 45 n. 33, 62 n. 3
de la Marche, Olivier, 30, 31 n. 19
desire, in Cetina's sonnets, 113–15
Development of the Sonnet, The (Spiller), 34
De vulgari eloquentia (Dante), 2, 37
Diálogo de la lengua (Valdés), 43
Diaz Larios, Luis F., 15 n. 2, 23, 30 n. 18, 31 n. 19
diestro braço trope, 22–23, 59, 139, 146, 173, 180
Discerning the Subject (Smith), 3 n. 5
discourse
  of arms and letters, 24
  blazon and anti-blazon in poetic, 8
  in Boscán's poetry, 71–72
  in Cetina's poetry, 110–14
  of courtiership, 61, 139–40
  of heroism, 40, 146, 150, 152, 154–56, 163 n. 32, 172, 173–74
  of just war, 30 n. 18
  of monarchy, 141–42
  of nobility, 51, 142
  of Petrarchism, 120
  poetics and, 2–4, 11–12, 17–18, 20, 23–24, 34–35, 57, 60, 81–82, 148 n. 18
  political and religious, 144
  of reason, 34–35, 37
  of the Reconquest, 43 n. 30
  social discourse, 95–96
  in song, 28 n. 17, 72–73

of sprezzatura, 38, 38 n. 25
of Stoicism, 126 n. 26
divine will, in Herrera's poetry, 141–51
dolce stil nuovo, 17–18
Don Quijote (Cervantes), 180
Dórida relation, in Cetina's work, 115–21
Durling, Robert, 64 n. 5, 112

Eclogue 2 (Garcilaso de la Vega), 144, 146, 152
Eclogue I (Vergil), 107, 128
Egle (Cinthio), 115
8 + 6 stanza form, 33 n. 21
El arte poética en romance castellano (The art of poetry in vernacular Castilian) (Sánchez de Lima), 48–49
elegy, 143, 164 n. 34
Elegy 2 (Garcilaso de la Vega), 96–97, 100
Elegy 3 (Herrera), 164 n. 34
Elias, Norbert, 3, 17, 17 n. 4, 28 n. 17
empire. *See also* imperialism
  in Cetina's poetry, 103–37
  of Charles V, 172
  discourses on, 41–43
  Hapsburg Empire, 59
  Philip II and, 15 n. 2
enargeia, 140, 169–70
Encina, Juan de, 20 n. 8
English sonnets, form of, 33 n. 21
Enríquez de Ribera, Fernando de, 150–52
"Entre osar y temer" (Cetina), 169
epic
  conditions fatal to (Schumpeter), 58 n. 44
  courtierization and, 60
  memorializing role of, 60
  sonnetization and, 14–15, 17, 19–20, 28 n. 17, 43, 58
  Spanish heroic lyric and role of, 1–2, 8–10, 147–52
Epistle 10 (Cetina), 131–35
"Epístola a Arias Montano" (Epistle to Arias Montano) (Aldana), 7 n. 15
"Epístola a Boscán" (Epistle to Boscán) (Garcilaso de la Vega), 96
"Epístola a Mendoza" (Epistle to Mendoza) (Boscán), 66 n. 8, 83 n. 22, 89 n. 25
Epístola Séptima (Seventh epistle) (López Pinciano), 47 n. 35
Erasmus, 56
Ercilla, Alonso de, 147

erotic desire
  in Boscán's poetry, 63–64
  in Cetina's poetry, 113–15, 134–35

fantasy, in Boscán's poetry, 63–64, 90–95
Ferdinand of Aragon, 41 n. 26, 44 n. 32, 46 n. 34, 56 n. 42, 57 n. 43
Ferdinand of Austria (younger brother of Charles V), 54 n. 38, 56 n. 42, 57 n. 43
Ficinian philosophy, Aldana and, 5
fighter poet, Acuña as, 14–15
First Book. *See Obras completas* (Boscán)
Flor, Fernando Rodríguez de la, 177
Flores de varia poesía (Cuevas), 105 n. 3
form
  in Acuña's poetry, 28–32
  coplas, 64, 103
  courtierization of, 61
  eclogue, 130, 152–53
  Herrera's scholarship on, 143, 147–48
  ideology of, 57–58
  in new lyric, 1–11, 48–52, 154, 173
  politics of, 14–58
  of songs, 68, 152
  sonnets, 61–62, 72, 102, 105–7, 108–10, 113, 150, 163
Foucault, Michel, 24
Fox, Dian, 9 n. 20
Freccero, John, 64 n. 5, 112
Frederick II (King), 32
friendship
  in Boscán's poetry, 73, 95–96
  in Garcilaso, 96, 96 n. 27
  Renaissance theories of, 18 n. 5

gallardo español motif, 146–47
Garcí Sánchez de Bajadoz, 54 n. 41
Gattinara, Mercurio de, 142 n. 10
Gelves, Count and Countess of, 141 n. 8, 173–74
germanías revolts, 41 n. 26
Girón de Rebolledo, Ana, 95
Godzich, Wlad, 28 n. 17
Góngora, Luis de, 33
Gonzaga, Fernando de, 104
González de Córdoba, Fernando, 172
Gracián, Baltasar, 158
Gramática de la lengua castellana (Nebrija), 42
Granada, as symbol, 42–44
Greene, Roland, 11 n. 24, 12 n. 26, 106 n. 9
Grossman, Allen, 1, 3–4, 176 n. 1

gunpowder revolution, 8
gun warfare, evolution of, 7–8, 142 n. 12

Hapsburg regime, Spanish lyric poetry and, 96–97, 106–7
Hapsburg-Valois wars, 104
harquebus, influence on poetry of, 7–8
Headley, John, 142 n. 10
Heidegger, Martin, 164
hendecasyllables
   Boscán's new art of, 41–52, 61 n. 2
   Castillejo's discussion of, 53
   López Pinciano's discussion of, 47 n. 35
heresy, in Spanish poetry, 53–54
Hermida Ruiz, Aurora, 99 n. 30
"heroic" Greek hexameter, *arte mayor* and, 47–48
heroic lyrics
   forms of, 152–58
   Herrera's attempts at, 138–74
   imitation and aesthetics of, 164–74
   odes as, 158–64
Herrera, Fernando de, 10–12, 177
   Boscán's work and, 47–48, 156–59
   "Canción en alabanza de la divina majestad, por la victoria del Señor don Juan," 158–60
   Cetina and, 104–6
   Elegy 3, 164 n. 34
   heroic lyrics of, 138–74
   "radiant" poetics of, 138–41
   Relación de la guerra de Cipre, 158
   Song 1, 161
   Song 2, 150–53, 166–67
   Sonnet 1, 167–70
   Sonnet 10, 171
   Sonnet 33, 170–71
   Sonnet 45, 170–71
   Sonnet 54, 162–64
   Sonnet 59, 171–73
   Sonnet 64, 163 n. 32
   sonnet form discussed by, 36–41, 154
history, Herrera's view of, 152–74
Homer, poetics of, 28 n. 17, 60, 147, 176, 180
homoeroticism
   Aldana and, 9 n. 20
   and friendship in the poetry of Boscán and Garcilaso, 95–102
Horace
   lyric poetry and influence of, 3–4, 12, 19, 28 n. 17, 60, 65–69, 73 n. 12, 76, 89, 176
   poetics of, 28 n. 17, 60, 103, 180

humanism
   in Boscán's poetry, 65, 66 n. 8
   Castilian culture and, 42
   in Herrera's writing, 155–56
   reason in sonnets and, 26 n. 15
Hurtado de Mendoza, Diego, 11, 22–25, 68, 83 n. 22, 89 n. 25, 105, 110–13
   Sonnet 20, 110–11
   Sonnet 21, 22–25

identity
   courtierization and, 59, 100, 108–10, 112
   imperial lyrics and, 41–43, 45, 51–52, 57, 124, 127–29
   masculine, 139, 172–73
   sonnetization and, 20–21
   Spanish sonnet and role of, 3, 11–12, 42–44, 51–52
imitatio
   Herrera's discussion of, 164–65
   Petrarchan aesthetics and, 73
   politics of form and, 27
   rational mind and, 27–28
   in Sonnet 45 (Acuña), 19–25
imperialism
   in Cetina's poetry, 103–37
   Herrera's heroic poetry and, 141–74
In Praise of Folly (Erasmus), 56
interiority
   in Castillejo's poetry, 54 n. 39
   in Cetina's poetry, 110–13
   in Spanish lyric poetry, 23, 39, 54 n. 39, 57
interpellation
   Acuña's poetry and, 17 n. 4, 22, 27, 32, 35, 82, 110
   Althusserian scenario of, 24
   in Boscán's work, 96, 103
invulnerabilis, classical ideal of, 10 n. 23
Isabel the Catholic, 41 n. 26
Isabel of Portugal, 41–42, 44 n. 32
Italianate new lyric, introduction in Spain of, 36–38, 48–52
Italian poetry
   Boscán and, 32 n. 20, 38 n. 25, 43, 48, 60, 68, 72
   Castillejo and, 46, 54–55
   Cetina and influence of, 105–6
   hendecasyllables in, 48, 103, 156
   Herrera and, 104–5, 153 n. 23, 156–58, 162 n. 31
   imperial lyrics and, 145
   lyric forms of, 17, 31, 36, 46, 48, 52, 101–2

metaphysics in, 25
sonnets in, 26, 34 n. 22
vita nuova, 25

Jackson, Virginia, 177–78
Jews, expulsion of, 42
jongleur, 28 n. 17, 50 n. 36
Juana of Castile (Queen), 41 n. 26
Juan of Austria, 142, 146, 159–60
just Christian war doctrine, Spanish lyric poetry and, 29–32

Kamen, Henry, 106 n. 10
Kittay, Jeffrey, 28 n. 17
knight-warrior poetry, 17–18

La Araucana (Ercilla), 147 n. 18
Laberinto de la fortuna, El (The labyrinth of fortune) (de Mena), 46–47
La Diana (Montemayor), 107 n. 11
La Goleta, battle for (1535), 97
"La Lira de Garcilaso contrahecha" (The lyre of Garcilaso, unstrung) (Acuña), 31–32
Langer, Ullrich, 18 n. 5, 95
language
  eficacia of, in Herrera's heroic lyrics, 140, 148–49
  Herrera's discussion of, 155–56
  structuring effects of, 34, 42
  virility and, 155–56
Lara Garrido, José, 143, 165 n. 35
Las obras de Garcilaso de la Vega con anotaciones (The poetry of Garcilaso de la Vega with annotations), 60–61, 138–39, 140 n. 5, 143–46, 149–52, 153 n. 22, 155–56, 159, 165, 169
Leal, Valdés, 6
Le Chevalier Déliberé (The steadfast knight) (de la Marche), 30
Leiva, Antonio de, 14–15, 172
Lepanto, victory at, 29, 30 n. 18, 40, 43 n. 31, 142, 142 n. 12, 146 n. 15
letrados, 19
"Letter to the Duchess of Soma" (Carta a la duquesa de Soma) (Boscán), 41, 44–45, 46 n. 34, 53, 60–62, 68–69, 72–73, 90, 173
Letter to the Pisos (Horace), 66–67
"Lily among Thorns" (March), 73 n. 12
loco amor, in Boscán's poetry, 64
López Bueno, Begoña, 104, 107 n. 12, 108 n. 13, 138, 165 n. 35, 168 n. 37

López Pinciano, Alonso, 47 n. 35
Lorenzo, Javier, 49, 106, 153
Loyola, Ignatius of, 6
Lucero, Diego Rodriguez, 53
Lutherans, 53
Lynch, John, 41 n. 26, 42 n. 27
lyric poetry
  definitions of, 2
  evolution of, 2–3, 176–80
  form and politics in, 28–32
  Herrera's view of, 152–74
  modern Spanish culture and, 1–2
  rational subjects in, 25–28
  status in early modern period of, 14–15

Macrí, Oreste, 147 n. 17, 173 n. 42
mannerism, in Herrera's poetry, 142 n. 12, 149 n. 19
Manrique, Jorge, 54 n. 40
March, Ausiàs, 46 n. 34, 60, 73, 105, 107 n. 12
masculinity, noble ideal of, 18 n. 5, 40, 51, 59–60, 140–52, 155–58, 166–67, 169
mathematics, sonnet form and, 34 n. 22
Medici, Lorenzo de', 38–41, 49, 106, 150, 153
Medico de su honra, El (Calderón de la Barca), 6
Memorial (Acuña), 15 n. 2
Mena, Juan de, 46–47, 54 n. 41
"Mientras por competir con tu cabello" (Góngora), 33
military service
  in Sonnet 45 (Acuña), 20–25
  in Sonnet 45 (Aldana), 5
  evolution of in Spain, 8
modernity
  double meanings and, 18
  form and politics and, 27–28
  lyric poetry and, 3, 7 n. 15, 13–14
  Petrarchism and, 10
  rational subjects and, 25
  Spanish poetry and, 1, 37, 173, 176, 180
monarchy
  Boscán's relations with, 46 n. 34
  comuneros revolts and, 41 n. 26
Montemayor, Jorge de, 107
More, Thomas, 173
  Herrera's discussion of *(Tomás Moro)*, 139 n. 2
Morreale, Margherita, 61
Morros Mestres, Bienvenido, 139 n. 2, 153 n. 23, 154 n. 24
mudanza
  in Boscán's poetry, 82, 125–26
  in Cetina's poetry, 125–26

Munárriz Peralta, Jesus, 176
Murrin, Michael, 8 n. 16
Muslims, forced conversion of, 42

nationalism, in Herrera's poetry, 142 n. 12
Navagero, Andrea, 38 n. 25, 41, 66 n. 8
Navarrete, Ignacio Enrique, 45 n. 33, 61, 76 n. 16, 87, 153 n. 23, 154 n. 25, 165 n. 35
Nebrija, Antonio de, 42
Neo-Platonic sublimation, 9, 164–74
Neo-Platonism
　in Boscán's poetry, 82, 96–102
　in Herrera, 164–74
　and heterosexuality, 18 n. 5
　and sublimation, 9
new art, defined, 1
new lyric
　defined, 1
　Garcilaso and Boscán's use of, 102
　Herrera's view of, 153–74
　modernity and, 3, 11–13
new poetry
　of Boscán, 40–51
　defined, 1
　introduction of, 36–38
　song-sonnet relationship in, 32 n. 20
New World
　Acuña and, 27 n. 16
　Cetina and, 103–5
　as topos, 27 n. 16
nobility
　Herrera and, 141–74
　idealization of in lyric poetry, 59, 141–74
　poetry and concepts of, 2–3

Obras completas (Boscán), 42, 95
　First Book, 60–61, 62–67
　Second Book, 61–62, 68–82
octava form, 33
ode
　defined by Herrera, 153
　used by Herrera, 158–64
Oppenheimer, Paul, 32 n. 20, 34 n. 22, 34–35
Origin and Originality (Quint), 114 n. 19
Orlando Furioso (Ariosto), 31 n. 19
Orphans of Petrarch (Navarrete), 87
osado español, motif, 142, 142 n. 11, 146, 154 n. 25, 169, 172

Pacheco, Francisco de, 141, 173
Parker, Geoffrey, 142 n. 10

Parker, Patricia, 155–56
pastoral imagery
　in Cetina's poetry, 107–28, 131–37
　in Vergil, 128–30
Pelayo, 144
perfect friendship (Langer), 95
Petrarch, Francesco. *See also* Petrarchan poetics
　Herrera and, 141 n. 8, 164–70
　influence of, 2, 64, 72–77, 84–87, 105, 112–13
　as literary model, 18, 25
　socialization of, 87–95
Petrarch and the English Sonnet Sequences (Roche), 86
Petrarchan poetics
　Acuña's poetry and, 18–25
　Boscán's poetry and, 43, 60–61, 72–77, 84–87, 104
　Cetina's poetry and, 105, 107, 109–13
　Herrera's poetry and, 138–39, 141 n. 8, 158, 164–70
　lyric poetry and, 2, 8–12, 36–37, 56 n. 42
　sixteenth-century sonnets and, 16–17
　socialization and, 87–89
　sonnet forms and, 33 n. 21
Phaeton myth, in Herrera's poetry, 169
Philip II (King), 44 n. 32, 107
　Acuña's poetry and reign of, 15, 29–32
　Herrera's poetry and reign of, 12, 140, 142–43, 147
　just Christian empire of, 29
　as "prudent" king, 147 n. 15
Philip the Fair of Burgundy, 44 n. 32
pie quebrado (broken foot) form, 55 n. 42, 63
poemi brevi, 32 n. 20, 36–37
poemi piccoli, emergence of, 14, 32–41
Poems 55–65 (Petrarch), 86–87
Poetics (Aristotle), 2
poiesis
　defined, 19 n. 8,
　Heidegger's ideas of, 165
　lyric poetry and, 3–4
　politics versus, 174
　reason and, 25–26
　in Sonnet 45 (Acuña), 19–24
politics
　in Acuña's lyric poetry, 28–32
　in Boscán's new poetry, 41–50
　Castillejo's "Reproof" and, 52–58
　in Herrera's poetry, 142–53
power
　form and politics in sonnets and role of, 28–32

informs Boscán's poetics, 42
  influence on Garcilaso's poetry, 100–102
  influence on Herrera's poetry, 141–52
  in Sonnet 45 (Acuña), 24–25
  tropes of in courtly poetry, 24–25
  tropes of in Vergil's poetry, 130–31
presentism, in Herrera's poetry, 142 n. 12
Prieto, Antonio, 106
Protestants, in Spanish poetry, 53
Psychic Life of Power, The, (Butler), 3 n. 5, 24, 100

Quint, David, 114 n. 19
Quintilian, 153
quintillas form, 33

"radiant" poetics, Herrera and, 138–41, 164–74
Ramón Resina, Joan, 43 n. 30
Randel, Mary Gaylord, 140, 142 n. 12
rational subjects, in Spanish lyric poetry, 25–28
reason
  in Acuña's Sonnet 30, 25–27
  in Boscán's poetry, 91–95
Reconquest
  Boscán's poetry and, 42–46, 59
  discourse of Christian, 2, 42
  second Reconquest, 40, 139, 146
reflexivity, in sonnet form, 33–34
Reichenberger, Arnold G., 66 n. 8
Relación de la guerra de Cipre (Herrera), 158
religion
  power and, in Herrera's poetry, 142–52
  in Spanish poetry, 53–54, 139–42
"Reprensión contra los poetas que escriben en metro italiano" (Reproof against those poets who write in Italian meters) (Castillejo), 53–58
Reyes Cano, Rogelio, 56 n. 42, 57 n. 43
Rime diverse di molti eccellentissimi authori nuovamente raccolte, 105
Rioja, Francisco de, 147 n. 16
Rivers, Elias, 6, 7 n. 15, 32 n. 20
Roche, Thomas P., 86
Rufo, Juan, 147
Ruiz Silva, Carlos, 7 n. 15
Ruscelli, 153

salvation
  in Boscán's poetry, 88–89, 93–95
  in the *Canzoniere*, 82, 85, 87–90, 94

Sánchez de Lima, Miguel, 28 n. 17, 49–50
Sannazaro, Jacopo, 11, 105, 107, 113–14
Scaliger, Julius Cesar, 153–54
Sebastian of Portugal, 142, 161
Second Book. *See Obras completas* (Boscán)
second lady, in Boscán's poems, 83–87
Sicilian court, sonnet form and influence of, 34 n. 22
Sidney, Philip, 34 n. 22, 88
Sighted Singer, The, (Grossman), 4 n. 6–7, 176 n. 1
silva poetry, 180
Smith, Paul, 3 n. 5
Smith, Paul Julian, 98 n. 29, 138 n. 1, 140
social structure
  in Acuña's poetry, 21–25
  in Boscán's new art, 41–52
song
  Acuña and, 31
  Boscán's courtierization of, 11, 59–61, 90–95, 175
  in Castilian culture, 10
  of Cetina, 105, 115–17, 120–21, 124, 126–27, 129–37
  early songs, 17 n. 4
  of Herrera, 12, 141, 143, 150, 152–56
  little songs, 32–40
  new art and, 1–2, 49, 103, 176, 180
  poiesis and, 19
  sonnet as derivative of, 2, 6–27, 23, 28 n. 17, 32 n. 20, 51–52
Sonnet 30 (Aldana), 34 n. 22
Sonnet 33 (Garcilaso), 96, 100–102, 108
Sonnet 33 (Herrera), 170–71
Sonnet 35 (Cetina), 131–35
Sonnet 45 (Acuña), 15–17
Sonnet 45 (Aldana), 4–11, 113 n. 17
Sonnet 45 (Herrera), 170–71
Sonnet 46 (Cetina), 131–35
Sonnet 54 (Herrera), 162–64
Sonnet 59 (Herrera), 171–73
Sonnet 64 (Herrera), 163 n. 32
Sonnet 72 (Cetina), 131–35
Sonnet 87 (Cetina), 131–35
Sonnet 88 (Cetina), 131–35
Sonnet 94 (Acuña), 29–32
Sonnet 97 (Cetina), 135–37
Sonnet 98 (Cetina), 131–35
Sonnet 109 (Cetina), 131–35
Sonnet 120 (Cetina), 131–35
Sonnet 140 (Cetina), 135–37
Sonnet 162 (Cetina), 122

Sonnet 191 (Cetina), 123–24
Sonnet 193 (Cetina), 135–37
Sonnet 212 (Cetina), 131–35
sonnet form
　defined by Herrera, 36, 38, 40
　elements of, 33–41
　ideology of, 57–58
　new lyric poets' dismissal of, 48–52, 179–80
　rational mind and, 25–28
　"reproof" in, 52–57
sonnetization
　in Acuña's work, 14–17
　Herrera and, 38, 40–41
　in new lyric, 11
Spain, cultural production in, 1–2
Spanish language
　Castilian culture and, 43
　Herrera's views on, 140, 148–49, 155–56
Spenser, Edmund, 88
Spiller, Michael R. G., 32 n. 20, 34, 34 n. 22
Spiritual Exercises (Loyola), 6
sprezzatura, 14, 16, 38, 98, 113
　Boscán's discussion of, 38 n. 25
　Cetina and, 113, 135
　courtierization and, 98
　Herrera's repudiation of, 38, 156–57
　role of power in, 24
　sonnets and, 52
stanza asymmetry, in sonnet form, 34 n. 22
state regimes
　in Boscán's poetry, 43–44
　courtierization of song and, 59
　poetry and, 4
Stewart, Susan, 4, 19 n. 7, 176
Stoicism
　Acuña and, 17 n. 5
　Boscán and, 81
subject
　in Acuña's writing, 30, 32–33, 35
　in Cetina's work, 105–6, 108–9, 130–37
　courtierization of, 18–25, 39–40, 96–97, 100
　of Herrera, 38
　imperial subject, 96–97, 100
　lyric poetry and role of, 3–4, 10, 48, 91, 102
　in Petrarch, 112
　politics of form and, 48, 51, 56–58
　post-structuralist theories of, 3 n. 5
　rational subjects, 25–28

subjectivity
　in Cetina's poetry, 105–6
　in sixteenth-century poetry, 10 n. 23
Tansillo, Luigi, 84, 105
Tasso, Torquato, 147
tercets, pressures of reason on, 26–28
terza rima poetic form, 33
Timaeus, 34 n. 22
Toledo, Don García de, 142
Torres Naharro, Bartolomé, 55
Tylus, Jane, 10 n. 23

Urrea, Jerónimo de, 31 n. 19, 136

Valdés, Juan de, 43
Vandalio poems (Cetina), 106–7, 114–37
vanitas painting, 6
Vega, Garcilaso de la, 11–12, 31, 54–56, 61, 95–102, 105, 177
　Eclogue 2, 144, 146, 152
　Elegy 2, 96–97, 100
　"Epístola a Boscán" (Epistle to Boscán), 96
　Herrera's attitude toward, 138, 146, 152–58
　historical narrative of, 152–53
　Las obras de Garcilaso de la Vega con anotaciones (The poetry of Garcilaso de la Vega with annotations) (Herrera), 60–61, 138–39, 140 n. 5, 143–46, 149–52, 153 n. 22, 155–56, 159, 165, 169
Vega, María José, 32 n. 20
vehemence, mannerist discourse of, 7 n. 14
Vergil, 107
　Cetina and, 128–30
Versos de Fernando de Herrera, 147 n. 16
　problems with, 171 n. 41
villancico form, 62
vision
　anamorphic in Sonnet 45 (Aldana), 9–10,
　Aldana's of Spain in Sonnet 45, 6–7, 9–10
　Boscán's assimilatory, 77–78, 109
　Counter-Reformation political, 164 n. 32
　Herrera's heroic, 140
visual effect, rhetoric of
　in Aldana, 6–10
　in Herrera, 138–40, 140 n. 4, 164–73
vita nuova, 25
volta (turn), in sonnet form, 26, 33–34, 102 n. 34, 163

Walters, D. Gareth, 7 n. 15

www.ingramcontent.com/pod-product-compliance
Lightning Source LLC
Chambersburg PA
CBHW031551300426
44111CB00006BA/266